A BASIC DICTIONARY

A Student's Reference

Compiled by E. W. Hobson, B. A.

Allied Publishing Group, Inc. 2003
Copyright © 1980 Schofield & Sims Ltd.

A Basic Dictionary

A Student's Reference

CONTENTS

Page

Preface   6

The Dictionary   7

Appendices

    Parts of Speech   137

    Capital Letters   138

    Common Abbreviations   139

    Calendar   144

    Roman Numerals   144

PREFACE

A Basic Dictionary contains a vocabulary of over 6,500 words and has been compiled to meet the needs of children in Elementary, Middle and High Schools.

To say that the dictionary is for use by one particular age group would be wrong, as abilities and needs vary from child to child within any age group.

The dictionary includes words that are in common use in both spoken and written English. There are also a great number of words that children hear on radio and television, especially those relating to the scientific, political, cultural and recreational activities that so many young people wish to discuss in speech and writing.

The clear layout is designed to encourage quick and easy reference. The definitions have been written to give accurate and easily understood meanings and to extend the child's vocabulary and knowledge. Where two words are spelled the same but are pronounced differently, the words are defined individually and the word is respelled in letters combined to convey sounds familiar to a child.

Abbreviations used in *A Basic Dictionary*

abbrev.	abbreviation		*L.*	Latin
adj.	adjective		*masc.*	masculine
adv.	adverb		*n.*	noun
conj.	conjunction		*pl.*	plural
e.g.	for example		*prep.*	preposition
esp.	especially		pron.	pronunciation
fem.	feminine		*pron.*	pronoun
Fr.	French		*R.*	Russian
Gk.	Greek		*sing.*	singular
inter.	interjection		*v.*	verb

A

abandon *v.* to give up; to forsake.
ABANDON *n.* lack of restraint.

abbess *n.* the female head of an abbey or a convent.

abbey *n.* a church, once part of a monastery.

abbot *n.* the head (male) of an abbey.

abbreviate *v.* to shorten. ABBREVIATION *n.*

abdicate *v.* to give up (a throne or high position). ABDICATION *n.*

abdomen *n.* the belly; the part of the body below the chest.

abduct *v.* to carry off by force; to kidnap.

ability *n.* skill or power to do things. *pl.* ABILITIES.

able *adj.* clever; talented; having the power or skill to do something.

abnormal *adj.* unusual; strange.

abolish *v.* to do away with; to end.

abrasion *n.* a graze, an injury made by rubbing or scraping.

abreast *adv.* 1 side by side. 2 up-to-date.

abroad *adv.* in another country.

abrupt *adj.* 1 very sudden; unexpected. 2 rude and hasty in speech or manner. ABRUPTLY *adv.*

abscess *n.* an inflamed boil or ulcer.

absence *n.* non-attendance; a lack.

absent *adj.* (pron. AB-sent) not present; away. ABSENT *v.* (pron. ab-SENT) to keep (oneself) away; to stay away.

absorb *v.* 1 to soak up. 2 to be interested in.

abstain *v.* to avoid doing; to keep away from.

absurd *adj.* ridiculous, unreasonable. ABSURDITY *n.*

abundance *n.* a large quantity; an excess.

abundant *adj.* plentiful.

abuse *n.* (pron. ab-USE) 1 a wrong use. 2 insulting language. ABUSE *v.* (pron. ab-UZE) to misuse; to harm.

accelerate *v.* to increase speed.

accent *n.* 1 stress; emphasis. 2 a manner of pronunciation. 3 a tone of voice.

accept *v.* to take something offered; to agree to. ACCEPTABLE *adj.* ACCEPTANCE *n.*

access *n.* the way in.

accident *n.* a mishap; an unexpected happening.

accidental *adj.* unintended; happening by chance.

accommodate *v.* 1 to fit in with. 2 to find room for.

accommodation *n.* 1 a lodging place. 2 a service.

accompany *v.* 1 to go with. 2 to play an instrument while someone sings or plays.

accomplish *v.* to complete; to achieve.

accord *v.* to be in agreement or harmony. ACCORD *n.* agreement; friendship.

account *n.* 1 a statement of money received and spent. 2 a bill. 3 a story or description. ACCOUNT (FOR) *v.* to explain; to be a reason for.

accumulate *v.* to gather more and more; to pile up.

accurate *adj.* exact; correct in detail.

accuse *v.* to blame. ACCUSER *n.*

accustom *v.* to become used to something.

ache *n.* 1 a continuous pain. 2 a longing; yearning. ACHE *v.* 1 to give continuous pain. 2 to yearn.

achieve *v.* to succeed in doing; to attain.

acid *adj.* sour; bitter. ACID *n.* a sour or corrosive substance.

acknowledge *v.* to admit the truth or the receipt of something.

acorn *n.* the fruit of the oak-tree.

acquaint (with) *v.* 1 to inform (somebody) of. 2 to make (oneself) familiar with.

acquire *v.* to obtain; to gain.

acquit *v.* to declare a person innocent.

acre *n.* a measure of land; an area of 4840 yd^2 (about 4000 m^2).

acrobat *n.* a gymnast; trapeze artist. ACROBATIC *adj.*

act *v.* 1 to do. 2 to play a part in. 3 to pretend. ACT *n.* 1 a deed. 2 a law made by a legislature. 3 a section of a stage play.

action *n.* 1 a style of movement. 2 a battle. 3 a thing done.

active *adj.* 1 lively; busy; energetic. 2 still working.

activity *n.* 1 an occupation. 2 alertness; quickness. *pl.* ACTIVITIES.

actor *n.* a male player on stage, radio, television or in films. *fem.* ACTRESS.

actual *adj.* real; existing. ACTUALLY *adv.*

acute *adj.* sharp; quick at understanding. ACUTENESS *n.* ACUTELY *adv.*

adamant *adj.* hard; stubborn.

adapt *v.* to fit in; to use in the best way.

add *v.* 1 to count up. 2 to join one thing to another. 3 to increase.

addition *n.* 1 the process of adding. 2 a thing joined on to another. ADDITIONAL *adj.*

address *v.* 1 to speak or write to. 2 to make a speech.
ADDRESS *n.* 1 a speech. 2 a residence or place of business. 3 manner or behavior.

adequate *adj.* enough; sufficient.
ADEQUACY *n.*

adhesive *adj.* sticky.
ADHESIVE *n.* a glue or a gum.

adjacent *adj.* next to; near by.

adjective *n.* a word which describes or qualifies a noun. ADJECTIVAL *adj.*

adjourn *v.* to put off; to postpone.
ADJOURNMENT *n.*

adjust *v.* to put in order; to make right; to adapt. ADJUSTMENT *n.*

admiral *n.* a naval officer commanding a fleet or squadron.

admire *v.* to be pleased with; to look up to.
ADMIRATION *n.*

admission *n.* 1 being allowed to enter.
2 entrance. 3 a confession.

admit *v.* 1 to allow to enter. 2 to acknowledge.
3 to confess.

adolescent *n.* a person approaching maturity.
ADOLESCENT *adj.* youthful; near-adult.

adopt *v.* 1 to be allowed to take another's child as one's own. 2 to choose. ADOPTION *n.*
ADOPTIVE *adj.*

adore *v.* to worship; to love very much.
ADORATION *n.* ADORABLE *adj.*

adrift *adj.* 1 floating without control.
2 unsettled.

adult *adj.* grown-up; responsible.
ADULT *n.* a man; woman.

advance *v.* to go forward.
ADVANCE *n.* progress.

advantage *n.* 1 ability or knowledge that places one above or before others. 2 a profit; benefit.
TO TAKE ADVANTAGE to act unfairly.

adventure *n.* an exciting experience.
ADVENTURE *v.* to dare; to do something risky.

adverb *n.* a word which tells more about a verb, adjective or other adverb.
ADVERBIAL *adj.*

adversary *n.* an opponent; an enemy.

advertise *v.* to make public or well known.

advertisement *n.* a public notice, as in a newspaper or on television. ADVERTISER *n.*

advice *n.* an opinion about what to do.

advise *v.* to give advice. ADVISER *n.*

aerosol *n.* a container capable of expelling liquid in a fine spray.

affect *v.* 1 to act upon. 2 to pretend.

affection *n.* love; great liking. AFFECTIONATE *adj.*

afford *v.* 1 to be able to buy or act without loss or injury. 2 to spare. 3 to supply or furnish.

afraid *adj.* frightened; alarmed.

afternoon *n.* the time of day between noon and evening.

again *adv.* once more; another time.

against *prep.* opposite to; facing.

age *n.* 1 the length of time a person or an animal has lived. 2 a particular period in history,
e.g. the Stone Age. AGE *v.* to grow old.

agent *n.* one who acts for another; a representative.

aggravate *v.* to make worse; to annoy.
AGGRAVATION *n.* AGGRAVATOR *n.*

agile *adj.* nimble; active.
AGILITY *n.* AGILELY *adv.*

agitate *v.* to shake; to stir up.
AGITATION *n.* AGITATOR *n.*

agony *n.* great pain; anguish. AGONIZING *adj.*

agree *v.* to be alike; to give consent; to accept.
AGREEMENT *n.*

agreeable *adj.* 1 pleasing; delightful. 2 willing.

agriculture *n.* the cultivation of the land.
AGRICULTURAL *adj.*

ahead *adv.* on in front; in advance.

aid *v.* to help. AID *n.* help; assistance.

aim *v.* to point at.
AIM *n.* an intention; a purpose.

air *n.* 1 the atmosphere. 2 a tune.
AIR *v.* to dry; to warm.

airborne *adj.* carried by the wind; in flight.

aircraft *n.* any flying machine.

airport *n.* place where passenger and freight aircraft land.

airtight *adj.* not allowing air to enter or escape.

aisle *n.* a passage between rows of seats as in a church, movie or theater.

alarm *v.* 1 to warn of danger. 2 to startle.
ALARM *n.* 1 a sudden warning. 2 fear.

album *n.* a book containing a collection of pictures, stamps, etc.

alcohol *n.* spirit formed in wine, beer, etc.
ALCOHOLIC *adj.*

alert *adj.* watchful; wide awake.
ALERT *n.* a warning.

algebra *n.* a branch of mathematics in which letters are used as numbers.

alien *n.* a foreigner. ALIEN *adj.* foreign.

alike *adj.* resembling; similar.
ALIKE *adv.* in the same way, manner or form.

alive *adj.* 1 living. 2 aware, alert.

all *adj.* the whole quantity, time, extent, etc.
ALL *adv.* wholly; completely.
ALL *n.* everyone; everything.

Allah *n.* the Muslim name for God.

allege *v.* to state; to declare without proof.

alligator *n.* a large reptile in the crocodile family.

allocate *v.* to share out; to distribute.

allow *v.* 1 to let; to permit. 2 to grant a payment. 3 to take into account.

ally *n.* a friend; partner. *pl.* ALLIES.
ALLY *v.* to unite with.

almighty *adj.* all-powerful. ALMIGHTY *n.* God.

almost *adv.* very nearly.

alone *adj.* single; solitary.
ALONE *adv.* by itself; separately.

aloud *adv.* in a voice loud enough to be heard.

alp *n.* a high mountain or pasture (esp. in Switzerland). ALPINE *adj.*

alphabet *n.* the letters of a language arranged in order; the "*ABC*". ALPHABETICAL *adj.*

also *adv.* in addition; as well.

alter *v.* to change. ALTERATION *n.*
ALTERABLE *adj.*

alternative *n.* offering the choice between two things.

although *conj.* though; otherwise; supposing.

altitude *n.* height, esp. above sea-level.

altogether *adv.* entirely; wholly.

always *adv.* at all times.

amateur *n.* a person who does things for pleasure as a hobby, and not professionally or for profit.

amaze *v.* to astonish; to astound.
AMAZEMENT *n.*

ambition *n.* a determination to win success or distinction. AMBITIOUS *adj.*

ambulance *n.* a vehicle for conveying the sick or injured.

ambush *v.* to lie in wait and then attack.
AMBUSH *n.* a surprise attack from a hiding place.

amen *n. & inter.* so be it *(Gk.).*

amend *v.* to improve; to set right.
AMENDMENT *n.*

American *adj.* belonging to America.
AMERICAN *n.* a citizen of the United States.

amiable *adj.* friendly.
AMIABILITY *n.* AMIABLY *adv.*

ammunition *n.* bombs, shells, cartridges for firearms, etc.

among *prep.* mixed with; making part of.

amount *n.* the quantity, value or sum.
AMOUNT (TO) *v.* to come to (a total); to add up to.

amphibian *n.* an animal able to live both on land and in water; a vehicle for use on both land and water. AMPHIBIOUS *adj.*

ample *adj.* quite enough, sufficient.
AMPLY *adv.*

amputate *v.* to cut off. AMPUTATION *n.*

amuse *v.* to please; to cause laughter.
AMUSEMENT *n.* AMUSING *adj.*

analyze *v.* to break up something into its separate parts.

ancestor *n.* a forefather, forbear.
ANCESTRAL *adj.*

ancestry *n.* line of descent, series of ancestors.

anchor *n.* a heavy metal hook which grips the sea-bed and holds a ship at its moorings.
ANCHOR *v.* to secure a ship with an anchor; to cast anchor.
TO WEIGH ANCHOR to haul up the anchor.

ancient *adj.* very old; of times long past.

and *conj.* also; together with. A word used to join words, phrases, clauses or sentences.

angel *n.* a heavenly messenger; a good and helpful person. ANGELIC *adj.*

anger *n.* displeasure; rage.
ANGER *v.* to vex; to make angry.

angle *n.* a corner; the space between two lines meeting at a point.
ANGLE *v.* to fish with a rod and line.

angry *adj.* annoyed; vexed. ANGRILY *adv.*

animal *n.* 1 a beast; a creature. 2 any living organism, including a human, that is not a plant.

ankle *n.* the joint connecting foot and leg.

anniversary *n.* the date of an annual event or celebration. *pl.* ANNIVERSARIES.

announce *v.* to make known. ANNOUNCEMENT *n.*

annoy *v.* to vex; to tease. ANNOYANCE *n.*

annual *adj.* happening yearly.
ANNUAL *n.* a plant that lives for only one year.
ANNUALLY *adv.*

anonymous *adj.* nameless; not known.
ANONYMITY *n.*

another *adj.* not the same; different.
ANOTHER *pron.* anyone else; one more.
pl. OTHERS.

answer *v.* to reply.
ANSWER *n.* a reply to a question.

ant *n.* a small, busy insect.

antarctic *n.* the south-polar region.
ANTARCTIC *adj.* concerning the south-polar region.

antelope *n.* African animal resembling a deer.

antenna *n.* 1 one of the feelers on the head of an insect. 2 a kind of aerial. *pl.* ANTENNAE.

anthem *n.* a song of praise.

anticipate *v.* to use in advance; to foresee; to look forward to.

antics *n. pl.* amusing or silly actions.

antique *adj.* old and rare.
ANTIQUE *n.* something old and rare.

anxiety *n.* worry; disquiet.

anxious *adj.* troubled; worried.

any *pron., adj. & adv.* one out of many; some; whichever you please.

anybody *pron.* any person, no matter who.

apart *adv.* aside; separately; independently.

apartheid *n.* the policy of keeping people of separate races apart.

ape *n.* a tailless monkey. APE *v.* to mimic.

apex *n.* tip; top; peak; vertex (of a triangle).

apologize *v.* to express regret.
APOLOGY *n.* APOLOGETIC *adj.*

apostle *n.* a messenger; a missionary.

apostrophe *n.* the sign (') used to show 1 the omission of a letter or letters (''don't'', for ''do not'') or 2 possession (the boy's hat).

apparent *adj.* easily seen or understood; plain, clear.

appeal *v.* to ask for help or sympathy.
APPEAL *n.* 1 an earnest request. 2 a request for a decision to be reconsidered.

appear *v.* 1 to come into sight. 2 to seem.
APPEARANCE *n.*

appetite *n.* a desire, especially for food.

applaud *v.* to show approval by clapping; to praise loudly. APPLAUSE *n.*

apple *n.* the fruit of the apple tree.

appliance *n.* a piece of apparatus or an instrument applied for a particular purpose.

application *n.* 1 a request. 2 attention to work; perseverance.

apply *v.* 1 APPLY FOR to ask for.
2 APPLY ONESELF TO to attend to.

appoint *v.* to choose a person for a post or job.
APPOINTMENT *n.*

appreciate *v.* 1 to value highly. 2 to understand. 3 to grow in value.

approach *v.* to come nearer; to be nearly equal to APPROACH *n.* the way leading to a place.

approve *v.* to be pleased with; to give permission. APPROVAL *n.*

approximate *adj.* very near; nearly correct.

April *n.* the fourth month of the year.

apron *n.* a garment worn to protect the clothes.

aqualung *n.* a diver's breathing apparatus carried on the back.

aquarium *n.* a tank for live fish.

aqueduct *n.* a bridge built to carry water or a canal across a valley; a conduit or pipe.

arable *adj.* (land) fit for plowing and growing crops.

arbitration *n.* settlement of a dispute by an independent person or committee.

arc *n.* a curve; part of a circle.

arch *n.* a curved structure upholding weight. *pl.* ARCHES.

archbishop *n.* a chief bishop.

archaeology *n.* the study of objects and remains from ancient times.

archer *n.* one who shoots with a bow and arrow.

architect *n.* one who plans and designs buildings.
ARCHITECTURAL *adj.* ARCHITECTURE *n.*

arctic *n.* the north-polar region.
ARCTIC *adj.* north-polar.

area *n.* 1 the size or extent of a surface. 2 a region.

argue *v.* to discuss; to debate; to dispute.
ARGUMENT *n.* ARGUMENTATIVE *adj.*

arm *n.* 1 an upper limb. 2 an inlet of the sea. 3 a weapon. ARM *v.* to equip with weapons.

armada *n.* a fleet of warships.

armistice *n.* an agreement to stop fighting for a time; a truce.

armor *n.* a protective covering for cars, tanks, etc., also for the body.

arms *n. pl.* weapons; firearms.

army *n.* a large number of trained soldiers. *pl.* ARMIES.

around *adv. & prep.* on all sides of; in every direction.

arrange *v.* 1 to put in proper order. 2 to make plans. ARRANGEMENT *n.*

arrest *v.* 1 to stop. 2 to take prisoner.
ARREST *n.*

arrive (at) *v.* to reach a destination; to come to (a conclusion). ARRIVAL *n.*

arrow *n.* a straight, barbed shaft shot from a bow; the sign →.

arson *n.* the crime of deliberately setting property on fire.

art *n.* skill, especially in painting, music, etc.

artery *n.* a blood-vessel carrying blood away from the heart. *pl.* ARTERIES.

article *n.* 1 a single thing. 2 an account in a newspaper or magazine.

artificial *adj.* not natural; manufactured.

artillery *n.* guns; cannon.

artist *n.* one skilled in any art. ARTISTIC *adj.*

ascend *v.* to climb up; to rise. ASCENSION *n.*

ascent *n.* 1 an upward movement. 2 a gradient.

ash *n.* 1 a common tree. 2 the powdery remains left after burning wood, coal, etc.

ashamed *adj.* feeling disgraced.

ask *v.* to inquire; to request; to invite.

asleep *adv.* sleeping, not awake.

aspect *n.* a view; an outlook; a facet.

assault *n.* a sudden attack.
ASSAULT *v.* to attack.

assemble *v.* 1 to gather or meet together. 2 to put (something) together. ASSEMBLY *n.*

assess *v.* to estimate the value or quality of.

asset *n.* a possession worth something.

assist *v.* to help. ASSISTANCE *n.* ASSISTANT *n.*

associate *v.* to join in with.
ASSOCIATE *n.* a companion.

association *n.* a society; a company.

assortment *n.* a mixture of different kinds; a variety.

assume *v.* to suppose; to pretend.

assured *adj.* certain; sure.

asthma *n.* a disease that makes breathing difficult.

astonish *v.* to surprise; to amaze.
ASTONISHMENT *n.*

astound *v.* to amaze; to shock with surprise. ASTOUNDING *adj.*

astrology *n.* fortune-telling by the position of the stars. ASTROLOGER *n.*

astronaut *n.* a person who travels in space.

astronomy *n.* the study of the stars and their movements. ASTRONOMER *n.*

asylum *n.* 1 a place of refuge or safety. 2 a home for the care of the mentally ill.

athlete *n.* a person active in sports.

atlas *n.* a book of maps. *pl.* ATLASES.

atmosphere *n.* 1 the air surrounding the Earth. 2 feeling; mood. ATMOSPHERIC *adj.*

atoll *n.* a coral reef enclosing a lagoon.

atom *n.* smallest part of an element; anything very small. ATOMIC *adj.*

attach *v.* 1 to fasten. 2 to make fond of. ATTACHMENT *n.*

attack *v.* to begin to fight; to assault.
ATTACK *n.* a battle; an onslaught. ATTACKER *n.*

attain *v.* to reach or gain after an effort. ATTAINMENT *n.*

attempt *v.* to try; to make an effort.
ATTEMPT *n.* an effort; an endeavor.

attend *v.* 1 to be present at (a meeting etc.). 2 ATTEND TO to consider.
ATTENDANCE *n.* presence.

attendant *n.* a servant or helper.

attention *n.* consideration; care.

attic *n.* a room under the roof of a house.

attitude *n.* a position of the body; a way of thinking or behaving.

attract *v.* to draw towards. ATTRACTION *n.*

attractive *adj.* pleasing; charming.

auction *n.* a sale in which goods are sold to one who bids or offers the highest price. AUCTION *v.*

audible *adj.* loud enough to hear. AUDIBLY *adv.*

audience *n.* 1 a group of listeners. 2 an interview.

audition *n.* a hearing given to a singer, speaker or actor as a test.

August *n.* the eighth month of the year.
AUGUST *adj.* (pron. aug-UST*)* noble; stately.

aunt *n.* 1 father's or mother's sister. 2 uncle's wife.

authentic *adj.* genuine; true. AUTHENTICITY *n.*

author *n.* 1 a writer of books or plays. 2 the creator of anything.

authority *n.* 1 legal power; right. 2 a person or group having official power. 3 a reliable source of knowledge.

autobiography *n.* the life story of a person, written by himself or herself.

autograph *n.* a person's own signature.

automatic *adj.* self-acting; acting mechanically and without thought.

automation *n.* the automatic control of machines by computers or other machines.

autumn *n.* third season of the year, between summer and winter.

available *adj.* within reach; able to be made use of.

avalanche *n.* a mass of ice, snow, and rock sliding down from a mountain.

avenge *v.* to take revenge for.

avenue *n.* a wide street.

average *adj.* ordinary; everyday.
AVERAGE *n.* the result obtained by adding several amounts and dividing by the number of amounts.

aviation *n.* the art of flying aircraft.

avoid *v.* to keep away from (something); to shun.
AVOIDANCE *n.* AVOIDABLE *adj.*

await *v.* to wait for; to expect.

awake *v.* to arouse; to wake up.
AWAKE *adj.* not asleep; alert. AWAKENING *n.*

award *v.* to give a prize or penalty.
AWARD *n.* a prize or an honor.

aware *adj.* conscious; watchful. AWARENESS *n.*

awe *n.* a feeling of reverence, fear or wonder.
AWE *v.* to fill with reverence, fear or wonder.
AWESOME *adj.* causing awe.

awful *adj.* terrible; dreadful.

awkward *adj.* 1 clumsy. 2 inconvenient.
3 embarrassing.

axe *v.* to chop down.
AXE *n.* a sharp-edged chopping tool.

axle *n.* a bar or rod on which a wheel rotates.

B

baby *n.* a very young child. *pl.* BABIES.

bachelor *n.* an unmarried man.

back *n.* the rear part of anything.
BACK *v.* 1 to go backward. 2 to support.
BACK *adv.* BACKWARDS *adv.*

backbone *n.* 1 the spine. 2 courage.

backward *adj.* 1 towards the back. 2 not very clever.

bacteria *n. pl.* disease germs or microbes.
sing. BACTERIUM.

bad *adj.* 1 wicked. 2 decayed. BADNESS *n.*

badge *n.* a special button worn by members of a society; a symbol; an emblem.

badger *n.* a burrowing, nocturnal, gray-coated wild animal. BADGER *v.* to bother; to tease.

baffle *v.* to puzzle; to bewilder. BAFFLING *adj.*

bag *n.* a container made of paper, fabric, etc., and having an opening top.
BAG *v.* 1 to put in a bag. 2 to swell; to bulge. 3 to droop; to hang in folds.

bail *v.* 1 to secure the release of an accused person by promising to pay a certain sum of money if the accused fails to appear for trial.
2 to ladle water out of a boat.
BAIL *n.* the sum forfeited if a prisoner breaks his or her bail.

bait *n.* a temptation; a lure; food put on a hook to catch fish or in a trap to catch animals.

bake *v.* to cook hard by heat; to cook in an oven.

balance *v.* 1 to keep steady; to keep upright.
2 to make things equal.
BALANCE *n.* 1 scales. 2 steadiness; stability.

balcony *n.* a platform projecting from a window or wall.

bald *adj.* 1 hairless. 2 bare. BALDNESS *n.*

bale *n.* a large bundle.

ball *n.* 1 a sphere; a spherical object.
2 an assembly for dancing.

ballad *n.* a simple song or poem telling a story.

ballerina *n.* a female ballet-dancer.

ballet *n.* a performance which is set to music but which is wholly dancing and mime, and without songs or speech.

balloon *n.* 1 a large airtight envelope which, when filled with gas lighter than air, rises skywards. 2 a small colored rubber bag filled with air and used as a toy or decoration.
BALLOON *v.* 1 to ascend in a balloon. 2 to swell out like a balloon.

ballot *n.* a system of secret voting.
BALLOT *v.* to vote.

bamboo *n.* giant, woody grasses.

ban *v.* to forbid; to prohibit.
BAN *n.* an order forbidding something.

banana *n.* a tropical tree; its fruit.

band *v.* to join together in a group.
BAND *n.* 1 a strip of cloth or other material.
2 a group of persons; a group of musicians.

bandit *n.* an outlaw who robs people.
BANDITRY *n.*

bang *v.* to strike noisily; to beat.
BANG *n.* a loud noise; a violent blow.

banish *v.* to drive away; to exile. BANISHMENT *n.*

bank *n.* 1 a place where money is kept and paid out. 2 the sides of a river or lake. 3 an earth mound, ridge or barrier.
BANK *v.* 1 to place money in a bank. 2 to raise an earth mound or barrier. 3 to fly an aircraft at an angle in turning.

bankrupt *n.* a person who, by legal declaration, is unable to pay his or her debts.

banner *n.* a flag; an ensign.

banquet *n.* a feast; a dinner with speeches.
BANQUET *v.* to feast.

baptize *v.* to christen and name. BAPTISMAL *adj.*

bar *n.* 1 a rigid rod. 2 any obstruction.
3 a counter where drinks are sold.
BAR *v.* 1 to hold back with bars. 2 to stop; to obstruct.

barbecue *n.* 1 a framework for roasting meat over a fire. 2 an open-air party where meat is roasted.

bare *adj.* 1 naked; uncovered. 2 empty.
BARENESS *n.*

bargain *v.* to argue about price or terms.
BARGAIN *n.* something bought or sold cheaply.

barge *n.* a flat-bottomed boat used on rivers and canals.

baritone *n.* 1 a male singer. 2 a deep-toned voice between tenor (high) and bass (low).

bark *n.* 1 the cry of a dog, fox, etc. 2 the outer covering of trees.
BARK *v.* 1 to utter a bark. 2 to speak sharply.

barley *n.* a grain; a cereal.

barn *n.* a farm building used for storage.

barometer *n.* an instrument which measures air pressure. BAROMETRIC *adj.*

barrack *n.* a building in which soldiers live.

barrel *n.* 1 a metal or wooden cask. 2 the tube of a gun.

barren *adj.* 1 fruitless. 2 bare.

barricade *n.* a barrier put up to block a street. BARRICADE *v.* to build a barrier.

barrier *n.* something standing in the way.

barter *n.* the exchange of goods for other goods. BARTER *v.* to exchange goods.

base *n.* the bottom; foundation; starting point. BASE *adj.* low; vile.

basement *n.* the floor below ground level in a building.

basin *n.* 1 a bowl. 2 a harbor. 3 the land drained by a river.

basis *n.* 1 a foundation. 2 the chief ingredient. BASIC *adj.*

basket *n.* a container with handle, made of cane, rushes or grasses.

bass *n.* 1 a fish. 2 (pron. BASE) a deep-toned voice.

bat *n.* 1 a club for striking a ball. 2 a night-flying animal. BAT *v.* to strike with a bat.

batch *n.* a number of persons or things. *pl.* BATCHES.

bath *n.* a large receptacle in which to bathe.

bathe *v.* 1 to wash. 2 to go swimming. BATHING *n.*

batter *v.* to strike again and again. BATTER *n.* 1 cooking ingredients beaten up with liquid. 2 the hitter in bat-and-ball games.

battery *n.* a device for making or storing electricity. *pl.* BATTERIES.

battle *v.* to struggle with; to fight. BATTLE *n.* a mass fight between two armies.

battlefield *n.* the place where a battle is fought.

battleship *n.* a heavily armed warship.

bawl *v.* to shout or cry out loudly. BAWL *n.* a loud cry; a continued yelling.

bay *n.* 1 an inlet of the sea. 2 a wall recess.

be *v.* 1 to live or exist. 2 to become.

beach *n.* the seashore; sands. BEACH *v.* to run a ship ashore.

beacon *n.* a warning signal light or fire; a lighthouse.

bead *n.* a small pierced ball of glass, wood or other material.

beak *n.* 1 a bird's bill. 2 a bill-like projection.

beam *n.* 1 a ray of light. 2 a long piece of timber. 3 a radio signal.
BEAM *v.* 1 to give light; to shine. 2 to send radio signals. 3 to smile brightly.

bean *n.* plant with long pods containing eatable seeds.

bear *n.* a large, flat-footed, furry animal. BEAR *v.* 1 to carry; to support. 2 to endure.

beard *n.* the hair grown on the cheeks and chin of a man. BEARD *v.* to defy.

bearing *n.* 1 behavior; manner. 2 a direction; an aim.

beast *n.* 1 a four-footed animal. 2 a brutal person.

beat *v.* 1 to strike. 2 to bang. 3 to defeat. 4 to throb. 5 to mark time in music. BEAT *n.* 1 a stroke; bang. 2 a police officer's round.

beaten *adj.* 1 defeated. 2 hammered into shape.

beautiful *adj.* lovely; pleasing to the eye or ear.

beauty *n.* a person or thing pleasing to the sight or hearing.

beckon *v.* to summon with a nod or wave.

become *v.* 1 to change into or begin to be. 2 to suit; to grace.

becoming *adj.* 1 suitable. 2 attractive.

bee *n.* a winged insect.

beech *n.* a large, nut-bearing tree with smooth, silvery bark.

beef *n.* meat from cattle.

beehive *n.* bees' home and store.

beer *n.* an alcoholic drink brewed from hops and malt.

beet *n.* a vegetable with a sweet, fleshy root. SUGARBEET a kind of beet from which sugar is extracted.

beetle *n.* an insect with horny wing-covers.

before *prep.* in front of; earlier or sooner. BEFORE *adv.* ahead of. BEFORE *conj.* sooner than.

beforehand *adv.* in advance; earlier; before the time.

beg *v.* 1 to implore. 2 to ask for help, food or money. BEGGAR *n.* one who begs.

begin *v.* to start; to commence.

beginning *n.* a start; origin.

behave *v.* to act properly or in some other way.

behavior *n.* conduct, good or bad; a way of behaving.

behold *v.* to look at; to see.

belief *n.* faith; confidence.

believe *v.* to trust; to accept something as true.

bell *n.* 1 a hollow metal object which will ring when struck. 2 any object designed to make a bell-like sound for calling attention.

bellow *v.* to roar; to shout loudly.
BELLOW *n.* a bull-like roar.

belly *n.* abdomen; the underside of an animal's body.

belong *v.* to be the property of; to be part of.

belongings *n. pl.* a person's possessions.

beloved *adj.* much loved; very dear.
BELOVED *n.* a loved one.

below *prep.* under, beneath; underneath.
BELOW *adv.* beneath, in a lower place.

belt *n.* 1 a flexible strap.

bench *n.* 1 a seat. 2 a work-table.

bend *v.* 1 to curve. 2 to bow or stoop. 3 to subdue.
BEND *n.* a curve, an angle or a turning.

benefit *n.* a gain; an advantage.
BENEFIT *v.* 1 to do good to (someone). 2 BENEFIT FROM to gain an advantage from.

benevolent *adj.* kind; generous.

bequeath *v.* to leave one's estate (to someone) by will; to hand down.

beret *n.* a flat, brimless woollen cap.

berry *n.* a small juicy fruit enclosing seeds.

berth *n.* 1 the place where a ship is tied up in port. 2 a sleeping-bunk in a ship or train.

beside *prep.* by the side of; next to; close to; adjacent to.

besides *adv.* moreover; furthermore; also; in addition.
BESIDES *prep.* over and above; in addition to.

betray *v.* to reveal information. BETRAYER *n.*

between *prep.* 1 in the space separating two persons or things. 2 shared by two or more; among. BETWEEN *adv.*

beverage *n.* a refreshing drink.

beware *v.* to be careful; to be cautious.

bewilder *v.* to puzzle; to confuse.
BEWILDERED *adj.*

beyond *prep.* on the farther side of; out of reach. BEYOND *adv.* at a distance.
BEYOND *n.* a distant place; the unknown.

bias *n.* a leaning towards; an influence.
BIAS *v.* to influence.

Bible *n.* the Holy Scriptures of the Christian Church.

bicycle *n.* a two-wheeled vehicle driven by pedals.

bid *v.* to invite; to make an offer.
BID *n.* price offered.

big *adj.* large; great; important. BIGNESS *n.*

bill *n.* 1 a proposed law. 2 an account of money owing; an invoice. 3 a bird's beak.
BILL *v.* 1 to announce; to advertise. 2 to send note of money owing.

binary *adj.* with 2 (not 10) as the base of a number system.

bind *v.* 1 to fasten or tie together. 2 to promise faithfully.

binding *n.* an outside cover. BINDING *adj.* firm.

binoculars *n. pl.* field glasses; opera glasses.

biography *n.* the written life story of a person. *pl.* BIOGRAPHIES.

biology *n.* the study of living things.
BIOLOGICAL *adj.*

biped *n.* a two-footed animal.

birch *n.* a tree with a smooth bark.

bird *n.* a creature with feathers and wings.

birth *n.* being born.

bisect *v.* to cut into two equal parts.
BISECTION *n.*

bishop *n.* 1 a clergyman of high rank. 2 a chess piece.

bison *n.* a wild ox or buffalo of North America and Europe.

bit *n.* 1 a small piece. 2 a boring tool. 3 the part of the bridle that goes into the horse's mouth.

bite *v.* 1 to cut or nip with the teeth. 2 to sting. 3 to take bait.
BITE *n.* 1 the piece bitten off. 2 a wound made by biting.

bitter *adj.* 1 opposite of sweet; one of the four tastes—sweet, salt, sour and bitter. 2 unpleasant.

black *adj.* 1 opposite of white; dark. 2 gloomy; mournful.

blackmail *n.* money, goods or services obtained from a person by threats of exposure.
BLACKMAIL *v.* to obtain anything from another by threats.

bladder *n.* 1 a bag-like organ, containing urine, in the body of a human or an animal. 2 a thin bag which can be inflated with air, as that in a football.

blade *n.* 1 the flat cutting part of a knife, sword, etc. 2 the broad part of an oar, a paddle, etc. 3 the flat part of a leaf or a shoulder-bone.

blame *v.* to find fault with; to hold responsible.
BLAME *n.* responsibility for a mistake.

blank *adj.* without any writing or marks; without expression. BLANK *n.* an empty space.
BLANKNESS *n.*

blanket *n.* a warm covering for a bed.

blast *n.* a sudden rush of air; an explosion.
BLAST *v.* 1 to blow up. 2 to break by explosion.

blaze *n.* a bright flame.
BLAZE *v.* to burn brightly. BLAZING *adj.*

bleach *v.* to make white.
BLEACH *n.* substance used to make something white.

bleak *adj.* cold and unsheltered; dull, cheerless.

bleed *v.* to lose blood.

blend *v.* to mix; to mingle. BLEND *n.* a mixture.

bless *v.* 1 to make holy. 2 to wish success and happiness to.

blind *adj.* 1 unable to see. 2 unable to look ahead. BLIND *v.* 1 to make sightless. 2 to dazzle.

bliss *n.* very great happiness. BLISSFUL *adj.*

blister *n.* 1 a painful, bubble-like swelling filled with fluid, on the skin. 2 a similar swelling on a plant-leaf, paintwork, etc.
BLISTER *v.* to cause a blister.

blizzard *n.* a violent storm of snow and wind.

block *n.* 1 a solid mass of material. 2 a row of connected buildings. 3 an obstruction.
BLOCK *v.* to obstruct.

blond *n.* a fair-haired man or boy.
fem. BLONDE.

blood *n.* a red liquid flowing in the arteries and veins of animals, such as birds and mammals.

bloom *n.* 1 a flower; blossom. 2 freshness; vigor.
BLOOM *v.* 1 to flower. 2 to flourish; to glow.

blossom *v.* to flower; to bloom.
BLOSSOM *n.* a flower; a bloom.

blow *v.* 1 to force air out of the mouth.
2 to cause air to move.
BLOW *n.* 1 a puff of air from the mouth.
2 a gust of wind. 3 a knock; a rap. 4 a shock; a disaster.

blubber *n.* whale fat. BLUBBER *v.* to weep noisily.

blue *adj.* 1 the color of a cloudless sky.
2 dismal; down-hearted.

bluff *n.* 1 a pretence. 2 a steep high bank or cliff.
BLUFF *v.* to deceive; to pretend.
BLUFF *adj.* 1 rough and hearty. 2 steep.

blunder *v.* to make a bad mistake.
BLUNDER *v.* a bad mistake; an oversight.
BLUNDERER *n.* BLUNDERING *adj.*

blunt *adj.* 1 without a sharp edge or point.
2 outspoken; candid; frank.
BLUNT *v.* to dull the edge or point; to deaden.

blur *v.* to dim; to make indistinct; to smudge.
BLUR *n.* a smudge.

blurt *v.* to speak hastily; to burst out with.

blush *v.* to flush; to become red-faced.
BLUSH *n.* a rosy glow.

boar *n.* a male pig.

board *n.* 1 a plank. 2 daily meals. 3 a committee.
BOARD *v.* 1 to cover with boards. 2 to supply with meals. 3 to enter a ship, train, bus, aircraft, etc.

boast *v.* to brag; to praise oneself.
BOAST *n.* bragging; self-praise. BOASTFUL *adj.*

boat *n.* a small vessel or ship.

body *n.* 1 the main part of a person or animal.
2 a group; a crowd. *pl.* BODIES.

bog *n.* a swamp; a marsh. BOGGY *adj.*

boil *v.* 1 to turn a liquid into a vapor; to cook by boiling. 2 to be angry.
BOIL *n.* a hard, painful swelling.

boiler *n.* a strong metal container in which steam is made or liquids are heated.

boisterous *adj.* rough; noisy; stormy.

bold *adj.* 1 brave; daring. 2 clear; well-marked.

bolt *n.* a metal fastening for a door.
BOLT *v.* 1 to fasten. 2 to run away. 3 to eat quickly.

bomb *n.* a metal case filled with explosives.
BOMB *v.* to attack with bombs.

bombard *v.* 1 to attack with bombs and shells.
2 to question again and again. BOMBARDMENT *n.*

bond *n.* 1 a contract; an agreement.
2 a link; a tie. BOND *v.* to join (together).

bone *n.* a hard substance forming the skeleton of an animal's body. BONY *adj.*

bonfire *n.* a large, open-air fire.

bonus *n.* an extra goodwill payment.

book *n.* written or printed sheets bound together.
BOOKSELLER *n.*

boom *n.* 1 a long spar. 2 a barrier across a harbor mouth. 3 a deep, hollow sound.
4 a sudden increase in trade, prosperity.
BOOM *v.* to make a deep, hollow sound.

boomerang *n.* Australian weapon, a curved throwing stick.

boot *n.* footwear reaching above the ankles.

border *n.* an edge; a boundary; a margin.
BORDERING *adj.*

bore *v.* 1 to pierce. 2 to weary.
BORE *n.* 1 a hole. 2 the width of a hole.
3 anything wearisome.

boredom *n.* dullness; weariness.

borrow *v.* to obtain on loan. BORROWER *n.*

boss *v.* to give orders to.
BOSS *n.* the manager; the person in charge.

botanist *n.* a person who studies plants.

botany *n.* the study of plants. BOTANICAL *adj.*

bother v. to be troublesome to; to annoy.
BOTHER n. trouble; worry.

bottle n. a hollow, narrow-necked container for liquids, usually made of glass or plastic.
BOTTLE v. to store or preserve in a bottle.

bottom n. the lowest part; base.

bough n. a branch of a tree.

boulder n. a large stone or rock.

bounce v. to spring suddenly; to rebound.
BOUNCE n. a rebound.

bound v. to leap; to spring.
BOUND n. 1 a leap. 2 a boundary.

boundary n. a line dividing one area from another.

bouquet n. 1 a bunch of flowers.
2 the perfume of wine.

bout n. a contest; a period.

bow v. 1 to bend the head or body forward in respect or greeting. 2 to give in; to submit.
BOW n. 1 a forward bending of the head or body. 2 the curved front part of a ship; its prow.

bow n. (pron. like "low") 1 a weapon for shooting arrows. 2 a looped knot in a tie or ribbon. 3 a stringed rod used to play various stringed instruments. 4 anything curved.

bowl n. a round dish to hold food or liquids.

box n. 1 a container made of wood, cardboard, metal, etc. 2 a blow, esp. on the ear.
pl. BOXES.
BOX v. 1 to encase. 2 to fight with fists.

boxer n. 1 a fighter with gloved fists. 2 a type of dog.

boy n. a male child.

brace v. to tighten or strengthen.
BRACE n. 1 a support. 2 a pair; a couple.
3 a tool for holding a bit for drilling holes.

bracket n. a small shelf or support.

brag n. boastful talk.
BRAG v. to boast. BRAGGING n.

braid v. to weave or plait together.
BRAID n. a cord or tape made by weaving different strands together. BRAIDED *adj.*

Braille n. a system of writing and printing for the blind, using raised marks which can be read by feeling.

brain n. the center of the nervous system.

brake n. an apparatus for stopping or slowing a moving vehicle.
BRAKE v. to check; to slow down.

bran n. husks of grain, separated from flour after grinding.

branch n. 1 the bough of a tree. 2 an offshoot of a business, bank, library, etc. *pl.* BRANCHES.
BRANCH v. to divide into or spread out.

brand n. 1 a mark made with a hot iron, as on cattle. 2 a burning or charred piece of wood; a fiery torch. 3 a trade mark.
BRAND v. to mark with a hot iron.

brass n. 1 a yellow alloy of copper and zinc.
2 brass, wind instruments.

brave adj. daring; courageous.

bravery n. courage; valor. BRAVELY adv.

brawl v. to quarrel.
BRAWL n. a noisy quarrel; a fight. BRAWLER. n.

breach n. 1 a break; a gap. 2 a quarrel.
BREACH v. to make a gap in; to break.

bread n. a food made from flour and water.

break v. to damage or spoil; to fracture.
BREAK n. a pause; an interruption.
BREAKAGE n. BREAKABLE *adj.*

breakfast n. the first meal of the day.
BREAKFAST v.

bream n. a river fish.

breast n. 1 the chest; bosom. 2 the front of anything.

breath n. 1 air drawn in and expelled by the lungs. 2 a breath of wind; a light wind or gentle breeze.

breathe v. 1 to draw breath into the lungs and expel it. 2 to whisper or utter. 3 to be alive.

breed v. to produce young; to rear.
BREED n. the race; the family.

breeze n. a light wind. BREEZY *adj.*

brew v. to make beer, tea, etc.
BREW n. a single brewing. BREWER n.
BREWERY n.

bribe n. money or a gift offered to gain a favor.
BRIBE v. to tempt with a bribe.

brick n. a fire-hardened and molded block of clay used as a building material.

bride n. a newly-married woman.

bridegroom n. a newly-married man.

bridge n. 1 a structure to carry traffic over a river, railway or road. 2 the raised structure of a ship from which the captain operates. 3 a card game. BRIDGE v. to span a gap.

bridle n. the headgear of a horse's harness; a check; a restraint. BRIDLE v.

brief adj. short, concise. BRIEFLY adv.

bright adj. 1 shining. 2 clever. 3 cheerful.
BRIGHTNESS n.

brighten v. to make or become bright.

brilliance n. great brightness or cleverness.

brilliant adj. 1 bright; sparkling. 2 very clever.

brim *n.* the edge of a bowl or drinking vessel.

brine *n.* salt water; pickle. BRINY *adj.*

bring *v.* to fetch; to carry.

brink *n.* the edge of a cliff or steep place.

brisk *adj.* active; lively; quick. BRISKLY *adv.*

bristle *n.* a stiff, coarse hair.
BRISTLE *v.* 1 to stand up straight like an angry animal's hair. 2 to show anger.

brittle *adj.* easy to break; fragile.

broad *adj.* wide; large; full.

broadcast *n.* a radio or television transmission.
BROADCAST *v.* 1 to transmit by radio or television. 2 to scatter.

broaden *v.* to make wide or wider.

brochure *n.* a small booklet.

bronchitis *n.* inflammation of the tubes of the lungs.

bronco *n.* a half-tamed horse.

bronze *n.* a red-brown alloy of copper and tin.
BRONZE *v.* to tan.
BRONZE *adj.* made of bronze; bronze-colored.

brood *n.* 1 a number of young birds hatched at the same time. 2 a swarm.
BROOD *v.* to worry for some time; to think anxiously.

brook *n.* a small stream.

broom *n.* 1 a sweeping brush with stiff bristles. 2 a yellow-flowered shrub.

brother *n.* 1 a son of the same parents as another person. 2 a friend; a comrade.
pl. BROTHERS or BRETHREN. BROTHERLY *adj.*

brow *n.* 1 the forehead. 2 the top of a hill.

brown *adj.* red, blue and yellow mixed.
BROWN *v.* 1 to make brown; to toast. 2 to tan; to sunburn.

bruise *n.* a skin injury caused by pressure or a blow. BRUISE *v.* to press; to crush.

brush *n.* 1 an implement for painting, sweeping or scrubbing. 2 a brief encounter.
3 a fox's tail. BRUSH *v.* 1 to sweep. 2 to touch in passing.

brutal *adj.* cruel; like a brute.

brute *n.* 1 a beast. 2 a cruel or savage person.

bubble *n.* a thin, ball-shaped film of liquid full of air.
BUBBLE *v.* 1 to rise in bubbles. 2 to flow with a gurgling noise.

buck *n.* the male of many animals—deer, goat, rabbit, etc.

bucket *n.* a container for carrying water, coal, etc.; a pail.

buckle *n.* a metal clasp.
BUCKLE *v.* 1 to bend. 2 to fasten with a buckle.

bud *n.* a leaf or flower not fully open.
BUD *v.* to begin growing.

budget *n.* a plan to show how money will be spent.

buff *n.* a pale yellow color. BUFF *v.* to polish.

buffalo *n.* a wild ox (see bison). *pl.* BUFFALOES.

buffer *n.* anything that softens a blow.

buffet *v.* to strike; to knock about.
BUFFET *n.* 1 a blow. 2 (pron. BU-fay) a refreshment bar.

bug *n.* 1 a small insect. 2 a hidden listening device.

bugle *n.* a small trumpet. BUGLER *n.*

bulb *n.* a large ball-shaped base of a plant stem, e.g. onion.

bulge *v.* to swell outwards.
BULGE *n.* a swelling. BULGING *adj.*

bulk *n.* the size; the volume; the greater part.

bull *n.* the male of cattle, elephants, whales, etc.

bulldozer *n.* a powerful caterpillar tractor used for levelling or clearing land.

bullet *n.* a missile shot from a rifle or pistol.

bulletin *n.* a short, news report.

bullion *n.* gold or silver in the form of bars.

bully *n.* one who frightens or ill-treats someone weaker. BULLY *v.* to frighten; to ill-treat.

bump *n.* 1 a knock; a collision. 2 a swelling.
BUMP *v.* to knock into.

bunch *n.* a cluster or group of things tied or growing together.
BUNCH *v.* to cluster; to gather together.

bundle *n.* a package; a parcel.
BUNDLE *v.* to bind together.

bungle *v.* to blunder; to do clumsily.

bunk *n.* a box-like bed; a sleeping berth in a ship or train.

buoy *n.* a large, anchored float to guide ships.
BUOY *v.* 1 to keep afloat. 2 to cheer; to comfort.

burden *n.* a load; a weight.
BURDEN *v.* to lay weight upon; to load.

burglar *n.* someone who breaks into a house or building to steal.

burial *n.* the burying of anything.

burn *n.* an injury or a mark caused by burning.
BURN *v.* to blaze; to set fire to; to destroy by fire.

burrow *n.* a hole in the earth dug by an animal as a home and shelter.
BURROW *v.* to make a hole underground.
BURROWING *adj.*

burst *v.* to fly into pieces; to explode.
BURST *n.* a splitting apart; a sudden spurt; an explosion.

bury v. to cover over; to hide in the earth.
TO BURY THE HATCHET to forgive and forget.
BURIAL v.

bus n. a passenger-carrying motor vehicle.

bush n. 1 a shrub. 2 wild, uncultivated country.

business n. occupation; work; trade; profession.
BUSINESS adj. concerning business.

bust n. a sculpture of the upper part of the body.

bustle n. fuss; noisy stir.
BUSTLE v. to hurry about fussily. BUSTLING adj.

busy adj. fully occupied; active; working hard.
BUSILY adv.

butcher n. a person who kills animals for meat;
one who sells meat.
BUTCHER v. to kill, to slaughter.

butt n. the thicker end of anything.
BUTT v. to push or strike with the head.

butter n. a yellow fatty food made from milk.
BUTTER v. 1 to spread (bread etc.) with butter.
2 BUTTER UP to flatter (someone).

button n. a round, flat disc or knob for fastening
clothing. BUTTON v. to fasten with buttons.

buy v. to purchase. BUYER n.

buzz n. 1 the humming sound made by a flying
insect. 2 the hum of many people in
conversation. BUZZ v. to hum.

bypass v. to go around, not through.
BYPASS n. a road around a town center.

C

cabbage n. a large, green vegetable.

cabin n. 1 a hut. 2 a room in a ship or
aeroplane.

cabinet n. a cupboard having drawers and
shelves.

cable n. 1 a strong rope, wire or chain. 2 covered
communications wires.

cackle n. 1 the noise of a hen or goose.
2 a giggle. CACKLE v. 1 to cluck. 2 to giggle.

cactus n. a prickly desert plant with swollen
stems.

café n. a coffee-house; a restaurant.

cage n. a barred enclosure for birds or animals.
CAGE v. to imprison.

calamity n. a disaster; a great misfortune.
pl. CALAMITIES.

calculate v. to count with numbers; to work out.
CALCULATION n. CALCULATOR n.

calendar n. a table showing the days, weeks and
months of a particular year; a list of events.

calf n. 1 the young of certain animals, such as
the cow, elephant, etc. 2 the back bulging part
of the leg below the knee. pl. CALVES.

call v. 1 to shout or cry out. 2 to name or
summon. 3 to visit.
CALL n. 1 a shout. 2 an invitation. 3 a visit.
CALLER n.

callous adj. unfeeling; hard-hearted.

calm adj. 1 still; windless. 2 not easily upset.
CALM v. to make peaceful; to quieten.

calorie n. 1 the energy value of food. 2 a unit
measure of heat.

camel n. a large, humped, domesticated animal.

camera n. a device for taking photographs,
videos, or movies.

camouflage v. to disguise an object by making it
merge into its background. CAMOUFLAGE n.

camp n. a group of inhabited tents. CAMPER n.

campaign n. 1 a series of military operations in
one area. 2 a series of efforts for a definite
purpose. CAMPAIGN v. to carry on a campaign.

can n. a small metal container.
CAN v. 1 to be able. 2 to preserve in airtight
metal containers.

canal n. an artificial waterway for ships, boats,
barges and drainage.

canary n. a yellow songbird. pl. CANARIES.
CANARY adj. bright yellow.

cancel v. to cross out; to withdraw; to call off.

cancer n. a harmful growth in the body.

candid adj. frank, honest and straightforward.

candle n. a cylinder of wax surrounding a wick,
for giving light by burning.

canine adj. to do with dogs.

cannibal n. a person who eats human flesh; an
animal which eats others of its own kind.

cannon n. a large gun. CANNON v. to collide.

canoe n. a light, open boat propelled by using a
paddle.
CANOE v. to sail or paddle a canoe. CANOEIST n.

canopy n. a light, overhead covering.
pl. CANOPIES.

canter n. an easy gallop.
CANTER v. to ride at an easy gallop.

canvas n. strong, coarse cloth for sails, tents, oil
paintings, etc.

canyon n. a deep, narrow gorge or valley.

cap n. 1 a soft, peaked head covering. 2 a cover
or top. CAP v. 1 to cover. 2 to outdo.

capable adj. able to do; efficient.

capacity n. 1 the amount that a container holds.
2 ability. pl. CAPACITIES.

cape n. 1 a headland. 2 a short cloak.

capital n. 1 a chief city. 2 money or goods used
for business. 3 a large letter used to begin a
sentence or name.

capsize *v.* to overturn.

capsule *n.* 1 a pill. 2 a seedpod. 3 part of a spacecraft.

captain *n.* 1 an officer qualified to command a ship or aircraft. 2 a military officer commanding a company. 3 the leader of a sports team.
CAPTAIN *v.* to lead; to command.

captive *n.* a prisoner.
CAPTIVE *adj.* kept as a prisoner; not free.

capture *v.* 1 to catch. 2 to imprison. 3 to attract or hold. CAPTOR *n.*

car *n.* a box like vehicle on wheels.

carcass (-ase) *n.* the body of an animal, esp. a dead body.

card *n.* a piece or sheet of very stiff paper.

cardinal *n.* a member of the Pope's Council.
CARDINAL *adj.* most important; chief.

care *n.* 1 attention. 2 worry. 3 caution.
CARE (FOR OR ABOUT) *v.* 1 to be interested.
2 to be concerned. 3 to watch over.

career *n.* a person's profession or course in life.
CAREER *v.* to move quickly and wildly.

careful *adj.* painstaking; watchful; cautious.
CAREFULLY *adv.*

careless *adj.* thoughtless; unconcerned; inaccurate. CARELESSNESS *n.*

cargo *n.* the load carried by a ship or aircraft; freight. *pl.* CARGOES.

carmine *adj. & n.* a purplish-red color.

carnation *n.* 1 a garden flower of the pink family. 2 a pink color.

carnival *n.* a merrymaking; festivity.

carol *n.* a joyous song; a Christmas hymn.
CAROL *v.* to sing gaily. CAROLLING *adj.*

carp *n.* a freshwater fish.
CARP (AT) *v.* to find fault with. CARPING *adj.*

carpenter *n.* a joiner; someone who works with wood.

carpet *n.* a woven floor covering.
CARPET *v.* to cover with carpet.

carriage *n.* 1 a wheeled vehicle. 2 a person's bearing. 3 the cost of transportation.

carrot *n.* an orange-colored root vegetable.

carry *v.* 1 to convey. 2 to transport.

cart *n.* a wagon.
CART *v.* to convey by cart or wagon. CARTER *n.*

cartoon *n.* a comic drawing or film.
CARTOONIST *n.* one who draws cartoons for a living.

carve *v.* 1 to shape by cutting; to sculpt.
2 to slice meat. CARVER *n.*

case *n.* 1 a container. 2 a lawsuit. 3 an example.
CASE *v.* to enclose.

cash *n.* coins or banknotes.
CASH *v.* to turn into money.

cast *v.* 1 to throw. 2 to shape in a mold.
3 to drop; to shed.
CAST *n.* 1 a throw. 2 anything molded.
3 the actors in a play, movie or television show.

castaway *n.* a shipwrecked sailor.

castle *n.* 1 a stronghold; a fortress. 2 a chess piece.

casual *adj.* due to chance; informal; off hand.

casualty *n.* 1 an accident. 2 the victim of an accident. *pl.* CASUALTIES.

cat *n.* a common domestic animal; a feline.

catalogue *n.* a complete list, usually in alphabetical or other order.
CATALOGUE *v.* to make a list.

catastrophe *n.* a sudden disaster.
CATASTROPHIC *adj.*

catch *v.* 1 to capture; to seize and hold. 2 to be in time for.
CATCH *n.* 1 a capture. 2 a fastening-clasp or hook.

cater *v.* to supply what is needed. CATERER *n.*

caterpillar *n.* the larva of a moth or butterfly; an endless belt with treads that is used to drive some vehicles.

catholic *adj.* world-wide; universal; general.
CATHOLIC *n.* a member of the Roman Catholic Church.

cattle *n. pl.* cows, bulls, calves, etc.

cauliflower *n.* a kind of cabbage with a large white flower head.

cause *n.* 1 a beginning. 2 a reason. 3 a purpose.
CAUSE *v.* to make happen.

caution *n.* 1 watchfulness; care. 2 a warning.
CAUTION *v.* to warn.

cavalry *n.* mounted soldiers.

cave *n.* a hole in a cliff or hillside.

cavern *n.* a large underground cave.

cavity *n.* a hollow place; a hole. *pl.* CAVITIES.

cease *v.* to stop; to come to an end.

cedar *n.* an evergreen cone-bearing tree.

ceiling *n.* 1 the top of a room. 2 the maximum altitude an aircraft can reach. 3 the upper limit.

celebrate *v.* to honor; to praise.

celebration *n.* a special festivity; merry-making.

celebrity *n.* a celebrated person.
pl. CELEBRITIES.

cell *n.* 1 a small room in a prison or monastery.
2 a small unit of living matter. 3 a unit in an electric battery.

cellar *n.* an underground room where coal, wine, etc., is stored.

cello *n.* (pron. CHEL-oh) a musical instrument like a violin but which is large and rests on the floor.

Celsius *adj.* a common temperature scale.

cement *n.* a mixture of quicklime and clay used with sand and water to make mortar.
CEMENT *v.* to join securely.

cemetery *n.* a burial ground.

censor *n.* an official who examines and prohibits offensive books, plays or films.
CENSOR *v.* to prohibit; to ban.
CENSORSHIP *n.*

censure *v.* to blame; to express disapproval.
CENSURE *n.* blame, reproof.

census *n.* an official counting of the population.

cent *n.* a coin which is one-hundredth part of a larger amount.

centigram *n.* one hundredth part of a gram; a measure of mass.

centiliter *n.* one hundredth part of a liter; a measure of volume or capacity.

centimeter *n.* one hundredth part of a meter.

central *adj.* 1 in the middle. 2 chief; leading.
CENTRALLY *adv.*

center *n.* the middle point or part.
CENTER *v.* a place in the middle.

century *n.* 100 years. *pl.* CENTURIES.

ceramic *n.* a decorative article made of clay or porcelain. CERAMIC *adj.*

cereal *n.* any grass grain used as food.

ceremony *n.* a solemn or stately celebration.
pl. CEREMONIES.

certain *adj.* sure; without any doubt.

certainly *adv.* willingly; surely.

certificate *n.* a written proof.

certify *v.* to inform truthfully and accurately; to guarantee.

chain *n.* 1 a length of joined links or rings. 2 a measure of length (22 yards). 3 a series of events.
CHAIN *v.* to bind; to secure with a chain.

chair *n.* a backed, four-legged seat for one.
CHAIR *v.* to preside over a meeting.

chalet *n.* (pron. SHAL-ay) a wooden house built in the Swiss style.

chalk *n.* soft, white limestone.
CHALK *v.* to mark with chalk. CHALKY *adj.*

challenge *v.* to question or doubt something; to dare (someone to do something).
CHALLENGE *n.* 1 a summons to a contest. 2 a query or an objection. CHALLENGER *n.*

champagne *n.* a sparkling white wine from the district of Champagne, in France.

champion *n.* 1 one who defends others. 2 a victor over all competitors.
CHAMPION *v.* to uphold; to defend.
CHAMPIONSHIP *n.*

chance *n.* 1 an unexpected or unplanned event. 2 an opportunity; a risk.
CHANCE *v.* to risk. CHANCY *adj.*

change *n.* 1 an alteration; a variation. 2 money received back from a sum offered.
CHANGE *v.* to alter; to substitute or exchange.

channel *n.* 1 a waterway. 2 a groove.
THE CHANNEL the English Channel.
CHANNEL *v.* 1 to groove. 2 to cut a canal.

chant *v.* to sing. CHANT *n.* a sacred song.

chaos *n.* (pron. KAY-oss) disorder.

chap *v.* to crack or to split open in cracks.
CHAP *n.* 1 a crack in the skin caused by frost, wind, etc. 2 a boy; a man. CHAPPED *adj.*

chapter *n.* a division of a book.

character *n.* 1 a person's own nature. 2 a reputation. 3 a person in a story or play.

characteristic *n.* a feature; a quality.

charge *v.* 1 to rush at. 2 to fill up. 3 to ask a price. 4 to accuse.
CHARGE *n.* 1 an onslaught. 2 a filling. 3 a price. 4 an accusation.

chariot *n.* a horsedrawn cart used in ancient warfare and racing.

charity *n.* 1 kindness or goodwill felt towards other people. 2 an institution that gives help to those in need.

charm *n.* 1 attractiveness. 2 a magic spell. 3 a good-luck object.
CHARM *v.* 1 to attract. 2 to delight.

chart *n.* 1 a map showing coasts, shoals, rocks, etc. 2 a diagram giving information (such as a weather chart).
CHART *v.* to plan; to show on a chart.

charter *n.* a document granting certain rights.
CHARTER *v.* to hire for a period.

chase *v.* to pursue; to hunt; to drive away.
CHASE *n.* a pursuit; the hunt.

chat *v.* to talk in an easy familiar way.
CHAT *n.* a friendly talk.

cheap *adj.* costing little; of poor value.
CHEAPNESS *n.*

cheat *v.* to be dishonest; to deceive.
CHEAT *n.* a person who cheats.

check *v.* 1 to hinder or stop. 2 to look for faults in. 3 to make sure.
CHECK *n.* 1 a hindrance. 2 a control. 3 a pattern of squares.

cheek *n.* 1 each side of the face. 2 impudence.

cheer *v.* 1 to applaud by shouting. 2 to gladden.
CHEER *n.* 1 a cry of applause or welcome.
2 happiness.

cheerful *adj.* happy and lively.
CHEERFULNESS *n.*

cheese *n.* a food made from milk curd, pressed and dried.

chef *n.* (pron. SHEF) a cook in a hotel or restaurant.

chemical *n.* a substance made by chemistry.
CHEMICAL *adj.* CHEMICALLY *adv.*

chemist *n.* a person skilled in chemistry.

cherry *n.* a small sweet stone-fruit. *pl.* CHERRIES.
CHERRY *adj.* reddish; ruddy.

chess *n.* a game for two played on a squared board. CHESSBOARD *n.*

chest *n.* 1 the upper front part of the body; the thorax. 2 a large box.

chew *v.* to crush or grind with the teeth; masticate.

chicken *n.* a young fowl.

chief *n.* a leader; a head.
CHIEF *adj.* most important.

child *n.* a young boy or girl. *pl.* CHILDREN.

chill *n.* 1 a coolness; a feeling of coldness.
2 a shivery cold. CHILL *v.* to make cold.

chime *n.* the music of bells.
CHIME *v.* to ring tunefully.

chimney *n.* a tubelike passage to carry smoke away; a flue.

chimpanzee *n.* an African ape.

chin *n.* the part of the face below the mouth.

china *n.* fine, thin porcelain.

chip *n.* a tiny piece.
CHIP *v.* to break off a fragment. CHIPPED *adj.*

chirp *n.* a shrill birdcall.
CHIRP *v.* to call like a young bird. CHIRPING *n.*

chisel *n.* a wood- or stone-cutting tool.
CHISEL *v.* to cut or carve with a chisel.

chocolate *n.* a sweet or drink made from cocoa.
CHOCOLATE *adj.* deep brown.

choice *n.* 1 anything chosen or selected.
2 a variety to choose from.
CHOICE *adj.* rare; excellent.

choir *n.* 1 a group of people trained to sing together. 2 that part of a church occupied by the choir; the chancel.

choke *v.* 1 to smother. 2 to block up. 3 to catch the breath.

choose *v.* to select; to decide between.

chop *v.* to cut with short downstrokes; to cut into small pieces.

chord *n.* 1 two or more musical notes in harmony. 2 a string of a musical instrument.
3 the straight line joining the ends of an arc of a circle.

chorus *n.* music which all join in singing.

chosen *adj.* picked; selected.

christen *v.* to baptize and name. CHRISTENING *n.*

Christian *adj.* concerning Christ and His teaching.
CHRISTIAN *n.* a believer in Christ's teaching.

Christmas *n.* the festival celebrating Christ's birth (December 25).

chuckle *v.* to laugh quietly.
CHUCKLE *n.* an amused laugh held back or suppressed.

church *n.* a building set apart for worship.

churchyard *n.* a burial ground adjacent to a church.

churn *n.* 1 a butter-making machine. 2 a large milk can. CHURN *v.* to make butter.

chute *n.* 1 a sloping trough or slide.
2 a shortened form for parachute.

cigarette *n.* tobacco rolled in paper for smoking.

cinema *n.* a motion-picture theater.

circle *n.* 1 a perfect ring. 2 a group of people who have a common interest.
CIRCLE *v.* to revolve.

circular *adj.* round; ring-like; moving in a circle.
CIRCULAR *n.* a notice or letter, many copies of which are distributed.

circulate *v.* to distribute; to go or spread around.

circumference *n.* the line enclosing a circle; the distance around anything circular in form.

circumstance *n.* a particular incident; a fact.

circus *n.* a traveling show of horse riders, acrobats, clowns, etc. *pl.* CIRCUSES.

citizen *n.* 1 an inhabitant of a town or city.
2 a member of a country or nation.

city *n.* an important town. *pl.* CITIES.

civic *adj.* concerned with a citizen or city.

civil *adj.* 1 concerned with a nation or community. 2 courteous.

civilian *n.* one not serving in the armed forces.

civilization *n.* socially and culturally developed communities and nations.

civilize *v.* to educate, enlighten and develop socially.

claim *v.* to demand as a right.
CLAIM *n.* a demand for something regarded as a right.

clamp *v.* to grip together.
CLAMP *n.* a device for holding things together firmly.

clan *n.* a tribe united under a chieftain.
CLANNISH *adj.*

clang *n.* the loud ringing sound of a heavy bell or cymbal.
CLANG *v.* to make a loud, ringing sound.

clap *v.* to strike the hands together in applause.
CLAP *n.* 1 the sound of clapping. 2 a peal of thunder. CLAPPING *adj.*

clarinet *n.* a musical wind instrument.

clasp *v.* 1 to grasp. 2 to embrace. 3 to buckle.
CLASP *n.* 1 a grasp. 2 an embrace. 3 a buckle.

class *n.* a group of persons or things of the same kind. CLASS *v.* to place in a class.

classic *n.* a model example; the best kind.
CLASSIC *adj.*

classify *v.* to sort into kinds or groups.

clatter *v.* to rattle noisily.
CLATTER *n.* a repeated rattling noise.

clause *n.* 1 a part of a sentence containing a verb. 2 a complete paragraph in an agreement.

claw *n.* an animal's hooked nail; a talon.
CLAW *v.* to tear or scratch with claws.

clay *n.* moist, sticky earth.

clean *v.* to free from dirt or smoke.
CLEAN *adj.* fresh; pure.
CLEAN *adv.* altogether; completely.

clear *v.* 1 to make or become clear. 2 to prove innocent. 3 to pass over or by without touching, esp. by jumping.
CLEAR *adj.* 1 distinct. 2 open. 3 transparent.

clerk *n.* a person employed in an office, bank, etc., to make entries, keep accounts, etc.

clever *adj.* quick to learn and understand; talented.

client *n.* someone who employs the services of a professional person.

cliff *n.* a steep rock-face.

climate *n.* the normal weather over a region or zone.

climax *n.* 1 the highest point; turning point. 2 the most exciting part of a book or film.

climb *v.* to ascend; to go up or down; to grow upwards. CLIMBER *n.*

cling (to) *v.* to hold firmly (to). CLINGING *adj.*

clip *v.* to cut; to trim. CLIP *n.* a fastener.

cloak *v.* to screen; to hide.
CLOAK *n.* a sleeveless outer garment.

clock *n.* an instrument for measuring time.

close *v.* (pron. KLOZE) 1 to shut. 2 to bring or come to an end. 3 to draw nearer.
CLOSE *n.* the end; conclusion. CLOSED *adj.*

close *adj.* (pron. KLOSE) 1 near. 2 hot and stuffy. 3 secret. CLOSENESS *n.* CLOSELY *adv.*

cloth *n.* a woven material.

clothe *v.* to dress; to provide with clothes.

clothing *n.* garments.

cloud *v.* to darken; to obscure.
CLOUD *n.* a mass of watery vapor, dust or smoke floating in the air.

club *n.* 1 a heavy stick or cudgel. 2 a stick used in golf, etc. 3 a society or its meeting-place.
CLUB *v.* to beat with a club.
TO CLUB TOGETHER to unite.

clue *n.* a hint or idea that helps to solve a puzzle or mystery.

clump *n.* a group of trees or plants.
CLUMP *v.* to walk heavily.

clumsy *adj.* awkward; tactless. CLUMSILY *adj.*

cluster *v.* to form a group.
CLUSTER *n.* a bunch; a group.

clutch *v.* to grasp at; to hold tightly.
CLUTCH *n.* 1 a grip. 2 a set of eggs. 3 a device for connecting two moving parts of a machine.

clutter *v.* to make untidy.
CLUTTER *n.* untidiness; disorder.

coach *v.* to teach.
COACH *n.* a teacher. COACHING *n.*

coal *n.* a hard, black mineral used as fuel.

coarse *adj.* 1 rough. 2 rude. COARSELY *adv.*

coast *n.* the land bordering a large body of water. COASTAL *adj.*

coat *v.* to cover; to spread over.
COAT *n.* 1 an outer garment. 2 an animal's fur or hair. 3 a layer of paint, etc.

coax *v.* to persuade gently. COAXING *n. & adj.*

cobra *n.* a poisonous, hooded snake.

cocaine *n.* an addictive drug; used medically a drug used to deaden pain.

cock *n.* a male bird.

cocoa *n.* 1 a drink made from the powdered seeds of the cacao-tree. 2 a powder used to make chocolate.

coconut *n.* a large nut, fruit of the coconut palm, containing a white liquid and edible tissue.

cocoon *n.* a silky case spun by many insects to protect themselves in the pupal stage.

cod *n.* a large, edible sea-fish.

code *n.* 1 a set of laws or rules. 2 words or signs having a secret meaning. 3 an agreed set of symbols.
CODE *v.* to give words a secret meaning.

coffee *n.* 1 the roasted and ground beans of the coffee tree. 2 a hot drink made from roasted and ground coffee beans.

cog *n.* a tooth on the rim of a wheel.

coil *v.* to wind in loops.
COIL *n.* a length wound in loops.

coin *n.* a metal piece of money.
COIN *v.* 1 to make into money; to mint.
2 to invent a new word or phrase.

coincide *v.* 1 to agree or fit exactly. 2 to happen at the same time. COINCIDENCE *n.*

cold *adj.* 1 low in temperature. 2 unfriendly.
COLD *n.* a chill.

collapse *n.* a sudden failure.
COLLAPSE *v.* to fall down; to give way.

collar *n.* a neckband.
COLLAR *v.* to seize; to grasp.

collect *v.* to gather together, to accumulate.

collection *n.* money collected; set of things collected.

collide *v.* to come into collision.

colon *n.* a punctuation mark (:).

colonel *n.* (pron. KER-nel) a senior military officer; ranked below a brigadier general.

colony *n.* 1 a settlement formed in a new land by emigrants, or a group of people forming a community in a town. 2 a settled swarm of insects, birds, etc.

color *v.* 1 to dye; to paint. 2 to exaggerate.
COLOR *n.* 1 any particular hue. 2 paint.

colossal *adj.* vast; very large.

colt *n.* a young horse. *fem.* FILLY.

column *n.* 1 an upright pillar. 2 a vertical row of numbers or printing. 3 troops in marching order.

coma *n.* a prolonged unconscious state.

comb *v.* 1 to draw a comb through. 2 to search very carefully.
COMB *n.* 1 a toothed implement for dressing the hair. 2 a cock's crest. 3 bees' storage place for honey.

combat *v.* to fight against; to oppose.
COMBAT *n.* a fight; a struggle.

combination *n.* a union of things or people.

combine *v.* (pron. kom-BINE) to unite; to join together.

come *v.* to move towards; to arrive.

comedian *n.* an actor who takes comic parts.
fem. COMEDIENNE.

comedy *n.* an amusing play, film or incident.

comet *n.* a spherical body, smaller than a planet, moving through space with a shining "tail" that always points towards the sun.

comfort *v.* to console; to cheer; to soothe.
COMFORT *n.* ease, contentment; consolation.

comfortable *adj.* cosy; happy; easy.

comic *adj.* funny; laughable.
COMIC *n.* a comic actor or person.

coming *adj.* approaching; future.

comma *n.* a punctuation mark indicating a short pause (,).

command *v.* to order; to be in command.
COMMAND *n.* an order.

commander *n.* someone who commands.

commando *n.* 1 a soldier trained for a special mission. 2 a small body of handpicked troops.

commence *v.* to begin.

comment *v.* to make remarks; to say.

commentary *n.* a series of comments.
pl. COMMENTARIES.

commentator *n.* someone who comments in written or spoken words.

commercial *adj.* concerning trade and commerce.

commit *v.* 1 to do; to perform (a crime).
2 to entrust (something to someone's care).
3 COMMIT TO to imprison.

committee *n.* a body of people chosen to deal with some special business.

common *adj.* 1 ordinary. 2 shared by many.
3 vulgar. COMMON *n.* an area of public land.

commonwealth *n.* a self-governing state or a group of such states.

commotion *n.* a noisy confusion; disturbance.

communicate *v.* to make known; to correspond with.

community *n.* a group of people living in one place. *pl.* COMMUNITIES.

compact *adj.* 1 closely packed. 2 concise.

companion *n.* a person who accompanies another; a friend; an associate.
COMPANIONSHIP *n.*

company *n.* a group of people; an assembly; a business. *pl.* COMPANIES.

compare *v.* to liken.

comparison *n.* likeness; similarity.

compass *n.* an instrument for showing magnetic north. COMPASS *v.* to go round; to encircle.

compasses *n. pl.* an instrument for drawing circles and arcs.

compel *v.* to force; to make. COMPELING *adj.*

compete *v.* to strive against others.

competition *n.* a contest; rivalry.
COMPETITOR *n.*

compile *v.* to collect; to make a book by collecting information. COMPILATION *n.*

complain *v.* to express dissatisfaction or discontent.

complaint *n.* 1 a grievance. 2 an ailment.

complete *adj.* whole; finished; thorough.
COMPLETE *v.* to finish.

complicate *v.* to entangle; to make difficult.

compliment *v.* to praise; to congratulate.
COMPLIMENT *n.* a tribute.

component *v.* one of the parts that forms a whole.

compose *v.* 1 to form by putting parts together. 2 to arrange.

composition *n.* 1 the act of composing. 2 a mixture.

compound *v.* (pron. kom-POUND) to mix; to combine.
COMPOUND *n.* (pron. KOM-pound) a mixture.

comprehension *n.* understanding.

comprehensive *adj.* wide; complete; all-embracing.

compress *v.* to press or squeeze tightly together; to reduce in length or size. COMPRESSION *n.*

compulsion *n.* a strong impulse.

compulsory *adj.* requiring to be done; enforced.

compute *v.* to calculate.

computer *n.* an electrical machine which can calculate and store and retrieve information.

concave *adj.* hollow, saucerlike in shape; opposite to convex.

conceal *v.* to hide; to keep secret.

concede *v.* to allow; to grant; to admit.

conceit *n.* vanity. CONCEITED *adj.*

conceive *v.* 1 to imagine; to think. 2 to become pregnant. CONCEIVABLE *adj.*

concentrate *v.* 1 to bring to one point. 2 to focus on. 3 to make stronger.

concern *v.* 1 CONCERN ONESELF IN to take interest in. 2 CONCERN ABOUT to be anxious about. CONCERN *n.* 1 interest. 2 anxiety.

concert *n.* a musical entertainment.

concise *adj.* brief; in a few words.

conclude *v.* 1 to finish; to bring to an end. 2 to decide.

conclusion *n.* 1 an end. 2 a decision.

concrete *adj.* real; definite.
CONCRETE *n.* a mixture of cement, gravel and water that is used in building.

concussion *n.* 1 a violent shock. 2 unconsciousness caused by a heavy blow.

condemn *v.* 1 to blame. 2 to sentence to punishment.

condensation *n.* 1 the changing of a vapor into a liquid. 2 reduction in volume or size.

condense *v.* 1 to reduce in size. 2 to change a vapor into a liquid.

condition *n.* state.

condone *v.* 1 to overlook an offense. 2 to forgive.

conduct *n.* 1 management. 2 behavior.
CONDUCT *v.* 1 to lead; to guide. 2 convey; to transmit. 3 to behave.

conductor *n.* 1 a guide; a leader. 2 a carrier; a transmitter.

cone *n.* 1 a solid body tapering from a circular base to a point. 2 the fruit of a conifer tree.
CONICAL *adj.* cone-shaped.

conference *n.* a meeting for discussion.

confess *v.* to make a confession; to admit.
CONFESSOR *n.*

confession *n.* an admission.

confidence *n.* trust; belief in; self-reliance.

confidential *adj.* secret; private; not to be told to others.

confinement *n.* 1 being confined; imprisonment. 2 being in bed for the birth of a child.

confirm *v.* 1 to strengthen. 2 to prove (something) to be true.

confirmation *n.* 1 proof; certainty. 2 admission to church membership.
CONFIRMATIVE *adj.*

confiscate *v.* 1 to take for public use. 2 to take forcibly.

conflict *n.* 1 a struggle. 2 a contest.
CONFLICT *v.* to disagree; to oppose.

conform *v.* to behave according to rule, custom or law; to comply

confront *v.* to face; to oppose.
CONFRONTING *adj.* CONFRONTATION *n.*

confuse *v.* 1 to mix up. 2 to bewilder.

confusion *n.* 1 a mixture; disorder. 2 embarrassment.

congratulate *v.* to offer good wishes to.

congregate *v.* to gather together; to assemble.

congregation *n.* a gathering of people for religious worship.

congress *n.* 1 an assembly of delegates. 2 Congress—the legislature of the United States of America.

conifer *n.* a cone-bearing tree. CONIFEROUS *adj.*

conjunction *n.* 1 a connection. 2 a word used to join sentences.

connect *v.* to join; to fasten; to link.
CONNECTION *n.*

conquer v. to defeat; to overcome.

conquest n. the act of conquering; capture.

conscience n. the sense of right and wrong.

conscientious adj. careful; thorough; honest.

conscious adj. awake; knowing; aware.

consecutive adj. following one after the other and in order.

consent v. to agree.
CONSENT n. permission; agreement.

conservation n. preservation; prevention of waste.

conservative adj. disliking change; moderate.
CONSERVATIVE n. a person or party opposed to rapid political and social change.

conserve v. to preserve; to keep from damage or loss. CONSERVE n. a preserve; jam.

consider v. to think about; to reflect; to allow for.

considerate adj. thoughtful for others.
CONSIDERATION n.

consignment n. a load; a shipment.

consist v. to be composed of.

console v. to give comfort to.
CONSOLATION n. comfort, relief.

consonant n. a letter denoting a speech sound other than a vowel.

conspiracy n. a plot. pl. CONSPIRACIES.
CONSPIRATOR n.

constant adj. unchanging; unceasing; faithful.

constantly adv. always; often.

constellation n. a group of stars forming a system and having a name.

consternation n. surprise and dismay.

constrict v. to press together tightly; to squeeze.

construct v. to make; to build; to fit together.

construction n. something constructed.

consult v. to seek information or advice.

consume v. 1 to use up. 2 to eat. 3 to destroy.

consumer n. a user; a buyer.

consumption n. the amount used.

contact v. to touch; to meet.
CONTACT n. an electrical connection.

contagious adj. catching; spread by touching.

contain v. to hold within; to enclose; to include.
CONTAINER n.

contaminate v. 1 to infect. 2 to make dirty or impure.

contemplate v. 1 to think about; to study. 2 to intend.

contempt n. scorn; disregard.

contend v. 1 to fight. 2 to argue. 3 to compete.
CONTENDER n.

content n. (pron. KON-tent) the amount contained.
CONTENT v. (pron. kon-TENT) to satisfy.
CONTENTED adj. satisfied; pleased.

contents n. pl. 1 that which is contained. 2 a list of matters written about in a book.

contest v. (pron. kon-TEST) to dispute; to compete; to argue against.
CONTEST n. (pron. KON-test) 1 a fight or struggle. 2 a competition.

continent n. one of the large land masses of the Earth's surface. CONTINENTAL adj.

continual adj. always happening; very frequent.

continuation n. an extension; an addition.

continue v. to go on; to prolong.

continuous adj. unbroken; non-stop.

contour n. an outline; a shape.

contractor n. a person who undertakes to do certain work or to supply goods.

contradict v. to deny (something); to speak against (someone). CONTRADICTION n.

contralto n. the lowest singing voice for women.

contrary adj. opposite; against.
CONTRARY n. the opposite or different opinion, intention or action.

contrast v. to compare so as to find or show differences.

contribute v. to give something; to help; to pay a share.

control v. to regulate; to guide
CONTROL n. authority; power.

convenient adj. handy; suitable.

convent n. religious community, esp. of nuns.

converge v. to approach a point from different directions, and as if to meet or join together.

conversation n. talk between two or more people.

convert v. (pron. kon-VERT) to change.
CONVERT n. (pron. KON-vert) one who has changed.

convex adj. curved outwards; the opposite of concave.

convict v. (pron. kon-VICT) to prove guilty.
CONVICT n. (pron. KON-vict) an imprisoned criminal.

conviction n. 1 a proving of guilt. 2 a firm belief.

convince v. to make someone feel sure; to satisfy.

convoy n. 1 a protected fleet of ships. 2 a column of vehicles.
CONVOY v. to guard on a journey.

cook *v.* to prepare food by heating.
COOK *n.* a person who cooks food.

cool *adj.* 1 slightly cold. 2 calm.
COOL *v.* 1 to make colder. 2 to become calmer.

cooly *adv.* calmly; without excitement.

cooperate (with) *v.* to work together; to help one another.

cooperation *n.* working together to help one another; mutual aid.

cooperative *adj.* ready to help.

cope *v.* to handle successfully.

copper *n.* a hard, reddish-brown metal.
COPPERY *adj.*

copy *v.* to imitate.
COPY *n.* an imitation. *pl.* COPIES.

cord *n.* strong, thick string, or rope.

cordon *n.* a line or ring of guards or police.
CORDON *v.* to close off an area.

core *n.* the inner part of anything.

cork *n.* the bark of the cork-oak and the stopper made from it.
CORK *v.* to stop or plug with a cork.

cormorant *n.* a diving sea-bird.

corn *n.* 1 the seeds of wheat, corn, barley, oats, etc.; cereals. 2 the kernels of sweet corn.
3 a painful hard growth on a toe.

corner *n.* the place where two lines, walls, streets, etc., meet.
CORNER *v.* to drive into a trap.

coronation *n.* the ceremony of crowning a king or queen.

corporal *n.* a non commissioned military officer.
CORPORAL *adj.* bodily.

corporation *n.* 1 a large trading concern. 2 the body of persons governing a city or town.

corpse *n.* a dead body.

correct *adj.* right; true; accurate.
CORRECT *v.* 1 to put right. 2 to mark for errors.
3 to punish.

correction *n.* 1 the correcting of something.
2 punishment.

correspond *v.* 1 to be similar (to).
2 CORRESPOND WITH to exchange letters.

correspondence *n.* 1 similarity. 2 letters.

corridor *n.* a passageway.

corrode *v.* to wear away; to destroy gradually.
CORROSION *n.* CORROSIVE *adj.*

corrupt *v.* 1 to decay. 2 to make another person dishonest. CORRUPT *adj.* 1 rotten. 2 dishonest.

cosmic rays *n. pl.* radioactive particles which reach the Earth from outer space.

cosmonaut *n.* a person who travels in space (*R*); an astronaut.

cost *v.* to have a price or value.
COST *n.* the price.

costly *adj.* highly-priced; expensive.

costume *n.* style of dress.

cosy *adj.* snug; comfortable.

cottage *n.* a small house, esp. in the country.

cotton *n.* 1 a plant bearing soft, white down.
2 thread or cloth made from this.

cough *n.* a sudden, noisy outburst of air from the lungs. COUGH *v.*

council *n.* a group of people appointed or elected to advise and make decisions.

councillor *n.* a member of a council.

counsel *v.* to advise.
COUNSEL *n.* 1 a lawyer, a barrister. 2 advice.

counselor *n.* an adviser; someone who counsels.

count *v.* to number; to calculate; to matter.
COUNT *n.* the act of counting.

counter *v.* to oppose.
COUNTER *n.* 1 a serving point in a shop or bank.
2 a small disc or token used in scoring.

countless *adj.* too many to count; very many.

country *n.* 1 any separate land or nation.
2 rural areas. *pl.* COUNTRIES.

county *n.* a division of a state or country.

couple *v.* to link two things together.
COUPLE *n.* a pair; two of a kind.

coupon *n.* a ticket exchangeable for something.

courage *n.* bravery; lack of fear.

courageous *adj.* brave; fearless.
COURAGEOUSLY *adv.*

courier *n.* a messenger.

course *n.* 1 the path or direction in which anything moves. 2 a part of a meal. 3 a line of bricks or stones in a wall.

court *v.* to try to please.
COURT *n.* 1 a place of justice. 2 a ruler's palace.
3 a yard. 4 a quadrangle for games such as tennis.

courteous *adj.* respectful; polite; considerate.

courtesy *n.* polite and considerate behavior.

cousin *n.* the son or daughter of an uncle or aunt.

cover *v.* 1 to spread over. 2 to hide.
3 to include.
COVER *n.* 1 something that covers. 2 a shelter or hiding-place.

cow *n.* female of cattle, elephants, whales, etc.
COW *v.* to make afraid; to intimidate.

coward *n.* a person without courage.

crab *n.* an edible shellfish with five pairs of legs.

crack *v.* 1 to split or break apart. 2 to make a sharp, snapping noise.
CRACK *n.* 1 a small opening or split. 2 a snapping noise. CRACKED *adj.*

cradle *n.* 1 a rocking bed for a baby. 2 a frame used as a support.
CRADLE *v.* to lay or rock in a cradle or in the arms.

craft *n.* 1 a skill. 2 a ship or an aircraft. 3 a trade.

craftily *adv.* cunningly.

crafty *adj.* sly; cunning.

cram *v.* to pack tightly; to overfill.

cramp *v.* to restrict; to tighten.
CRAMP *n.* a sudden, severe pain in a muscle.

crane *n.* 1 a machine for raising and lowering heavy weights. 2 a long-necked wading bird.

crank *v.* to wind; to turn a handle.
CRANK *n.* 1 a bend; turn. 2 a person with strange ideas.

crash *n.* 1 the loud noise of things breaking. 2 a sudden failure or ruin, esp. in business.
CRASH *v.* 1 to break noisily. 2 to fail. 3 to collide.

crater *n.* 1 the mouth of a volcano. 2 a hollow in the ground caused by an explosion.

crave *v.* to beg for; to long for.

crawl *v.* to creep on hands and knees.
CRAWL *n.* a swimming stroke.

crayon *n.* 1 a pencil or stick of colored chalk. 2 a drawing made with crayons.

craze *n.* a popular fashion; a fad.

crazy *adj.* mad; foolish.

creak *n.* a sharp, grating sound.
CREAK *v.* to make such a noise.

cream *n* 1 the rich, fatty substance which rises to the surface on milk. 2 the best part of anything.
CREAMY *adj.*

crease *n.* a line or mark made by folding.

create *v.* 1 to make; to invent. 2 to make a fuss.
CREATION *n.*

creature *n.* a living person or animal.

credit *n.* 1 a good reputation. 2 allowing a deferred payment. CREDIT *v.* to believe; to trust.

creditor *n.* a person to whom a debt is owed.

creek *n.* a narrow coastal inlet; a small stream.

creep *v.* 1 to move close to the ground. 2 to move silently on tiptoe. 3 to grow along the ground or up a wall.

cremate *v.* to burn (a body) to ashes.

crescent *adj.* shaped like a new moon.

crest *n.* 1 a tuft or comb on a bird's head. 2 a design on a coat of arms. 3 the top of a hill or wave.

crevice *n.* a crack or narrow opening, esp. in rock.

crew *n.* 1 the people manning a ship, aircraft or train. 2 a gang; a mob.

crib *n.* a young child's bed; a manger.
CRIB *v.* to cheat; to copy unfairly.

cricket *n.* 1 a small jumping, chirping insect. 2 an outdoor game for two teams, played with ball, bats and wickets.

crime *n.* an offense or offenses against the law; sin.

criminal *adj.* concerned with crime.
CRIMINAL *n.* someone who has committed a crime.

crimson *adj.* a deep red color.

cringe *v.* to crouch; to shrink from in fear.

cripple *v.* to disable; to ruin.

crisis *n.* a turning point; a time of emergency. *pl.* CRISES (pron. CRY-sees).

critic *n.* a person who examines and judges; a faultfinder.

criticism *n.* an opinion; a judgment; disapproval.

criticize *v.* to examine and judge; to find fault with.

crocodile *n.* a large four-footed aquatic reptile with a scaly skin (see ALLIGATOR).

crook *n.* 1 a hook; a hooked staff. 2 a criminal.

crooked *adj.* 1 bent. 2 dishonest.

crop *v.* 1 to harvest. 2 to cut short.
CROP *n.* 1 the produce of field or farm. 2 a riding whip. 3 the first stomach of many birds.

cross *n.* 1 anything X-shaped. 2 a monument.
CROSS *v.* 1 to pass from one side to the other. 2 to oppose. 3 to make angry.
CROSS *adj.* annoyed. CROSSLY *adv.*

crouch *v.* to stoop with the knees bent; to bend down. CROUCH *n.* stooping; bending.

crow *v.* 1 to boast. 2 to make a sound like a cock.
CROW *n.* 1 a large black bird. 2 a cock's cry.

crowd *n.* a large number of persons or things.
CROWD *v.* 1 to pack closely together; to cram. 2 to gather in a large number.

crown *n.* 1 the headdress worn by a king or queen on special occasions. 2 the top of many objects.
CROWN *v.* 1 to place a crown on. 2 to reward.

crucify v. to put to death on a cross.

crude adj. raw; rough; coarse. CRUDELY adv.

cruel adj. liking to cause pain. CRUELLY adv.

cruelty n. cruel action or behavior.

cruise v. to sail about; to travel at random.
CRUISE n. a sea voyage for pleasure

cruiser n. a fast warship.

crumb n. a small fragment, esp. of bread.
CRUMB v. to cover with crumbs.

crumble v. to break into crumbs.

crumple v. to crush out of shape.
CRUMPLE n. a wrinkle; a crease.

crunch v. 1 to crush with the teeth. 2 to grind
underfoot.
CRUNCH n. the noise of chewing or grinding.

crusade v. to fight or campaign for a cause.
CRUSADE n. 1 a war between Christians and
Muslims in the Middle Ages. 2 activity in
support of a cause.

crush v. 1 to squeeze together or squash.
2 to overcome; to ruin.
CRUSH n. a closely-packed crowd.

crust n. a hard coating, rind or shell.

cry v. 1 to shed tears. 2 to shout; to yell.
CRY n. a sob; a shout. pl. CRIES.

crying adj. 1 shedding tears. 2 calling for notice.
CRYING n. the act or sound of crying.

crystal n. 1 a glasslike stone having all its faces
flat. 2 a gem.
CRYSTAL adj. clear; transparent.

cub n. the young of such animals as the bear,
fox, lion, etc.

cube n. a solid body with six equal square sides
or faces.

cubic adj. 1 having the shape of a cube.
2 having volume, capacity.

cubicle n. a small partitioned compartment.

cuckoo n. a bird that lays its eggs in the nests of
other birds.

cucumber n. a long, green fruit eaten as salad.

cue n. 1 a sign; a hint. 2 a tapering stick used in
playing billiards and pool.

cuff n. 1 a slap. 2 the end of a sleeve.
CUFF v. to strike with the open hand.

culprit n. an offender; a guilty person.

cultivate v. 1 to prepare the ground and grow
crops. 2 to develop or improve. 3 to give
attention to. CULTIVATION n.

cumulus n. white, woolly clouds heaped one
above the other. pl. CUMULI.

cunning adj. skillful; crafty in a sly way.
CUNNING n. skill; deceit.

cup n. 1 a small drinking vessel, usually with a
handle. 2 ornamental cup used as a prize or
trophy.
CUP v. to place the hands in the form of a cup.

curator n. a person in charge of a museum, an
art gallery, etc.

curb v. to check; to restrain.
CURB n. a check; a bridle. CURBING adj.

cure v. 1 to heal; to restore. 2 to preserve food
by salting and drying.
CURE n. 1 a remedy. 2 a recovery. CURABLE adj.

curfew n. an order to remain indoors after a
stated time.

curiosity n. 1 eagerness to find out.
2 inquisitiveness. 3 a strange or rare thing.
pl. CURIOSITIES.

curious adj. 1 inquisitive. 2 eager to know.
3 strange or odd. CURIOUSLY adv.

curl v. to twist into ringlets; to bend into a curve.
CURL n. 1 a ringlet. 2 a curving line or
movement.

currency n. money in use in a country.

current n. the flowing of a liquid (stream) or air
(wind) or of electricity.
CURRENT adj. 1 popular; in circulation.
2 the present time; now.

curriculum n. a set course of study at a school or
college.

curry n. a seasoning of mixed spices; a dish
spiced with curry.

curse v. 1 to wish evil upon; to swear.
2 to harm. CURSE n. 1 an utterance wishing evil.
2 a great evil (e.g. warfare, epidemic. etc.)
causing suffering.

curtain n. 1 a cloth hung to screen a window.
2 the cloth concealing the stage from the
audience in a theatre.
CURTAIN v. to enclose or provide with a curtain.

curve n. a line that bends without angles.
CURVE v. to bend or shape to form a curve.

cushion n. a bag stuffed with soft material, a
pillow. CUSHION v. to lessen a shock or blow.

custody n. 1 care; safe keeping.
2 imprisonment before trial.

custom n. a habit; usual practice.
CUSTOMS n. pl. a tax on imports.

customer n. a regular buyer; a client.

cut v. to open, divide or slit with anything sharp.
CUT n. 1 a wound from a sharp edge.
2 a piece of meat.

cuticle n. the outer layer of skin; skin at base of
finger-nail or toe-nail.

cutlery n. knives, forks and spoons.

cycle *n.* 1 a series of events that is repeated constantly. 2 a bicycle, tricycle or motorcycle. CYCLE *v.* to ride a bicycle. CYCLIST *n.*

cyclone *n.* a violent storm in which the wind moves round a center of low atmospheric pressure.

cylinder *n.* 1 a roll-shaped object. 2 part of a gasoline or diesel engine.

cymbals *n. pl.* a pair of round brass plates used as a musical instrument.

D

dab *v.* to pat or touch gently and quickly. DAB *n.* 1 a gentle pat. 2 a small blob or smear. 3 a flat fish.

daffodil *n.* a yellow spring flower, grown from a bulb.

dagger *n.* a weapon with a short, pointed blade.

daily *adj.* every day. DAILY *n.* a newspaper published every weekday. *pl.* DAILIES.

dainty *adj.* small and delicate; pretty. DAINTY *n.* a delicacy.

dairy *n.* a building for keeping, processing or selling milk. *pl.* DAIRIES.

daisy *n.* a common wild flower with small white petals and a yellow center.

dam *v.* to hold back by means of a dam. DAM *n.* 1 a bank or wall to hold back water. 2 a mother, esp. of animals.

damage *v.* to cause injury; to hurt. DAMAGE *n.* injury, breakage or loss.

damp *n.* DAMPNESS *n.* moisture; slight wetness. DAMP *v.* 1 to moisten. 2 to discourage.

dance *v.* 1 to move rhythmically to music. 2 to leap or jump about in a lively manner. DANCE *n.* 1 the act of dancing. 2 a social gathering at which people dance. DANCER *n.*

dandelion *n.* a yellow-flowered wild plant.

danger *n.* a risk or peril.

dangerous *adj.* unsafe; very risky. DANGEROUSLY *adv.*

Danish *adj.* of or belonging to Denmark. DANISH *n.* language of Denmark; the Danes.

dare *v.* to attempt; to challenge. DARE *n.* a challenge.

daring *adj.* bold; fearless. DARING *n.* boldness.

dark *adj.* without light; gloomy.

darkness *n.* 1 absence of light. 2 night.

dart *v.* to move quickly and suddenly. DART *n.* 1 a quick, sudden movement. 2 a small arrow thrown by hand.

dash *v.* 1 to rush suddenly. 2 to throw violently. DASH *n.* 1 a rush. 2 a small amount. 3 a punctuation mark (-).

data *n. pl.* facts; information.

date *n.* 1 the day, month and year. 2 the time of an event. 3 the fruit of the date-palm. DATE *v.* to give a date to.

daughter *n.* a person's female child.

dawn *v.* 1 to begin to grow light. 2 to grow clear. DAWN *n.* 1 the first light of day; daybreak. 2 a beginning.

day *n.* 1 the time between sunrise and sunset. 2 the twenty-four hours from one midnight to the next.

daze *v.* to confuse; to bewilder. DAZE *n.* a dazed state. DAZED *adj.*

dazzle *v.* 1 to blind with light. 2 to confuse. DAZZLE *n.* a confusing or blinding light.

dead *adj.* no longer alive; lifeless. DEAD *n. pl.* persons no longer alive.

deaf *adj.* unable or unwilling to hear. DEAFNESS *n.* inability to hear.

deal *v.* 1 to trade or do business with. 2 to hand out. 3 to deliver. DEAL *n.* a business arrangement.

dear *adj.* 1 much loved; lovable. 2 costly; expensive. DEAR *n.* beloved; favorite.

death *n.* the end of life.

debate *v.* 1 to discuss. 2 to consider alternatives. DEBATE *n.* a discussion; a public argument.

debris *n.* remains of something broken to pieces; wreckage; trash.

debt *n.* 1 money owing. 2 a duty or obligation. DEBTOR *n.*

decade *n.* a period of ten years.

decapitate *v.* to cut off the head of.

decay *v.* to rot; to wither. DECAY *n.* a wasting away; a ruined state. DECAYED *adj.*

deceit *n.* misrepresentation; trick.

December *n.* the twelfth month of the year.

decent *adj.* 1 proper; respectable. 2 satisfactory; passable. DECENTLY *adv.*

deception *n.* 1 a trick; a fraud. 2 the act of deceiving.

deciduous *adj.* 1 shedding periodically. 2 losing leaves annually.

decimal *adj.* numbered by tens or tenths. DECIMAL *n.* a fraction in terms of tenths.

decipher *v.* 1 to translate (a secret message). 2 to find the meaning of.

decision *n.* 1 the act of deciding. 2 conclusion reached. 3 firmness.

deck *n.* the floor of a ship.
DECK *v.* to decorate; to adorn.

declare *v.* 1 to announce or make known publicly. 2 to state at customs the goods carried. DECLARATION *n.*

decline *v.* 1 to refuse. 2 to slope down. 3 to weaken or worsen.
DECLINE *n.* 1 a downward slope. 2 a weakening.

decorate *v.* 1 to make beautiful. 2 to paint or wallpaper. 3 to give a medal or title. DECORATOR *n.*

decrease *v.* to make or become less.
DECREASE *n.* a reduction; a lessening.

dedicate *v.* to devote to a particular purpose; to make sacred.

deduct *v.* to subtract; to take away.

deduction *n.* 1 the amount taken away. 2 the conclusion reached by reasoning.

deed *n.* 1 an action; something done. 2 a legal document.

deep *adj.* 1 reaching far down or far back. 2 intense or strong. 3 secretive; hard to understand. THE DEEP *n.* the ocean.

deer *n.* a swift-running, cud-chewing, cloven-hoofed, four-footed mammal (the males have horns). DEER *pl.*

defeat *v.* to beat in battle or contest; to conquer. DEFEAT *n.* the loss of a battle or contest.

defect *n.* (pron. DE-fect) a fault; a flaw. DEFECT *v.* (pron. de-FECT) to desert.

defend *v.* 1 to guard or protect against attack. 2 to argue in favor of.

defense *n.* 1 a means of protection. 2 fortifications. 3 argument against an accusation.

defiant *adj.* openly disobedient; challenging. DEFIANTLY *adv.*

definite *adj.* exact, distinct; not doubtful. DEFINITELY *adv.*

definition *n.* 1 an explanation of the exact meaning of a word. 2 clearness; sharpness.

deflect *v.* to turn (something) aside or to change its course.

deft *adj.* quick and skillful. DEFTLY *adv.*

defy *v.* to challenge; to resist openly.

degree *n.* 1 a unit of measurement of temperature, angles, etc. 2 a step or stage. 3 a qualification given by a college or university.

delay *v.* to postpone; to hinder.
DELAY *n.* a postponement; a hindrance.

delegate *v.* 1 to appoint and send as a representative. 2 to entrust (duties or responsibilities) to others.
DELEGATE *n.* a person appointed to represent.

delegation *n.* 1 a group of delegates. 2 the act of delegating.

delete *v.* to erase or cross out. DELETION *n.*

deliberate *adj.* 1 intentional; done on purpose. DELIBERATE *v.* to discuss or think over carefully.

delicate *adj.* 1 fine; dainty; not strong. 2 sensitive. DELICATELY *adv.*

delicious *adj.* very pleasing to taste and eat. DELICIOUSLY *adv.*

delight *v.* 1 to give pleasure to (someone) or to receive pleasure from. 2 DELIGHT IN to take pleasure in. DELIGHT *n.* great pleasure; joy.

deliver *v.* 1 to hand over. 2 to rescue; to set free. 3 to help in the birth of.

delivery *n.* the act of delivering.

delta *n.* a triangle of land formed by the mouths of a large river.

deluge *n.* 1 a great flood or downpour. 2 a great quantity.
DELUGE *v.* to overwhelm with a great quantity.

demand *v.* to claim (something from someone) as a right; to ask firmly (for).
DEMAND *n.* an urgent request or claim.

democracy *n.* government by representatives freely elected by the people.

demolish *v.* to destroy; to pull down.

demonstrate *v.* 1 to show clearly; to prove. 2 to take part in a demonstration.

demonstration *n.* 1 a practical display or explanation. 2 an organized expression of opinion or feeling by a procession or meeting.

den *n.* 1 a wild animal's lair. 2 a small private room or study.

denial *n.* 1 the refusal of a request. 2 a contradiction.

denominator *n.* the number below the line in a fraction.

denote *v.* 1 to stand for or to mean. 2 to indicate.

dense *adj.* 1 closely-packed. 2 stupid.

density *n.* 1 proportion of mass to volume. 2 crowded state.

dent *n.* a hollow in a surface caused by a blow or pressure. DENT *v.* to make a dent.

dentist *n.* a person qualified and skilled in the care of the teeth. DENTAL *adj.*

deny *v.* 1 to say something is untrue. 2 to refuse a request.

depart *v.* to go away; to leave; to set out.

department *n.* a separate part, division or section.

departure *n.* going away; leaving; setting out.

depend on or **upon** *v.* to rely on; to trust.

deposit *v.* 1 to put or set something down. 2 to place money in a bank. 3 to give in part payment.
DEPOSIT *n.* 1 a layer of solid matter. 2 money placed in a bank. 3 money given as part payment.

depress *v.* 1 to make sad or lower (a person's spirit). 2 to press down or in.

depression *n.* 1 mood of sadness or low spirits. 2 a hollow place on a surface. 3 an area of low atmospheric pressure. 4 a low level of trade, economy and employment.

deprive *v.* to take away (something) from (someone); to prevent (someone) from having.
DEPRIVATION *n.*

depth *n.* distance downwards or inwards.

deputy *n.* a person acting in place of another.

derelict *adj.* forsaken; abandoned.
DERELICT *n.* abandoned property, esp. a ship.

descend *v.* 1 to come or go down; to climb down. 2 to pass from one generation to another.

descendant *n.* a person or thing descended from another.

describe *v.* 1 to give a description of. 2 to mark out.

description *n.* a written or spoken account or report.

desert *v.* (pron. di-ZERT) to abandon; to run away from.
DESERT *n.* (pron. DEZ-ert) an area of dry, barren wasteland.

deserted *adj.* abandoned; forsaken.

deserve *v.* to earn; to be worthy of.

design *v.* to make a plan or pattern of something.
DESIGN *n.* 1 a plan; a pattern. 2 an intention.

desirable *adj.* worth having; sought after; pleasing.

desire *v.* to long or wish for.
DESIRE *n.* a longing; a wish.

desolate *adj.* 1 alone; solitary. 2 uninhabited; deserted. 3 neglected; dreary. 4 forlorn; wretched.

despair *v.* to give up hope.
DESPAIR *n.* loss of hope.

desperate *adj.* 1 almost without hope. 2 reckless.

despise *v.* to feel contempt for.

despite *prep.* in spite of.

dessert *n.* fruit or sweet dish served at the end of a meal.

destination *n.* the place to which a person or thing is going.

destitute *adj.* living in poverty without any means of support.
DESTITUTION *n.* poverty, need.

destroy *v.* 1 to break up; to spoil. 2 to kill.

detach *v.* to unfasten, to disconnect.

detail *n.* a small part; an item.
DETAIL *v.* to give all the facts.

detain *v.* 1 to keep back; to keep waiting. 2 to keep in custody.

detect *v.* to discover; to find out.

detective *n.* a police or private investigator.

detergent *n.* a chemical preparation used for washing and cleaning.

deteriorate *v.* to become worse.

determine *v.* to decide; to settle.
DETERMINED *adj.*

detest *v.* to hate or dislike deeply.

detonate *v.* to explode or cause to explode.
DETONATION *n.*

detour *n.* a roundabout way; a deviation.

devastate *v.* 1 to lay waste. 2 to destroy completely. DEVASTATING *adj.*

develop *v.* to grow or improve gradually.

development *n.* 1 gradual growth. 2 new facts affecting a situation. 3 a planned area of housing or buildings.

device *n.* 1 an invention; a contrivance. 2 a plan; a trick. 3 an emblem.

devil *n.* 1 an evil spirit. 2 a wicked person.

devote (to) *v.* 1 to give (one's) full attention to. 2 to dedicate (oneself) to.

devour *v.* to eat greedily; to consume.

dew *n.* drops of moisture which form on the ground, leaves and grass during the night when water vapor in cold air condenses.

diagnose *v.* 1 to discover the nature of an illness from a study of the symptoms. 2 to trace the cause of any trouble.

diagonal *n.* a straight line drawn between opposite corners.

diagram *n.* a plan or sketch drawn to explain something.

dial *n.* the face of a watch, clock or instrument.
DIAL *v.* to call a number on a telephone.

dialect *n.* a way of speech used in a particular district or part of a country.

diameter *n.* 1 a straight line passing from side to side through the center of a circle. 2 the length of such a line.

diamond *n.* an extremely hard and precious stone.

diary *n.* a daily record of events.

dictate *v.* 1 to say or read aloud for another person to write down or record. 2 to command or give orders firmly. DICTATION *n.* DICTATOR *n.*

dictionary *n*. a book listing words in alphabetical order with their meanings.

die *v*. 1 to cease living. 2 to wither.
DIE *n*. a block for making coins or patterns.

diesel *n*. 1 an engine using diesel oil.
2 a locomotive driven by a diesel engine.

diet *n*. 1 the kind of food normally eaten by a particular person, community or animal.
2 a set course of food, usually arranged for medical reasons or to lose weight.
DIET *v*. to eat certain kinds of food only.

differ *v*. 1 to be different. 2 to disagree.

difference *n*. 1 anything which makes one thing unlike another. 2 a quarrel or disagreement.

different *adj*. unlike; not the same.

difficult *adj*. 1 not easy; hard to do. 2 hard to get along with.

difficulty *n*. 1 anything hard to do or understand.
2 a problem or an obstacle.
pl. DIFFICULTIES.

dig *v*. 1 to turn soil with a spade or machine.
2 to prod or to poke.
DIG *n*. an archaeological excavation.

digest *v*. 1 to dissolve (food in the stomach).
2 to think over carefully.
DIGEST *n*. a short version.

digit *n*. 1 any of the numbers from 0 to 9.
2 a finger or toe.

digital *adj*. concerning or using digits, as in a computer.

dignified *adj*. noble; stately; showing dignity.

dignity *n*. worthiness; excellence; high rank and position.

diligent *adj*. hard-working; persevering.

dilute *v*. to weaken the strength of (esp. a liquid by adding another liquid). DILUTION *n*.

dim *adj*. not bright or clear; faint, indistinct.
DIM *v*. to make or become dim.
DIMLY *adv*. faintly; indistinctly.

dimension *n*. the measurement of length, breadth (width) or depth.

diminish *v*. to make, or become, less.
DIMINISHED *adj*.

dimple *n*. a small hollow in the cheek or chin.
DIMPLE *v*. to mark with dimples.

dinner *n*. the main meal of the day.

dinosaur *n*. any of various huge prehistoric reptiles.

dip *v*. 1 to put in and out of a liquid; to immerse. 2 to slope downwards.
DIP *n*. 1 a quick immersion. 2 a downward slope.

diploma *n*. a certificate confirming that a person has graduated from a school or has gained an honor or a privilege.

diplomacy *n*. skill in negotiating or managing.

diplomat *n*. a skilled negotiator, esp. for a government.

diplomatic *adj*. tactful; skilled in diplomacy.

direct *adj*. 1 straight, straightforward,
2 outspoken.
DIRECT *v*. 1 to aim. 2 to give directions.

direction *n*. 1 the way anything goes or moves.
2 an order or a command. 3 instructions.

directly *adv*. 1 in a direct manner. 2 at once; immediately.

director *n*. a person who directs.

directory *n*. a book in which names are listed, in alphabetical order, with addresses, e.g. a telephone directory. *pl*. DIRECTORIES.

dirt *n*. mud, earth, filth; anything unclean.
DIRTY *adj*.

disability *n*. a thing that disables or disqualifies.
pl. DISABILITIES.

disable *v*. to make powerless; to cripple.

disadvantage *n*. an unfavorable circumstance; a drawback.

disagree *v*. to fail to agree; to differ; to quarrel.

disagreeable *adj*. unpleasant; bad-tempered.

disagreement *n*. a failure to agree; a difference; a quarrel.

disappear *v*. to go out of sight, to become obsolete; to cease to exist.

disappearance *n*. vanishing; going out of existence.

disappoint *v*. to fail to fulfill hopes and desires of (someone).

disappointing *adj*. causing disappointment; failing to please.

disapprove *n*. to show dislike; to have a poor opinion of.

disarm *v*. to take someone's weapons away; to win over.

disaster *n*. a great misfortune; a sudden calamity.

disc; disk *n*. 1 a flat circular object. 2 a plastic disc, with a recording on it, for a record player or disc player.

discard *v*. to throw away; to reject.

discharge *v*. 1 to dismiss; to release. 2 to fire a gun. DISCHARGE *n*. 1 dismissal. 2 gunfire.

disciple *n*. a follower; someone who believes in a person's teaching.

discipline *n*. obedience to orders; training and self-control.
DISCIPLINE *v*. to bring under control; to train; to teach.

disclose *v*. to show; to uncover; to reveal.

discomfort *n.* lack of comfort; uneasiness.

disconnect *v.* to remove a connection; to detach. DISCONNECTED *adj.*

discontinue *v.* to stop; to bring to an end. DISCONTINUED *adj.* DISCONTINUANCE *n.*

discount *n.* (pron. DIS-count) an amount deducted from an account.
DISCOUNT *v.* (pron. dis-COUNT) to reduce; to disregard.

discourage *v.* to try to prevent; to dishearten. DISCOURAGEMENT *n.*

discover *v.* to find out; to find by chance.

discovery *n.* 1 anything discovered. 2 the act of discovering.

discredit *v.* 1 to disbelieve. 2 to dishonor. DISCREDIT *n.*

discreet *adj.* careful in speech and action. DISCREETLY *adv.*

discretion *n.* 1 sound judgment. 2 freedom to act as one thinks fit.

discriminate (between) *v.* to make or see differences (between); to show unfair preference for.

discrimination *v.* 1 good judgment. 2 a difference in the way two persons are treated.

discuss *v.* to talk about; to debate.

discussion *n.* a conversation or debate on a subject.

disease *n.* 1 an illness. 2 an unhealthy condition of the body or mind, or of plants, etc.

disengage *v.* 1 to release. 2 to free or detach something.

disfigure *v.* to spoil the appearance or beauty of.

disgrace *v.* to bring shame upon; to dishonor. DISGRACE *n.* loss of favor, dishonor.

disgraceful *adj.* shameful; causing disgrace.

disguise *v.* to alter the appearance of (someone or something) in order to deceive; to hide the truth of.

disgust *v.* to cause a strong feeling of dislike. DISGUST *n.* a strong feeling of dislike.

dish *n.* 1 a plate for holding food. 2 a particular kind of food. DISH *v.* to serve out.

dishonest *adj.* not honest.

disintegrate *v.* to fall to pieces; to break up; to crumble.

dislike *v.* to have no liking for; to disapprove of. DISLIKE *n.* displeasure; disapproval.

dislocate *v.* to put out of joint; to put out of order.

dismal *adj.* gloomy; cheerless; sad.

dismay *v.* to fill with alarm. DISMAY *n.* a feeling of alarm and consternation.

dismiss *v.* to send away; to discharge. DISMISSED *adj.*

disobedient *adj.* refusing or failing to obey.

disobey *v.* to refuse or ignore an instruction or order.

disorder *v.* to upset or confuse. DISORDER *n.* 1 lack of order; confusion. 2 illness.

disperse *v.* to scatter; to go in different directions. DISPERSED *adj.*

display *v.* to show; to exhibit. DISPLAY *n.* a show or an exhibition.

dispute *n.* an argument; a quarrel. DISPUTE *v.* to argue; to quarrel.

disqualify *v.* to take away permission or qualification. DISQUALIFIED *adj.*

disregard *v.* to ignore. DISREGARD *n.* lack of attention.

disrepair *n.* bad condition due to lack of repairs.

disrupt *v.* to break up; to cause confusion.

dissatisfaction *n.* discontent. DISSATISFIED *adj.*

dissect *v.* to cut up for examination. DISSECTION *n.*

dissolve *v.* 1 to break up or melt in a liquid. 2 to bring to an end.

dissuade *v.* to advise or persuade (someone) against doing (something).

distance *n.* 1 the space between two points. 2 a faroff place or point.

distant *adj.* 1 far away; remote. 2 shy; reserved in manner.

distaste *n.* dislike; disgust. DISTASTEFUL *adj.*

distill *v.* to condense the vapor from a heated liquid.

distinct *adj.* 1 clearly seen or heard; plain. 2 separate; different.

distinction *n.* 1 a difference between things. 2 a mark of honor or outstanding merit.

distinguish *v.* 1 to make or notice a difference (between one thing and another). 2 DISTINGUISH ONESELF to gain distinction (for oneself).

distinguished *adj.* famous; important.

distort *v.* 1 to turn or twist out of shape. 2 to misrepresent. DISTORTED *adj.*

distract *v.* to draw a person's attention from one thing to another. DISTRACTED *adj.*

distress *v.* to cause pain or sorrow to. DISTRESS *n.* 1 a great pain, sorrow or worry. 2 danger or difficulty.

distribute *v.* to give out to or share (something) among a number of people.

distribution *n.* distributing; sharing.

distributor *n.* a person who distributes or shares.

district *n.* an area or a region; part of a country or town.

distrust *v.* to have no trust in; to doubt.
DISTRUST *n.* lack of trust; doubt.

disturb *v.* 1 to upset the quiet or calm of. 2 to worry; to bother.

disturbance *n.* the act of disturbing; disorder.

ditch *n.* a narrow trench.
DITCH *v.* to make or repair ditches.

ditto *n.* the same; as before; also.

dive *v.* 1 to plunge head first into (water). 2 to descend underwater. 3 to descend steeply and fast (bird or aircraft). DIVER *n.*

diversion *n.* 1 an alternative route. 2 an amusement or a relaxation.

divert *v.* 1 to turn (something) in another direction. 2 to amuse or entertain.

divide *v.* 1 to separate or cut into parts. 2 to find out how many times one number contains another.

dividend *n.* 1 a share of the profit from a business. 2 a number that is to be divided.

divine *adj.* belonging to God; holy.
DIVINE *v.* to predict; to discover.

division *n.* 1 the process of dividing. 2 a separate section; a barrier.

divorce *n.* 1 the legal ending of a marriage. 2 separation.
DIVORCE *v.* 1 to end a marriage by law. 2 to separate.

divulge *v.* to make (something) known; to reveal a secret.

dizziness *n.* faintness; giddiness. DIZZY *adj.*
DIZZILY *adv.*

do *v.* 1 to perform or carry out (any action). 2 to make or produce. 3 to be suitable.

docile *adj.* tame; easily managed; obedient.

dock *n.* the place where ships berth to load and unload or to be repaired.
DOCK *v.* to bring a ship into dock; to moor one spacecraft to another when in orbit.

doctor *n.* 1 a person qualified to treat the sick and injured; a medical practitioner. 2 a person who has received the highest degree from a university.

document *n.* a paper containing written information or evidence.

documentary *adj.* in the form of a document.
DOCUMENTARY *n.* a television program or film which deals with facts about a subject.

dodge *v.* to avoid (something) by moving quickly.
DODGE *n.* 1 a movement to avoid something. 2 a trick.

doe *n.* the female of many animals, such as deer, rabbit, etc.

dog *n.* a common domestic animal, related to the fox and wolf. DOG *v.* to follow closely.

doldrums *n. pl.* 1 the equatorial ocean region where there is little wind. 2 low spirits.

doll *n.* a toy in the form of a baby or person.

dollar *n.* a unit of money ($1) equivalent to 100 cents, in the U.S., Canada, Australia and other countries.

dolphin *n.* a marine, fishlike mammal similar to a porpoise.

dome *n.* the top of a tower or roof in the shape of a half-sphere.

domestic *adj.* 1 to do with the family or home. 2 tame (domestic animals).

dominate *v.* to have a very strong influence over; to rule over. DOMINATED *adj.*

dominion *n.* a country or territory under the control of a king, queen, lord or government.

donate *v.* to give (something) to someone; to make a gift. DONATION *n.*

donkey *n.* 1 an ass, which is a long-eared, horse-like animal. 2 an obstinate or stupid person.

doodle *v.* to draw or scribble aimlessly.

doom *v.* to pass sentence on; to condemn; to ruin. DOOM *n.* judgment; ruin; fate.
DOOMED *adj.* ruined; condemned; fated.

door *n.* a hinged or sliding barrier of wood, metal or glass at the entrance to a building, room, closet, etc., which can be opened and closed.

dope *n.* a drug that affects the mind or senses.
DOPE *v.* to drug.

dormitory *n.* a large bedroom with many beds.
pl. DORMITORIES.

dose *n.* the amount of medicine to be taken at one time. DOSE *v.* to give (medicine) in doses to (someone).

dot *n.* a small spot. DOT *v.* to mark with small spots. DOTTED *adj.*

double *v.* 1 to become, or make, twice as much. 2 to fold in two.
DOUBLE *n.* 1 twice as much. 2 a person or thing very much like another.

doubt *v.* to be uncertain or undecided about; to distrust. DOUBT *n.* uncertainty; distrust.

dough *n.* flour which has been moistened and kneaded ready for baking.

dove *n.* a bird of the pigeon family.

down *n.* 1 soft, short hairs or feathers.
DOWN *adv.* to, or in, a lower place, size or amount; the opposite of UP.
DOWN *adj.* directed downward.
DOWN *prep.* downward, along or through.

doze *v.* to sleep lightly; to be half asleep.
DOZE *n.* a short, light sleep; a nap.

dozen *n.* a group of twelve things, twelve of anything.

drab *adj.* of dull color; dull; dreary.

draft *v.* 1 to prepare (a letter, statement or plan). 2 to pick people for some special purpose.
DRAFT *n.* 1 a rough copy of a letter, statement or plan. 2 a picked body of people.

drag *v.* to haul or pull along slowly.

dragon *n.* an imaginary firebreathing monster.

drain *v.* 1 to draw off (liquid). 2 to use up or exhaust.
DRAIN *n.* a pipe, ditch or sewer for carrying away water or waste.

drama *n.* 1 a play for theater, television or radio. 2 an exciting series of events.

drape *v.* to hang or cover with cloth or other fabric.
DRAPE *n.* a piece of cloth or fabric draped over something. DRAPED *adj.*

drastic *adj.* having a strong or powerful effect.

draw *v.* 1 to pull. 2 to attract. 3 to make a sketch, picture or design. 4 to end a game with equal scores.
DRAW *n.* 1 an attraction. 2 a drawn game (of soccer, etc.)

drawing *n.* a sketch, picture or design.

dread *v.* to fear greatly. DREAD *n.* a great fear.

dream *n.* 1 the thoughts and images that come during sleep. 2 something that is much desired or a recalled memory.
DREAM *v.* to experience dreams. DREAMER *n.*
DREAMILY *adj.*

dreary *adj.* dull, boring, cheerless, gloomy.

dredge *v.* to bring up mud or sand from the bottom of a harbor, river or channel; to deepen.

drench *v.* to make very wet; to soak through.
DRENCHED *adj.*

dress *v.* to put on clothes. 2 to bandage.
DRESS *n.* clothing; a frock.

dribble *v.* 1 to let flow in drops; to let saliva or liquid trickle from the mouth. 2 to bounce a basketball with one hand; to keep a ball moving along by giving it light taps with the feet.

drift *v.* to wander or float along; to be driven into heaps; to move off course.
DRIFT *n.* a heap of sand or snow caused by the wind.

drill *n.* 1 a special tool for boring holes. 2 an exercise in marching or a routine operation.
DRILL *v.* 1 to bore a hole. 2 to exercise, or follow a routine.

drink *v.* to swallow a liquid.
DRINK *n.* liquid for drinking.

drip *v.* to fall in drops.
DRIP *n.* a drop or the sound made by falling drops.

drive *v.* 1 to force or urge along. 2 to guide and control. DRIVE *n.* 1 a journey by car. 2 a road. 3 a campaign. DRIVER *n.*

drizzle *n.* fine or gentle rain.
DRIZZLE *v.* to rain gently.

drone *n.* 1 the male honeybee. 2 a low humming sound.
DRONE *v.* 1 to make a low humming sound. 2 to speak in a monotonous manner.

droop *v.* 1 to sag or hang limply. 2 to grow weak or faint. DROOPING *adj.*

drop *n.* 1 a tiny bead of liquid; a small quantity. 2 a fall. DROP *v.* 1 to fall in drops. 2 to fall or allow to fall. DROPPING *n.*

drought *n.* a long period of dry weather; a serious lack of rain or water.

drown *v.* 1 to die under water from lack of air. 2 to flood or overwhelm. DROWNING *adj.* & *n.*

drug *n.* a substance used in medicine; a substance which dulls pain or affects the senses (see DOPE).
DRUG *v.* to dose with a drug. DRUGGED *adj.*

drum *n.* 1 a musical percussion instrument with skin stretched over open ends. 2 a cylinder-shaped container.
DRUM *v.* to beat, or bang, on a drum; to beat or tap continuously.

dry *v.* to make or become dry.
DRY *adj.* 1 waterless. 2 thirsty. 3 uninteresting.

dual *adj.* double; forming a pair.

duck *n.* 1 a small web-footed water bird; a female duck (see DRAKE). 2 no-score by a batsman in cricket.
DUCK *v.* to lower the head suddenly; to dip in water suddenly.

due *n.* a right; that which is owing.
DUE *adj.* 1 owing. 2 suitable. 3 expected.

duel *n.* a fight or contest.

duet *n.* music performed by two singers or players.

duke *n.* a nobleman of the highest rank *fem.* DUCHESS.

dull *adj.* not bright or clear; not lively; uninteresting.
DULL *v.* to make or become dull.

duly *adv.* properly; punctually.

dumb *adj.* stupid.

dummy *n.* an imitation object; a sham package. DUMMY *adj.* not real; sham.

dump *v.* to throw away; to tip out. DUMP *n.* a garbage or storage heap.

dune *n.* a low hill of sand.

dung *n.* animal excreta; manure.

dungeon *n.* an underground cell for prisoners.

duplicate *n.* an exact copy. DUPLICATE *v.* to make an exact copy or copies of.

duplicator *n.* a machine which makes printed copies.

duration *n.* the length of time that something lasts or continues.

during *prep.* throughout; in the course of.

dusk *n.* twilight, nightfall.

dust *n.* fine dry particles of dirt carried in the air; any finely powdered particles of solid matter (e.g. coal, chalk, gold dust). DUSTY *adj.*

duty *n.* 1 anything a person has to do or ought to do. 2 a tax on goods.

dwarf *n.* an animal, plant or person much below ordinary size. DWARF *v.* to stunt in growth, to make look small by comparison.

dwell *v.* 1 to live in; to reside. 2 to speak for some time about.

dye *v.* to change the color of a material etc., by using a dye. DYE *n.* a coloring substance.

dynamite *n.* a powerful explosive. DYNAMITE *v.* to blow up with dynamite.

E

each *adj. & pron.* every one of a number taken singly or separately.

eager *adj.* keen; enthusiastic. EAGERLY *adv.*

eagle *n.* a large and powerful bird of prey.

ear *n.* 1 the organ of hearing. 2 a spike, or head, of corn.

earl *n.* a nobleman ranking between a marquis and a viscount. *fem.* COUNTESS. EARLDOM *n.*

early *adj.* long ago; in bygone days; in the first part of the day. EARLY *adv.* before the usual time; beforehand.

earn *v.* to gain (money) by work; to deserve.

earnest *adj.* serious, conscientious; determined.

Earth *n.* the world; the planet we live on.

earth *n.* 1 soil. 2 ground. 3 a fox's den.

earthquake *n.* underground shock waves which make the earth tremble.

earwig *n.* a small, dark-colored insect with a pincer-like tail.

ease *n.* rest, comfort; freedom from pain.

easel *n.* a frame to support a picture, blackboard, etc.

easily *adv.* without difficulty.

east *n.* the point on the horizon where the sun rises. EAST *adj.* in or to the east. EASTWARD *adv.* towards the east.

Easter *n.* festival of Christ's resurrection.

easy *adj.* comfortable; not difficult.

eat *v.* to chew and swallow food.

ebb *v.* to go back; to recede. EBB *n.* 1 flowing away of the tide. 2 a decrease; a decline.

ebony *n.* a black, heavy hardwood.

eccentric *adj.* odd; strange; not normal.

echo *v.* to throw back or reflect a sound. ECHO *n.* a sound reflected. *pl.* ECHOES.

echoing *adj.* reflecting; resounding.

eclipse *n.* a darkening of the face of the sun or moon. ECLIPSE *v.* 1 to darken; to overshadow. 2 to surpass. ECLIPSING *adj.*

economic *adj.* concerned with economics.

economical *adj.* thrifty, careful in spending.

economics *n.* the study or science of management of the money and resources of an organization or nation.

economy *n.* the management of resources and financial affairs; thrift.

ecstasy *n.* a feeling of great joy and delight.

edge *n.* 1 the rim or border. 2 the cutting side of a blade. EDGE *v.* 1 to sharpen. 2 to move gradually.

edible *adj.* fit to eat; wholesome.

edifice *n.* a large building or structure.

edit *v.* to correct the recorded material of others to make it suitable for printing, or broadcasting by television or radio.

editor *n.* 1 a person who chooses what is to be included in a book, newspaper, film, etc. 2 one who prepares the work of others for publication.

editorial *n.* an important article written by an editor, or an article giving his views.

educate *v.* to teach; to train; to discipline; to provide education for.

education *n.* the process of educating people; instruction; training.

eel *n.* a long, snake-like fish.

eerie *adj.* strange, weird; causing awe or fear. EERILY *adv.*

effect *n.* the result of an action; consequence.
EFFECT *v.* to bring about.

effective *adj.* 1 able to produce a desired effect.
2 impressive.

efficient *adj.* competent; skillful; satisfactory in use. EFFICIENCY *n.* competence, skill.

effort *n.* an attempt; exertion.

effortless *adj.* without effort; with ease.

eggs *n. pl.* the rounded bodies with a thin shell laid by birds, reptiles, etc., from which their young are hatched.
EGG *v.* to urge on; to stir into action.

eight *n.* the number that is one more than seven, the symbol 8.

either *adj.* one or the other of two persons or things.

eject *v.* to throw out, to expel.

elaborate *adj.* very detailed; complicated; highly decorated.
ELABORATE *v.* 1 to work out in detail.
2 to explain. 3 to exaggerate.

elapse *v.* to pass; to slip by, esp. time.

elastic *adj.* 1 able to stretch and spring back again. 2 not rigid.
ELASTIC *n.* a material containing rubber which stretches and springs back easily.

elate *v.* to raise the spirits of; to make (someone) glad. ELATED *adj.*

elbow *n.* 1 the joint where the arm bends.
2 an angle; a sharp bend.
ELBOW *v.* to push with the elbow; to jostle.

elder *n. & adj.* the older of two persons.
ELDER *n.* 1 a senior member of a tribe or of certain churches. 2 a large shrub which produces clusters of purple berries.

elderly *adj.* past middle age.

eldest *adj.* the oldest of three or more persons.

elect *v.* to choose by voting; to select.
ELECT *n.* specially chosen.

election *n.* the process of choosing, usually by voting.

elector *n.* a person who has a vote at an election.

electorate *n.* all the people entitled to vote.

electric *adj.* charged with electricity; capable of making electricity; operated or produced by electricity.

electrical *adj.* having to do with electricity.

electrician *n.* a person skilled in dealing with electricity or electrical equipment.

electricity *n.* a form of energy which produces light, heat and power; a flow of electrons.

electron *n.* a minute electric charge, a part of an atom.

electronics *n.* the science concerned with the behavior of electrons and with devices to make use of them.

elegance *n.* grace; refinement.

elegant *adj.* graceful; refined; in good taste.

element *n.* 1 the simplest form of anything.
2 a chemical substance that cannot be split up into simple substances. ELEMENTARY *adj.*

elephant *n.* the largest land animal, which has a trunk and two ivory tusks.

elevate *v.* to raise; to improve.

elevation *n.* 1 the act of raising. 2 a height.
3 a promotion.

elevator *n.* 1 a machine for raising people, coal, grain, etc., to a higher level. 2 the part of an aircraft which makes it climb or dive.

eleven *adj. & n.* the number one more than ten, the symbol 11.

elf *n.* a mischievous fairy. *pl.* ELVES.

eligible *adj.* suitable; qualified.

eliminate *v.* to remove; to get rid of.

elimination *n.* removal; expulsion.

elm *n.* a tall rough-barked tree.

elongate *v.* to lengthen; to extend.

elope *v.* to run away, esp. with a lover.
ELOPEMENT *n.*

eloquence *n.* fluent and persuasive speech.

else *adv.* otherwise; if not.

elsewhere *adv.* in another place; not here.

elude *v.* to dodge; to avoid; to escape.

elusive *adj.* hard to catch or grasp; evasive.

emancipate *v.* to set free; to liberate.
EMANCIPATED *adj.*

embalm *v.* to preserve (a dead body).

embankment *n.* a wall or bank, of earth or stone, to hold back water or to carry a road or railway.

embargo *n.* an official prohibition.

embark *v.* 1 to go on board a ship or an aircraft.
2 EMBARK ON to start on anything.
EMBARKATION *n.*

embarrass *v.* 1 to make someone feel ill at ease.
2 to hinder. EMBARASSING *adj.*

embarrassment *n.* the state of being embarrassed; discomfort.

embassy *n.* 1 an ambassador and his or her staff. 2 an ambassador's official residence.
pl. EMBASSIES.

embezzle *v.* to steal money by fraud from a person who trusts you. EMBEZZLEMENT *n.*
EMBEZZLER *n.*

embitter *v.* to make bitter; to cause ill feeling.

emblem *n.* a badge; a sign; a symbol.

embrace *v.* 1 to clasp in the arms; to hug.
2 to include. EMBRACE *n.* a clasp, a hug.

embroider *v.* 1 to ornament with needlework.
2 to add to a story; to elaborate.

embroidery *n.* ornamental needlework.

embryo *n.* the beginning; the earliest stage.

emerald *n.* a green and precious stone.
EMERALD *adj.* green.

emerge *v.* to arise or come out of; to come to
light.

emergency *n.* a situation needing immediate
action, an unexpected happening.

emigrant *n.* a person who emigrates.

emigrate *v.* to leave one's own country and settle
in that of another.

emigration *n.* a departure to settle in another
country.

emit *v.* to give, or send, out.

emotion *n.* a strong feeling—joy, pity, fear, love,
hatred, etc.

emotional *adj.* excitable; sensitive; full of feeling.

emperor *n.* the ruler of an empire.
fem. EMPRESS.

emphasis *n.* 1 the stress put on particular words
or syllables when speaking. 2 the importance
given to something.

emphasize *v.* to lay stress on (something).

emphatic *adj.* expressed with emphasis; firm and
forceful.

empire *n.* a group of countries or states under
one ruler or government.

employ *v.* 1 to use or make use of. 2 to provide
work for.

employee *n.* a person who works for an
employer.

employer *n.* a person who employs others.

employment *n.* work; a job; an occupation.

empty *v.* to take everything out.
EMPTY *adj.* containing nothing.

enable *v.* to make able; to supply with the
means.

enamel *n.* a smooth, hard coating; a gloss paint;
the hard coating on the teeth.
ENAMEL *v.* to coat with enamel.

enchant *v.* to put a charm or spell on; to delight.

enclose *v.* 1 to surround. 2 to close or shut in;
to contain inside.

encore *v.* to ask for a performance or item to be
repeated.
ENCORE *n.* a repetition of a performance or
item.

encounter *v.* 1 to meet by chance. 2 to meet (an
enemy).
ENCOUNTER *n.* 1 a chance meeting. 2 a fight.

encourage *v.* 1 to give hope, courage or
confidence. 2 to urge someone to do something.
ENCOURAGEMENT *n.*

encyclopedia *n.* a reference book giving
information of general knowledge or of one
particular subject.

end *n.* 1 the last part; the finish. 2 the death.
3 the aim or purpose.
END *v.* 1 to finish. 2 to destroy.

endanger *v.* to put in danger.

endeavor *v.* to try; to attempt to do.
ENDEAVOR *n.* an attempt.

ending *n.* the result; conclusion.

endless *adj.* everlasting; unending.

endorse *v.* to approve; to confirm; to write one's
signature, indicating approval or acceptance, on
the back of a document. ENDORSEMENT *n.*

endow *v.* 1 to give land or money to (an
institution). 2 to give a quality to (a person).

endure *v.* 1 to bear, or accept, with patience.
2 to last. ENDURING *adj.*

enemy *n.* a foe; an adversary. *pl.* ENEMIES.

energetic *adj.* very active; vigorous.
ENERGETICALLY *adv.*

energy *n.* force; vigor. *pl.* ENERGIES.

enforce *v.* to put (a law) into force; to compel
someone to obey.

engage *v.* 1 to employ. 2 to promise. 3 to begin
fighting. 4 to interlock (two or more parts), esp.
machinery.

engagement *n.* 1 an appointment. 2 a promise
to marry. 3 a fight.

engaging *adj.* attractive; pleasing; interesting.

engine *n.* a machine which produces power.

engineer *n.* a person who designs, makes or
operates machinery.

English *adj.* belonging to England or its people.
ENGLISH *n.* 1 the language of the British people.
2 the people of England.

engrave *v.* to cut letters or designs on (hard
material).

engraving *n.* 1 the process of engraving.
2 a picture printed from an engraved plate.

enjoy *v.* 1 to like; to find pleasure in.
2 to experience.

enjoyable *adj.* able to be enjoyed.

enjoyment *n.* pleasure.

enlighten *v.* 1 to throw light on.
2 to give information or an explanation to
(someone).

enlist *v.* 1 to join up for military service. 2 to obtain the help of.

enmity *n.* hatred; hostility.

enormous *adj.* very large; immense; huge. ENORMOUSLY *adv.*

enough *adj.* sufficient; ample. ENOUGH *n.* a sufficient quantity.

enrage *v.* to make angry; to infuriate.

enrich *v.* to make rich.

enroll *v.* to enter a name in a register or list; to enlist.

ensign *n.* 1 a flag; a banner. 2 lowest rank of navy officer.

enter *v.* 1 to go or come into. 2 to record in a book or list.

enterprise *n.* 1 a bold venture. 2 readiness to try a new thing.

enterprising *adj.* full of enterprise; showing courage or imagination.

entertain *v.* 1 to amuse. 2 to consider. 3 to treat as a guest. ENTERTAINER *n.*

entertaining *adj.* amusing. ENTERTAINING *n.* catering for guests.

enthusiasm *n.* eagerness; great interest.

enthusiastic *adj.* acting with enthusiasm.

entice *v.* to tempt; to lure.

enticement *n.* a temptation; an attraction; a bribe.

entire *adj.* complete; whole.

entirely *adv.* completely; wholly.

entrance *n.* (pron. EN-trance) a place of entering; a doorway; a gateway.

entrance *v.* (pron. en-TRANCE) to charm; to delight.

entrant *n.* one who enters.

entry *n.* 1 the act of entering. 2 an entrance. 3 an item entered in a book or record.

enumerate *v.* 1 to count. 2 to name one by one.

envelop *v.* to wrap up; to enclose.

envelope *n.* a folded cover or wrapper, esp. for a letter.

enviable *adj.* worth envying; desirable.

envious *adj.* showing or feeling envy. ENVIOUSLY *adv.*

environment *n.* surroundings; conditions.

envoy *n.* a special messenger or representative.

envy *v.* to be jealous of. ENVY *n.* jealousy.

epic *n.* a long poem telling of heroic deeds.

epidemic *n.* a quickly-spreading outbreak of disease, crime, etc.

episode *n.* an interesting event; one incident in a series of incidents.

epitaph *n.* words inscribed on a tomb telling about the dead person.

equal *adj.* of the same size, number, value, etc.

equality *n.* the state of being equal.

equally *adv.* to the same extent.

equation *n.* a mathematical statement in which two things are regarded as being equal.

equator *n.* an imaginary line around the Earth, midway between the North and South Poles.

equatorial *adj.* having to do with the equator; on or near the equator.

equestrian *adj.* having to do with horses or horse-riding. EQUESTRIAN *n.* a person riding on horseback.

equilateral *adj.* having all sides equal.

equinox *n.* the time each year when the sun crosses the equator making day and night equal in length (about March 20th and September 22nd).

equip *v.* to supply or outfit with everything needed for a particular purpose.

equipment *n.* what is needed for a particular task or purpose.

equivalent *adj.* equal in value, meaning, usefulness, strength, etc. EQUIVALENT *n.*

era *n.* a period of time, dating from some particular point in history; an age.

eradicate *v.* to root out; to get rid of completely.

erase *v.* to rub or scrape out; to get rid of.

erect *v.* to build; to construct. ERECT *adj.* upright.

erode *v.* to wear away; to eat away. ERODED *adj.*

erosion *n.* a wearing down; an eating away.

err *v.* to be mistaken; to do wrong.

errand *n.* a short journey to take a message or to deliver or collect something.

erratic *adj.* wandering; uncertain; unreliable. ERRATICALLY *adv.*

error *n.* a mistake; a blunder.

erupt *v.* to break or burst out violently.

eruption *n.* 1 an outburst; a breaking out. 2 a skin rash.

escalator *n.* a moving staircase.

escapade *n.* a mischievous prank or adventure.

escape *v.* 1 to get away. 2 to avoid. 3 to leak.

escape *n.* 1 the art of escaping. 2 an avoidance. 3 a leak.

escort *v.* to go with and protect. ESCORT *n.* an accompanying guard or guide.

Eskimo *n.* one of a people living on the coastlands of the Arctic regions.

espionage *n.* spying or using spies.

essay *n.* a written composition.

essential *adj.* absolutely necessary; important. ESSENTIALLY *adv.*

establish *v.* 1 to settle firmly; to set up. 2 to prove.

estate *n.* lands; property owned by a person or company.

esteem *v.* to value highly; to respect. ESTEEM *n.* regard; respect.

estimate *v.* to judge; to calculate. ESTIMATE *n.* a judgment; a calculation to decide size, value, etc.

estimation *n.* a judgment; a calculation.

estuary *n.* a river mouth.

etc. *abbrev. et cetera*—a Latin phrase meaning "and the others."

etch *v.* to engrave on a metal plate, glass, etc. using acid. ETCHED *adj.*

etching *n.* a print from an etched plate.

eternal *adj.* lasting for ever; unchanging.

eternity *n.* 1 all time. 2 a very long time.

ether *n.* 1 the clear, upper air. 2 a colorless liquid used as an anesthetic and as a solvent for fats.

Europe *n.* the smallest of the five continents. EUROPEAN *adj.* to do with Europe. EUROPEAN *n.* an inhabitant of Europe.

evacuate *v.* to leave; to empty; to withdraw from. EVACUATED *adj.* EVACUATION *n.*

evade *v.* to avoid; to dodge; to escape from.

evaporate *v.* to turn into vapor; to vanish. EVAPORATED *adj.*

evasion *n.* a means of avoidance; an excuse.

eve *n.* the close of the day; evening; the time just before an important event.

even *adj.* 1 level; smooth. 2 exactly divisible by two. EVEN *v.* to make level or smooth.

evening *n.* the close of the day.

event *n.* 1 something that happens. 2 an item in a sports program.

eventful *adj.* full of events; exciting.

eventual *adj.* happening as a result; final.

eventually *adv.* in the end; at last.

ever *adv.* always; at all times.

every *adj.* each one of a number and without exception.

evict *v.* to turn out or expel. EVICTION *n.*

evidence *n.* 1 proof. 2 the statement of a witness. 3 clear sign; or indication.

evident *adj.* plain; clearly seen and understood.

evil *n.* sin; wickedness. EVIL *adj.* wicked, unpleasant.

ewe *n.* a female sheep. *masc.* RAM.

exact *adj.* true; accurate. EXACT *v.* to enforce payment of (a debt, a fine, etc.).

exactly *adv.* just right; correctly; quite.

exaggerate *v.* to make something seem greater than it actually is; to overstate.

exalt *v.* to praise highly. EXALTED *adj.*

examination *n.* 1 a close inspection. 2 a test of knowledge or ability. 3 an investigation.

examine *v.* 1 to inspect closely. 2 to test.

example *n.* 1 a sample or specimen. 2 a model. 3 a warning.

exasperate *v.* to make very angry; to irritate. EXASPERATING *adj.*

excavate *v.* to dig or scoop out; to uncover buried ruins. EXCAVATION *n.*

excavator *n.* 1 a machine used for excavating. 2 someone who excavates.

exceed *v.* to be greater than; to go beyond.

excel *v.* to be better than; to be very good at; to do very well.

excellence *n.* high quality; great merit. EXCELLENT *adj.*

except *v.* to leave out; to omit. EXCEPT *prep.* leaving out; omitting.

exception *n.* something left out; something different from the rest.

exceptional *adj.* unusual; abnormal.

excerpt *n.* an extract from a book, play, musical work, etc.

excess *n.* 1 the extra amount; surplus. 2 going beyond what is reasonable.

excessive *adj.* too much; beyond what is right and proper.

exchange *v.* to give one thing in return for another. EXCHANGE *n.* 1 the act of exchanging. 2 an official building where merchants meet.

excise *n.* a tax on some goods.

excitable *adj.* easily excited.

excite *v.* to rouse; to stir up. EXCITING *adj.*

excitement *n.* the state of being excited; eager expectation.

exclaim *v.* to speak, or cry out, suddenly.

exclamation *n.* a sudden shout or cry; a punctuation mark to indicate surprise (!).

exclude *v.* to shut out; to leave out; to prevent (someone) from sharing (something); to ignore.

exclusion *n.* shutting or leaving out.

excursion *n.* a pleasure trip; an outing.

excuse *v.* (pron. ex-KUZE) to free from blame; to overlook a fault.
EXCUSE *n.* (pron. ex-KUSE) a reason given for having done something wrong.

execute *n.* 1 to do; to carry out.
2 to put to death.

execution *n.* 1 the deed; carrying out.
2 putting to death.

exempt *v.* to free from; to excuse.

exercise *v.* to train (the body or mind) by practice or drill. EXERCISE *n.*

exert *v.* to bring into action, to make active.
EXERTION *n.*

exhaust *v.* to use up completely.
EXHAUST *n.* 1 the used gases or steam from an engine. 2 the pipe which lets out waste gases or steam from an engine.

exhaustion *n.* extreme tiredness; weariness.

exhibit *v.* to show; to display; to show in public.

exhibition *n.* a public show; a display.

exile *v.* to banish, to expel (someone) from his or her own country. EXILE *n.*

exist *v.* to live; to be. EXISTENCE *n.*

exit *n.* 1 a way out. 2 a departure.
EXIT *v.* to go out; to leave.

exodus *n.* the departure of a large number of people.

exonerate *v.* to free from blame.

exorbitant *adj.* going beyond what is reasonable; excessive.

exotic *adj.* introduced from abroad; unusual; exceptional; rare.

expand *v.* 1 to make or grow larger. 2 to open out.

expanse *n.* a wide area.

expansion *n.* an increase in size; growing; stretching or spreading.

expect *v.* to look forward to; to wait for.

expedite *v.* to hasten.

expedition *n.* a journey with a purpose.

expel *v.* to drive or force out; to send away.

expenditure *n.* the money spent.

expense *n.* the cost.

expensive *adj.* costly.

experience *n.* 1 skill and knowledge gained by doing and seeing. 2 anything that happens to a person. EXPERIENCE *v.* to undergo.

experiment *v.* to test or try out.
EXPERIMENT *n.* a test; a trial.

experimental *adj.* based on experiments; used for experiments.

expert *n.* a specialist; skilled person.
EXPERT *adj.* specialized; skilled.

expire *v.* 1 to die; to come to an end.
2 to breathe out.

explain *v.* to make clear or easy to understand; to give reasons for.

explanation *n.* a spoken or written statement that explains something.

explode *v.* to blow up with a loud noise; to burst out.

exploit *v.* (pron. ex-PLOIT) to make use of selfishly; to use to advantage.
EXPLOIT *n.* (pron. EX-ploit) a daring deed; an achievement.

exploration *n.* a search.

explore *v.* 1 to make a journey of exploration.
2 to examine the possibilities (of); to search.
EXPLORER *n.*

explosion *n.* 1 a sudden burst or blowup with a loud noise. 2 a violent outburst.

explosive *n.* something that will explode.
EXPLOSIVE *adj.* liable to explode.

exports *n. pl.* (pron. EX-ports) goods sent abroad.
EXPORT *v.* (pron. ex-PORT) to send (goods) abroad. EXPORTER *n.*

expose *v.* 1 to uncover. 2 to endanger. 3 to show up. EXPOSURE *n.*

express *v.* to state; to declare; to put into words.
EXPRESS *adj.* 1 speedy. 2 definite.

expression *n.* 1 the manner in which anything is spoken, sung or written. 2 the look on a person's face.

expulsion *n.* a driving out; banishment.

exquisite *adj.* 1 delicate; of great beauty.
2 of unusual quality.

extend *v.* to stretch; to enlarge; to hold out.

extension *n.* lengthening; an addition.

extensive *adj.* wide; large; spacious.

exterior *n.* the outside.
EXTERIOR *adj.* outer; external.

exterminate *v.* to destroy completely; to kill off.

external *adj.* outside; lying on the outside.

extinct *adj.* dead; no longer active; no longer existing. EXTINCTION *n.* destruction.

extinguish *v.* to put an end to; to put out.

extinguisher *n.* a device for putting out fires.

extra *adj.* additional; more than is usual.
EXTRA *adv.* additionally.
EXTRA *n.* something additional.

extract *v.* (pron. ex-TRAKT) to draw or pull out; to squeeze out.
EXTRACT *n.* (pron. EX-trakt) a part that has been taken away from the whole; a part of a story, a play, an article, etc.

extraordinary *adj.* unusual; surprising; special.

extravagance *n.* lavish expenditure or waste.

extravagant *adj.* wasteful; going beyond reasonable limits.

extreme *adj.* farthest; not moderate; severe.
EXTREME *n.* the opposite end; the farthest point, the limit. EXTREMELY *adv.*

eye *n.* 1 the organ of sight. 2 a small hole, as in a needle. EYE *v.* to gaze at or watch carefully.

F

fable *n.* a story with a lesson or moral; a legend.
FABLED *adj.*

fabric *n.* 1 a woven material. 2 structure; walls, floors and roof of a building.

fabulous *adj.* legendary; astounding; marvellous.

face *n.* 1 the front part of the head.
2 the front of anything.
FACE *v.* 1 to turn towards. 2 to meet boldly.

facet *n.* 1 a small polished face or surface of a gem. 2 one aspect.

facial *adj.* having to do with the face.

facsimile *n.* an exact copy.

fact *n.* something known to be true.

faction *n.* 1 a disconnected party or group.
2 strife.

factor *n.* 1 a fact contributing to a result.
2 a number which divides into another number exactly.

factory *n.* a building in which goods are made.

fad *n.* a passing interest; a fancy.

fade *v.* to grow faint; to lose color or strength.
FADED *adj.*

Fahrenheit *n.* a scale of temperature, on which water freezes at 32° and boils at 212°.

fail *v.* to be unsuccessful; to disappoint; to let down.

failure *n.* 1 lack of success. 2 a person or thing that fails.

faint *adj.* 1 dim; not clear. 2 feeble, weak.
FAINT *v.* to lose consciousness for a short time.

fair *adj.* 1 just; honest. 2 light-colored.
3 free from rain. 4 pleasing.
FAIR *n.* a trade exhibition; a market with amusements.

fairly *adv.* justly; moderately.

fairness *n.* rightness; justice.

fairy *n.* an imaginary small person with magical powers. *pl.* FAIRIES. FAIRY *adj.* delicate; dainty.

faith *n.* trust; belief.

faithful *adj.* 1 loyal; true. 2 accurate.

fake *n.* an imitation; a sham.
FAKE *v.* to cheat by making an imitation; to pretend.

falcon *n.* a bird of prey, of the hawk family.

fall *v.* to drop; to descend; to decrease.
FALL *n.* a drop; a descent; a decrease.

false *adj.* 1 untrue; incorrect. 2 deceitful.
3 artificial.

falsehood *n.* a lie; an untruth.

falsify *v.* to alter for a dishonest purpose; to misrepresent.

falter *v.* 1 to stumble; to waver. 2 to speak hesitantly.

fame *n.* the condition of being well known; renown; reputation.

familiar *adj.* well known; intimate; impudent.

family *n.* 1 members of a household. 2 a group of plants, animals, etc., of the same kind.
pl. FAMILIES.

famine *n.* an extreme shortage of food.

famous *adj.* very well known; celebrated.

fan *n.* 1 an appliance for creating air currents.
2 a supporter. FAN *v.* to stir the air.

fanatic *n.* a person who is very enthusiastic about something.

fancy *v.* to suppose; to imagine; to have a liking for. FANCY *n.* an idea; a liking.
pl. FANCIES. FANCY *adj.* ornamental.

fang *n.* a long pointed tooth.

fantastic *adj.* fanciful; unusual; odd; extraordinary.

fantasy *n.* 1 something imagined; a daydream.
2 a story that is fantastic in content.

far *adj.* distant; remote.

farce *n.* 1 a silly but amusing play. 2 a silly or useless procedure.

fare *n.* 1 the charge made for a journey.
2 a passenger who pays.
FARE *v.* to proceed well or badly.

farewell *n.* a goodbye or leavetaking.

farm *n.* the land and buildings used for growing crops or raising animals.
FARM *v.* to work and cultivate the land; to raise animals. FARMER *n.*

farther *adv.* at a greater distance; in addition.
FARTHER *adj.* more distant; more advanced.

fascinate *v.* 1 to charm. 2 to put a spell on. FASCINATING *adj.* FASCINATION *n.*

fashion *n.* the most popular style of clothes or way of doing something. FASHION *v.* to make; to shape.

fashionable *n.* following the latest fashion.

fast *adj.* 1 rapid. 2 firm; secure. FAST *v.* to go without food. FAST *n.* a period during which little or no food is eaten.

fasten *v.* to fix or tie together; to make secure. FASTENER *n.*

fastening *n.* anything that fastens things together.

fat *n.* an oily substance in animals. FAT *adj.* 1 plump. 2 rich. 3 greasy.

fatal *adj.* causing death or disaster. FATALLY *adv.*

fatality *n.* a disaster which causes death; a calamity. *pl.* FATALITIES.

fate *n.* a power which is thought to determine the future.

father *n.* 1 a male parent. 2 a priest. FATHERLY *adj.*

fathom *n.* a measure of depth (6 feet or 1.8 meters).

fatigue *n.* tiredness; exhaustion. FATIGUE *v.* to tire (someone) out.

fatten *v.* to make or become fat.

fault *n.* a defect; a flaw. FAULT *v.* to blame.

fauna *n.* the animal life of a region.

favor *v.* to treat kindly; to prefer. FAVOR *n.* a kindness; a good wish.

favorable *adj.* giving or showing approval; in favor of; promising.

favorite *n.* a well-liked person or thing; pet. FAVORITE *adj.* preferred above others.

fawn *n.* 1 a young deer. 2 a light yellowish-brown color. FAWN *v.* to seek favor.

fear *n.* a feeling of alarm; dread; terror. FEAR *v.* to be afraid (of). FEARED *adj.*

fearful *adj.* full of fear.

fearless *adj.* courageous; bold.

feast *n.* 1 a banquet; a rich meal. 2 a holiday; a religious anniversary. FEAST *v.* to take part in a banquet.

feat *n.* a difficult or brave deed.

feather *n.* a fringed quill which grows on a bird. FEATHERED *adj.*

feature *n.* 1 a part of the face. 2 a characteristic quality. FEATURE *v.* to make prominent.

February *n.* the second month of the year.

federation *n.* a group of states which are united nationally but independent internally. FEDERAL *adj.*

fee *n.* a payment for services.

feeble *adj.* weak; without energy or vigor.

feed *v.* 1 to give or eat food. 2 to supply with.

feel *v.* 1 to examine by touch. 2 to be conscious of. FEEL *n.* a sense of touch.

feeler *n.* an insect's organ of touch.

feeling *n.* 1 the sense of touch. 2 an emotion such as hope, fear, sympathy, etc.

feign *v.* to pretend.

feint *n.* a pretense; a deceptive action. FEINT *v.* to take a deceptive action.

feline *adj.* catlike; stealthy. FELINE *n.* a member of the cat family.

fell *v.* to knock down; to cut down.

felony *n.* a serious crime.

felt *v.* past tense of FEEL. FELT *n.* a fabric made from shrunk and pressed wool, hair or fur.

female *n.* 1 a woman or girl. 2 an animal able to produce young. 3 a fruitbearing plant.

feminine *adj.* womanly; having to do with women.

femur *n.* the thighbone.

fence *n.* a barrier of wood, metal or wire, supported by posts, and enclosing a field or garden. FENCE *v.* 1 to enclose by means of a fence. 2 to fight with swords.

fender *n.* an object to prevent a damaging collision, e.g. ropes or matting over the side of a ship.

ferment *v.* (pron. fer-MENT) to cause the process of fermentation; to excite. FERMENT *n.* (pron. FER-ment) 1 a substance that causes fermentation, such as yeast. 2 a state of excitement.

fern *n.* a plant with broad feathery leaves or fronds.

ferocious *adj.* savage; fierce; cruel.

ferocity *n.* fierce cruelty.

ferry *v.* to convey over water. FERRY *n.* 1 a boat or aircraft which ferries passengers or freight. 2 a crossing place for a boat.

fertile *adj.* fruitful; productive; full of ideas.

fertilize *v.* to make fertile; to enrich.

fertilizer *n.* manure or chemicals put into the soil to make it more fertile.

festival *n.* a feast; a day or period of rejoicing.

festive *adj.* in glad mood; joyful.

fetch *v.* to go and get.

fetter *n.* a chain or shackle for the feet.
FETTER *v.* to chain; to hinder.

feud *n.* a lasting quarrel between two persons, families, tribes, etc. FEUD *v.* to quarrel.

fever *n.* 1 an illness causing high temperature. 2 excitement.

few *adj.* not many. FEW *n.* a small number.

fiasco *n.* a complete failure.

fiber *n.* a thread of mineral or vegetable tissue from which fabrics are manufactured.

fiction *n.* a story which is not true; a thing invented or imagined; not factual. FICTIONAL *adj.*

fictitious *adj.* imagined; false; invented.

fidget *v.* to move restlessly. FIDGETY *adj.*

field *n.* 1 an area of enclosed pasture or cultivated land. 2 a sports playing area. 3 an area of interest.

fiend *n.* a devil; a monster; a wicked person. FIENDISH *adj.*

fierce *adj.* violent; savage. FIERCELY *adv.*

fiery *adj.* 1 like a fire; flaming; burning. 2 quick-tempered.

fifteen *n.* a number (15).

fifty *n.* a number (50).

fight *v.* 1 to struggle with. 2 to battle with. FIGHT *n.* a combat; a battle. FIGHTER *n.*

figure *n.* 1 a human shape; image. 2 the symbol of a number.
FIGURE *v.* to imagine; to write numbers; to calculate.

filament *n.* a very fine thread or wire.

file *n.* 1 a steel tool with a rough surface used for smoothing wood or metal. 2 a folder or case in which papers or documents are stored. 3 a single line of people.
FILE *v.* 1 to use a file. 2 to place in a file. 3 to move one behind the other.

fill *v.* to become, or make, full; to occupy all the space in. FILL *n.* a full supply.

film *n.* 1 a thin skin, layer or coating. 2 a strip of celluloid on which photographs are taken.
FILM *v.* 1 to coat thinly. 2 to photograph.

filter *v.* to pass (liquid, light or air) through a filter.
FILTER *n.* a strainer; a device for purifying.

fin *n.* 1 one of the organs which enable a fish to swim and balance itself. 2 a finlike projection on a cycle engine, an aircraft, etc.

final *adj.* at the end, coming last; decisive.
FINAL *n.* the last in a series of examinations, games, etc.

finally *adv.* lastly, in conclusion.

finance *n.* 1 the management of money matters. 2 money. FINANCE *v.* to provide money for.

financial *adj.* concerned with money matters.

financier *n.* a person who arranges finance.

find *v.* 1 to discover by chance. 2 to search for and discover. FIND *n.* a discovery.

fine *adj.* 1 very thin; delicate. 2 of very good quality; excellent. FINELY *adv.*
FINE *n.* money paid as a penalty.
FINE *v.* to impose a penalty on (someone).

finger *n.* one of the five parts at the end of the hand. FINGER *v.* to touch with the fingers.

finish *v.* to bring to an end; to complete.
FINISH *n.* 1 the end; completion. 2 perfection.
FINISHED *adj.*

Finn *n.* an inhabitant of Finland.
FINNISH *n.* the language of Finland.
FINNISH *adj.* of Finland.

fir *n.* an evergreen, cone-bearing tree.

fire *n.* 1 flame and heat from burning. 2 eagerness; excitement.
FIRE *v.* 1 to cause to burn. 2 to excite. 3 to discharge from a gun.

firm *adj.* solid; fixed.
FIRM *n.* a business concern; a company.

first *adj.* coming before all others.
FIRST *adv.* before anything else.
FIRST *n.* a person or thing that is first.

fish *n.* a water animal having backbone, fins and gills. FISH *v.* to catch fish. FISHERMAN *n.*

fist *n.* a hand with fingers tightly clenched.

fit *v.* to agree exactly (with); to be suitable (for).
FIT *n.* a sudden seizure or spasm.
FIT *adj.* 1 suitable. 2 in good health.

fitness *n.* 1 suitability. 2 healthiness.

fitting *adj.* suitable; appropriate.
FITTING *n.* a fixture.

five *n.* the number one more than four (5).

fix *v.* 1 to make (something) firm; to secure. 2 FIX ON to decide on.
FIX *n.* an awkward situation.

flag *n.* a standard or ensign.
FLAG *v.* 1 to signal with flags. 2. to become tired.

flagrant *adj.* openly wicked; notorious.

flair *n.* instinct; aptitude.

flake *n.* a thin layer or scale.
FLAKE *v.* to come off in flakes.

flame *n.* 1 the burning gas from a fire; a blaze. 2 anger; enthusiasm.
FLAME *v.* 1 to burn with a flame; to blaze. 2 to show anger or enthusiasm

flammable *adj.* easily set on fire (see INFLAMMABLE).

flank *n.* the side of anything.
FLANK *v.* to be at one side of; to attack on one side.

flannel *n.* a soft loosely-woven woollen cloth.

flap *v.* to move up and down or from side to side; to flutter.

flare *v.* 1 to blaze; to flame. 2 to widen gradually (e.g. flared trousers).
FLARE *n.* 1 a bright, unsteady flame. 2 a signal light.

flash *n.* 1 a sudden bright light. 2 a moment.
FLASH *v.* to shine out suddenly.

flat *adj.* 1 level; even. 2 dull, uninteresting.
FLAT *n.* below the true pitch in music (sign *b*)

flatter *v.* to praise insincerely.

flaunt *v.* to show off.

flavor *n.* the taste.
FLAVOR *v.* to give flavor to; to season.

flavoring *n.* anything used to give a special taste to food.

flaw *n.* a fault; a crack; a defect.
FLAWLESS *adj.* without fault.

flax *n.* a plant whose fibers are woven into linen.

flea *n.* a small, wingless, jumping insect.

fledgling *n.* a young bird just able to fly.

flee *v.* to run away from.

fleece *n.* the woolly covering of a sheep.
FLEECE *v.* 1 to shear (a sheep). 2 to rob.

fleet *n.* a group of ships, aircraft, trucks, etc.
FLEET *adj.* quick; swift.

flesh *n.*1 the soft muscular tissues between the skin and bones of the body. 2 meat.

flex *n.* a flexible insulated wire which conveys electric currents. FLEX *v.* to bend.

flexible *adj.* easily bent; adaptable.
FLEXIBILITY *n.*

flicker *v.* to shine or burn unsteadily.
FLICKER *n.* an unsteady light.

flight *n.* 1 the act of flying; the distance flown. 2 a group of birds or aircraft flying together. 3 a series of steps or stairs.

flimsy *adj.* frail, thin.

flinch *v.* to draw back; to wince.

fling *v.* to throw violently; to hurl.
FLING *n.* 1 a throw. 2 a lively dance.

flint *n.* hard stone found in pebbly lumps.

float *v.* 1 to stay on the surface of a liquid. 2 to set going or launch.
FLOAT *n.* anything that floats on the surface of a liquid.

floating *adj.* 1 buoyant. 2 fluctuating.

flock *n.* 1 a group of animals or birds. 2 a gathering of people.
FLOCK *v.* to crowd together.

floe *n.* a sheet of floating ice.

flog *v.* to beat with a whip or stick.

flood *n.* 1 an overflow of water, etc. 2 an abundance of anything. 3 the flowing in of the tide.
FLOOD *v.* 1 to cover, or fill, with water. 2 to overwhelm. FLOODING *n.*

floor *n.* 1 the lower surface of a room. 2 a story of a building.
FLOOR *v.* 1 to lay a floor. 2 to knock to the ground. 3 to puzzle.

flora *n.* the plants of a particular region.

floral *adj.* made of or concerning flowers.

florist *n.* a person who grows or sells flowers for a living.

flounder *v.* to struggle helplessly.
FLOUNDER *n.* a small flatfish.

flour *n.* finely-ground wheat used for making bread, etc.

flourish *v.* 1 to grow vigorously; to prosper. 2 to wave or throw (something) about.
FLOURISH *n.* 1 a waving about. 2 a fanfare. 3 an ornamental curve.

flourishing *adj.* thriving; prosperous.

flow *v.* to move along easily; to glide.
FLOW *n.* 1 the act of flowing. 2 a steady supply.

flower *n.* 1 the part of a plant or tree from which the seed or fruit develops; bloom. 2 the best part of anything.
FLOWER *v.* to bloom; to blossom.

fluctuate *v.* to rise and fall; to vary irregularly.

flue *n.* a pipe or duct to carry air, smoke or fumes; a ventilating shaft.

fluent *adj.* 1 speaking or writing easily and skillfully. 2 graceful and easy in movement.
FLUENCY *n.*

fluid *n.* something which flows, such as a liquid or gas. FLUID *adj.* capable of flowing.

fluke *n.* an unexpected and lucky success.

flush *v.* 1 to clean by a flow of water. 2 to blush.
FLUSH *n.* 1 a sudden flow of water. 2 a blush.
FLUSH *adj.* full; level with the top.

fluster *v.* to confuse; to agitate.
FLUSTER *n.* confusion; agitation.
FLUSTERED *adj.*

flute *n.* 1 a musical wind instrument with finger holes. 2 a groove cut in a pillar.

flutter *v.* to flap (the wings); to move about quickly.
FLUTTER *n.* 1 a quick beating (of wings etc.). 2 a state of excitement.

fly *v.* 1 to move through the air with wings or in an aircraft; to pilot an aircraft.
2 to move swiftly; to flee.
FLY *n.* a two-winged insect such as the housefly. *pl.* FLIES.

foam *n.* froth or bubbles on liquid.
FOAM *v.* 1 to form or produce foam. 2 to be angry.

focus *n.* 1 the point at which rays of light meet. 2 a center point. *pl.* FOCI.
FOCUS *v.* 1 to adjust the eyes or a lens to get a clear image. 2 to draw attention to.

foe *n.* an enemy.

fog *n.* clouds of water droplets suspended in the atmosphere, either reducing visibility or causing almost complete obscurity.

foil *n.* 1 a thin sheet of metal. 2 a fencing sword.
FOIL *v.* to outwit; to baffle.

fold *v.* to double something over on itself; to enclose. FOLD *n.* the part folded over.

foliage *n.* the leaves of plants or trees.

folklore *n.* traditional legends, customs and beliefs.

follow *v.* 1 to go or come after. 2 to support. 3 to understand.

following *n.* all those who support.
FOLLOWING *adj.* that which follows.

folly *n.* foolishness; a foolish act. *pl.* FOLLIES.

fond *adj.* affectionate; loving. FONDNESS *n.*
FONDLY *adv.*

fondle *v.* to caress.

food *n.* 1 anything eaten. 2 nourishment for animals and plants.

fool *n.* a foolish person. FOOL *v.* to deceive.

foolish *adj.* unwise; stupid. FOOLISHLY *adv.*

foot *n.* 1 the lower part of the leg from the ankle down. 2 a measure of length; 12 inches or about 30 cm. 3 the bottom or base of anything. *pl.* FEET.

for *prep.* 1 in place of. 2 on behalf of. 3 in support of. 4 meant for. FOR *conj.* because.

forage *v.* to search for food, etc.
FORAGE *n.* food for horses, cattle, etc.

forbid *v.* to order (someone) not to do (something).

force *v.* to compel (someone); to break (something) open.
FORCE *n.* 1 strength; power. 2 compulsion. 3 an organized group of people.
FORCEFUL *adj.* strong; determined.

ford *n.* a shallow place where a river can be crossed on foot or in a vehicle.
FORD *v.* to wade across a river.

fore *n.* the front part. FORE *adj.* in front of.

forearm *n.* (pron. FORE-arm) the arm between the wrist and the elbow.
FOREARM *v.* (pron. fore-ARM) to prepare beforehand.

forecast *n.* a prediction of what may be expected
FORECAST *v.* to predict or estimate probable events.

forefather *n.* an ancestor.

forehead *n.* the part of the face above the eyebrows; the brow.

foreign *adj.* 1 belonging to or concerning another country. 2 alien; strange.
FOREIGNER *n.*

foresight *n.* 1 seeing beforehand. 2 care in preparing for future needs. FORESEE *v.*

forest *n.* a large area of land covered with trees.

forfeit *v.* to give up or lose (something) as a penalty.
FORFEIT *n.* something given up as a fine, penalty or punishment.

forge *n.* a workshop where metal is heated and shaped.
FORGE *v.* 1 to shape by heating and hammering. 2 to make a copy intending to deceive.

forgery *n.* a copy made with intent to deceive.

forget *v.* to fail to remember; to overlook; to neglect.

forgive *v.* to pardon; to be merciful (to someone).

forgiveness *n.* readiness to pardon.

forgotten *adj.* 1 not remembered. 2 neglected.

fork *n.* 1 a pronged implement for eating or, larger, for digging. 2 the point where a road, stream or tree divides into two or more branches.
FORK *v.* 1 to use a fork on (something). 2 to branch from.

form *n.* the shape; appearance.

formal *adj.* 1 according to rule and custom. 2 dignified; exact.

formation *n.* an arrangement in a particular form.

former *adj.* before in time or order.
FORMER *n.* the first of two.

formerly *adv.* at an earlier time; once.

formidable *adj.* to be dreaded; hard to overcome.

formula *n.* 1 a set form of words or symbols representing a rule or statement. 2 a recipe.

forsake *v.* to leave or desert (someone); to give up (something).

fort *n.* a fortified place or stronghold.

forth *adv.* onwards; forward.

forthcoming *adj.* happening soon; about to appear.

fortifications *n. pl.* defensive walls, towers, trenches, etc.

fortify *v.* 1 to defend against attack by making fortifications. 2 to strengthen (a place) against attack.

fortnight *n.* two weeks.

fortunate *adj.* lucky; prosperous.

fortune *n.* 1 good or bad luck; chance. 2 wealth; success.

forty *n.* a number (40).

forum *n.* 1 an occasion or a meeting place for discussion. 2 a marketplace in ancient Rome.

forward *adj.* 1 in front; advanced. 2 impudent. FORWARD *adv.* toward the front.

fossil *n.* the preserved remains of prehistoric animal or plant life found in rocks.

foul *adj.* 1 dirty; disgusting; obscene. 2 stormy; rough. 3 unfair. FOUL *n.* a breaking of the rules of a game. FOUL *v.* 1 to dirty. 2 to entangle (a rope etc.). 3 to break a rule in sports.

found *v.* to start (something); to establish.

foundation *n.* 1 the base or groundwork of a structure; basis. 2 an institution or establishment.

foundry *n.* a factory or workshop where molten metal is formed or cast in molds.

fountain *n.* a spring of water; an artificial jet of water.

four *n.* the number one more than three (4).

fourteen *n.* a number (14).

fowl *n.* a domestic bird, cock or hen; poultry.

fox *n.* a cunning wild doglike mammal. FOX *v.* to deceive; to puzzle (someone).

fraction *n.* 1 any part of a unit. 2 a fragment, piece or part of anything.

fracture *n.* a break, a crack. FRACTURE *v.* to break, to crack (something).

fragile *adj.* easily broken or damaged.

fragment *n.* a part broken off; an incomplete part.

fragrance *n.* a sweet smell or perfume.

fragrant *adj.* sweet smelling.

frail *adj.* weak; fragile.

frame *v.* 1 to put a frame around. 2 to put together; to construct. FRAME *n.* an outline, a skeleton or a basic structure.

framework *n.* 1 the frame around which something is built. 2 a system.

franchise *n.* 1 the right to vote. 2 a right or privilege granted.

frank *adj.* outspoken; sincere; candid.

frantic *adj.* wildly excited; showing frenzy.

fraud *n.* 1 trickery; deceit. 2 someone or something that is not genuine.

fraudulent *adj.* 1 obtained by trickery. 2 deceitful.

freak *n.* something very odd. FREAK *adj.* unusual (happening).

free *adj.* 1 having personal rights and liberty. 2 open; frank. 3 generous. 4 costing nothing. FREE *v.* to release; to set (someone) free.

freedom *n.* liberty; independence.

freeze *v.* 1 to change into ice; to change from a liquid into a solid by chilling. 2 to become suddenly still or rigid. 3 to fix (prices or wages) at a certain level.

freight *n.* goods carried by sea, air, road or rail.

freighter *n.* a cargo ship, aircraft, or train.

French *adj.* belonging to France or its people. FRENCH *n.* the language or people of France.

frenzy *n.* wild excitement or fury.

frequency *n.* 1 the repeated happening of (an action, an event) 2 the rate at which something occurs.

frequent *adj.* happening often. FREQUENT *v.* to visit often.

frequently *adv.* many times; often.

fresco *n.* a picture painted on a wall.

fresh *adj.* 1 new; recent. 2 clean; refreshing. 3 vivid; lively.

friction *n.* 1 the resistance between things rubbing together. 2 disagreement; bad feeling.

Friday *n.* the sixth day of the week.

friend *n.* a person attached to another by affection; a companion. FRIENDSHIP *n.*

friendliness *n.* affection; goodwill.

friendly *adj.* attached; affectionate.

frigate *n.* 1 a small, fast warship. 2 a fast sailing warship in earlier times.

fright *n.* sudden fear; terror.

frighten *v.* to terrify; to make afraid.

fringe *n.* 1 a border of loose threads. 2 an edge; a margin.

frisk *v.* 1 to romp and skip playfully. 2 to search a person for weapons.

frivolous *adj.* 1 trivial; not serious. 2 playful.

frog *n.* a small amphibious creature which grows from a tadpole.

from *prep.* starting from; out of; because of; at a distance of.

front *n.* the foremost part of anything; the face. FRONT *v.* to face; to look towards.

frontier *n.* the border or boundary between countries.

frost *n.* 1 an air temperature below freezing-point. 2 frozen dew or water vapor. FROSTY *adj.*

frown *v.* to wrinkle the forehead in anger or disapproval.

fruit *n.* 1 the seed-producing organ of a plant. 2 produce, e.g. apples, pears, etc.

frustrate *v.* to prevent (someone) from doing (something); to defeat.

fry *v.* to cook in hot fat or oil.

fuel *n.* any substance used to provide a source of heat or other energy.

fugitive *n.* a person who runs away or flees from something.

fulcrum *n.* the point or pivot on which a lever balances.

fulfill *v.* to carry out (what is promised or expected); to complete satisfactorily.

fulfilled *adj.* carried out as promised or expected.

full *adj.* complete; filled, unable to hold any more.

fun *n.* amusement. FUNNY *adj.*

function *v.* to work correctly; to operate. FUNCTION *n.* a ceremony or event; activity.

fundamental *adj.* essential; necessary. FUNDAMENTAL *n.* an essential and necessary part.

funeral *n.* a burial or cremation ceremony.

fungus *n.* 1. a soft, spongy plant growth such as a mushroom or toadstool. 2 a disease-growth on animals and plants.

funnel *n.* 1 a tube with a cone-shaped filler for pouring liquids through a small opening. 2 a chimney on a ship or locomotive.

fur *n.* the soft hair of certain animals.

furious *adj.* very angry; raging.

furlong *n.* an eighth of a mile (220 yards or 201 meters).

furnace *n.* an enclosed fire which produces intense heat to melt metal, provide hot water or supply heat for an engine, house, etc.

furnish *v.* to supply with furniture; to provide what is needed. FURNISHED *adj.*

furniture *n.* the larger, and often movable, articles in a room, house, office, etc., e.g. chairs, tables, bookshelves, etc.

further *adj.* 1 in addition. 2 more distant. FURTHER *adv.* 1 at a greater distance. 2 also; besides. FURTHER *v.* 1 to help (something) forward. 2 to encourage.

fury *n.* rage; violent anger.

fuse *v.* 1 to melt by intense heat. 2 to join together; to blend. 3 to cause an electric circuit to fail. FUSE *n.* 1 a safety device to protect electrical apparatus. 2 a device to time the detonation of an explosive.

fuselage *n.* the body of an aircraft.

fuss *n.* excitement or concern over trifling matters. FUSS (OVER) *v.* to worry over small things.

future *n.* the time still to come; events which will happen. FUTURE *adj.* about to be; still to happen.

G

gadget *n.* a small and useful device.

gag *n.* something placed in or over a person's mouth to keep it open or to prevent the person from speaking. GAG *v.* to silence with a gag.

gaily *adv.* happily and cheerfully.

gain *n.* an increase in wealth, profit or power. GAIN *v.* to earn; to profit; to win.

gala *n.* a festivity.

gale *n.* a strong wind; a storm.

gallant *adj.* brave; chivalrous; noble. GALLANTLY *adv.*

gallery *n.* 1 a long narrow passage. 2 a theater balcony. 3 a room in which paintings, etc., are exhibited.

galley *n.* 1 an ancient ship using sails and oars, usually rowed by slaves. 2 a ship's kitchen.

gallon *n.* a measure of capacity. 8 pints (approx. 4.5 liters).

gallop *n.* the fastest pace of a horse. GALLOP *v.* to move rapidly in leaps.

gamble *v.* to bet; to take a chance. GAMBLE *n.* a risk.

game *n.* 1 any form of organized sport or play; amusement. 2 wild animals or birds which are hunted for sport or food.

gander *n.* a male goose.

gang *n.* a group of people working, playing or going about together, sometimes for criminal purposes.

gangster *n.* a member of a gang of criminals.

gap *n.* 1 an opening; a break. 2 an interval.

garage *n.* a building where motor vehicles are kept; a business which sells and repairs motor vehicles.

garbage *n.* refuse; trash.

garden *n.* a place where flowers, shrubs, vegetables, etc., are cultivated.
GARDEN *v.* to work in a garden.

garment *n.* an article of clothing.

garrison *n.* 1 the troops defending a town. 2 the base or depot of a particular unit, regiment, etc.
GARRISON *v.* to provide with defending troops.

gas *n.* an elastic fluid that does not become solid or liquid at ordinary temperatures, e.g. nitrogen, helium, *pl.* GASES
GAS *v.* to injure or poison with gas.

gash *v.* to cut deeply. GASH *n.* a deep cut.

gasp *v.* to breathe with difficulty; to struggle for breath.
GASP *n.* a gulp; a sudden catching of the breath.

gate *n.* a hinged barrier to control an entrance or exit.

gather *v.* 1 to assemble; to collect; to bring together. 2 to understand. 3 to draw fabric together in folds.

gathering *n.* an assembly.

gaudy *adj.* bright and showy.

gauge *n.* an instrument for measuring, testing or estimating.
GAUGE *v.* to measure, test or estimate.

gaunt *adj.* thin; haggard; grim.

gay *adj.* lively; cheerful; full of fun.

gaze (at) *v.* to look at intently.
GAZE *n.* an intent look.

gear *n.* 1 equipment; tools. 2 toothed wheels for transferring motion in machinery, as in the gearbox of a motor vehicle.

gem *n.* a precious stone; something of great value.

gender *n.* the classification of a noun or pronoun as masculine, feminine or neuter.

general *adj.* 1 concerning everybody or everything. 2 not special; widespread.
GENERAL *n.* a high-ranking military officer.

generally *adv.* in most cases; commonly.

generate *v.* to produce; to set going.

generator *n.* a machine for producing electricity, steam, gases, etc.

generous *adj.* 1 liberal; giving freely. 2 kind; forgiving.

genial *adj.* good-natured; pleasant; friendly.

genius *n.* 1 exceptional power or ability. 2 a person who is highly intelligent and talented.

gently *adj.* 1 mild; kind; not rough or violent. 2 soft; light.

gently *adv.* mildly; without violence.

genuine *adj.* real; sincere; authentic.

geography *n.* the study of the Earth's surface, products, climate, inhabitants, etc.

geology *n.* the study of the Earth's crust and its rocks and minerals.

geometry *n.* a branch of mathematics that is the study of lines, angles and figures.

germ *n.* 1 the beginning of a living thing. 2 a beginning. 3 a microbe which may cause disease.

German *adj.* belonging to Germany or its people.
GERMAN *n.* the language or an inhabitant of Germany.

germinate *v.* to begin to grow; to sprout.

gesture *n.* an expressive movement of the body, especially of the hands and arms.

get *v.* 1 to obtain. 2 to catch. 3 to arrive. 4 to become.

ghastly *adj.* pale; hideous; deathlike.

ghost *n.* a spirit, supposed to be of a dead person.

giant *n.* a person, animal or plant of great height or size.
GIANT *adj.* unusually large; gigantic; monstrous.

gift *n.* 1 something given; a donation; a present. 2 a natural ability or talent.

gigantic *adj.* giant; huge; enormous.

giggle *v.* to laugh in a silly manner.
GIGGLE *n.* a silly laugh.

gild *v.* to cover with gold leaf or gold paint; to make bright.

gill *n.* the breathing organ of a fish.

ginger *n.* a tropical plant with a hot spicy root.

gypsy, gipsy *n.* a wandering person who lives in a caravan.

giraffe *n.* an African animal with very long legs and a long neck.

girder *n.* a strong beam of concrete, metal or wood supporting a bridge, floor or roof.

girl *n.* a female child or young woman.

give *v.* 1 to hand over; to donate. 2 to begin to break or crack; to yield.

glacial *adj.* having to do with glaciers; icy.

glacier *n.* a slow-moving mass of ice.

glad *adj.* happy; pleased; joyful.

gladiator *n.* a man trained, in Roman times, to fight in an arena with other men or with wild animals.

glamour *n.* charm; attraction; beauty.

glance *n.* a brief look.
GLANCE (AT) *v.* to look briefly at.

gland *n.* an organ of the body which stores and gives off used-up substances from the blood.

glare *v.* 1 to shine with a dazzling light. 2 to stare fiercely.
GLARE *n.* 1 a dazzling light. 2 a fierce stare.

glass *n.* 1 a transparent substance made from sand and soda. 2 a vessel made of glass.
GLASSY *adj.*

glaze *n.* a glasslike surface applied to pottery, porcelain, earthenware, etc.

gleam *n.* a brief flash of light.
GLEAM *v.* to glow; to flash.

glide *v.* 1 to move smoothly and slowly. 2 to fly an aircraft without an engine.
GLIDE *n.* a smooth, slow motion.

glimmer *v.* to shine faintly and unsteadily.
GLIMMER *n.* a faint, unsteady light.

glimpse *n.* a quick look or glance.
GLIMPSE *v.* to have a quick or incomplete view of.

glitter *v.* to sparkle; to glisten.

gloat *v.* to look at or to think about greedily, evilly or selfishly.

global *adj.* worldwide; affecting everybody.

globe *n.* a ball; a sphere; the Earth.

gloom *n.* 1 dimness. 2 sadness; depression.

glorify *v.* to praise highly; to honor; to worship.

glorious *adj.* 1 splendid; magnificent. 2 famous; renowned.

glory *n.* 1 splendor; magnificence. 2 fame; renown.

gloss *n.* a smooth, shiny surface.

glossary *n.* a list of words and their meanings.

glove *n.* a covering for the hand.

glow *v.* 1 to throw out light and heat without flame. 2 to feel hot and flushed.

glowing *adj.* 1 warm and bright. 2 hot and flushed. 3 enthusiastic.

glue *adj.* an adhesive.

glum *adj.* gloomy; downcast.

gnarled *adj.* twisted and knotty.

gnash *v.* to grind the teeth.

gnat *n.* a small biting insect.

gnaw *v.* to bite at bit by bit; to chew.

gnome *n.* a dwarf; a goblin.

go *v.* 1 to move from one place to another; to depart from. 2 to become.
GO *n.* 1 energy; activity. 2 an attempt.

goal *n.* anything aimed at or wished for.

goat *n.* an animal of the sheep family with horns and long hair.

goblin *n.* a mischievous fairy.

God *n.* the Creator; the Supreme Being.
GOD *n.* an idol; anything worshiped.
fem. GODDESS.

gold *n.* a yellow precious metal.
GOLD, GOLDEN *adj.* like, or made of, gold.

golf *n.* an outdoor game played with clubs and a small ball. GOLFER *n.*

good *adj.* 1 kind. 2 true. 3 well behaved. 4 enjoyable. 5 clever; skillful.
GOOD *n.* welfare; that which is right.

goodness *n.* 1 honesty. 2 kindliness. 3 nourishment.

goodwill *n.* 1 friendliness; kindly feeling. 2 the value of the success and reputation of a business.

goose *n.* a large bird with webbed feet.
pl. GEESE. *masc.* GANDER.

gooseberry *n.* a thorny shrub bearing an edible green or red hairy fruit. *pl.* GOOSEBERRIES.

gorge *n.* a deep valley.

gorgeous *adj.* splendid; fine; magnificent.

gorilla *n.* an African ape, the largest kind of ape.

gospel *n.* an account of the life and teaching of Christ; one of the first four books in the New Testament.

gossip *n.* 1 idle talk, chatter or rumor. 2 a person who gossips.
GOSSIP *v.* to talk and chatter idly.

Gothic *adj.* belonging to a style of architecture having high and pointed arches.

govern *v.* to rule; to control; to influence.

government *n.* 1 rule; control; authority. 2 the body of people chosen to rule a country.

grab *v.* to seize or grasp something suddenly.

grace *n.* 1 beauty, style, elegance. 2 a prayer or blessing. GRACE *v.* to give charm to; to honor.

graceful *adj.* beautiful in appearance and manner.

gracious *adj.* graceful; gentle; courteous.
GRACIOUSLY *adv.*

grade *n.* step or degree in quality, rank or scale.
GRADE *v.* to arrange in order.

gradual *adj.* by degrees; going slowly but surely.
GRADUALLY *adv.*

graduate *v.* 1 to arrange in order or mark in degrees. 2 to obtain a school degree.
GRADUATE *n.* a person who has obtained a school degree.

grain *n.* 1 the seed of barley, oats, wheat, etc. 2 a small particle. 3 the lines of fiber making the pattern in wood.

gram *n.* the thousandth part of a kilogram.

grammar *n.* the study of the rules for correctly using words.

grand *adj.* fine; great; splendid.

granite *n.* a very hard rock used in building.

grant *v.* to give; to allow.
GRANT *n.* an allowance; a payment.

grape *n.* the fruit of the vine.

graph *n.* a diagram which shows variations in quantity (e.g. temperature, rainfall, income, expenditure) and from which information can be extracted.

graphite *n.* a soft, black form of carbon used in making pencil leads.

grasp *v.* 1 to grip; to seize firmly.
2 to understand.
GRASP *n.* 1 a grip. 2 an understanding.

grass *n.* the common green plants which provide food for cattle and are mowed to form lawns, etc.

grateful *adj.* thankful; appreciative.

gratitude *n.* thankfulness; appreciation.

grave *n.* a burial place.
GRAVE *adj.* serious; solemn; important.
GRAVELY *adv.* seriously; solemnly.

gravel *n.* small stones or pebbles; a mixture of sand and pebbles.

gravity *n.* 1 the force by which all bodies are drawn towards the Earth's center.
2 seriousness; importance.

gravy *n.* the juices that come from meat that is cooking; a sauce made from these juices.

gray *adj.* ash-colored. gray-colored; dull.
GRAY *n.* a mixture of black and white; the color gray.

graze *v.* 1 to feed on growing grass. 2 to touch lightly. GRAZE *n.* a slight wound or scrape.

grease *n.* a thick fatty or oily substance used as a lubricant.
GREASE *v.* to smear with grease; to lubricate.

great *adj.* 1 of large amount, size, weight, etc.
2 important. 3 of remarkable ability or skill.
4 notable.

greed *n.* excessive and selfish desire for food, possessions or wealth.

Greek *adj.* belonging to Greece or its people.
GREEK *n.* the language or an inhabitant of Greece.

green *adj.* 1 the color of grass and most growing plants; the color between blue and yellow in the spectrum (rainbow). 2 fresh; unripe; new.
GREEN *n.* ground covered with grass; a lawn.

greenhouse *n.* a glass house where plants are grown.

greet *v.* to welcome.

greeting *n.* a welcome; a salutation.

grid *n.* 1 a system of numbered squares on a map forming the basis for references.
2 a network of power lines for the distribution of electricity. 3 a grating.

gridiron *n.* a grill for cooking.

grief *n.* 1 deep sorrow; anguish. 2 disaster.

grieve *v.* to mourn; to feel sorrow (for); to make (someone) sorrowful.

grill *v.* to cook on a grill.
GRILL *n.* a gridiron.

grim *adj.* stern; dismal; sinister.

grimy *adj.* dirty; dusty.

grin *v.* to smile broadly; to smile scornfully.
GRIN *n.* a broad or scornful smile.

grind *v.* 1 to crush to powder or small particles.
2 to sharpen or polish by grinding.
GROUND *adj.* made smooth by grinding.

grip *v.* to grasp or hold firmly.
GRIP *n.* a firm hold.

groan *v.* to make a moaning sound expressing pain, grief or disapproval.
GROAN *n.* a moaning sound.

groom *n.* 1 a bridegroom. 2 a person who is in charge of horses.
GROOM *v.* 1 to feed, brush and care for horses.
2 to make oneself neat in appearance.
3 to prepare a person for a job or a position.

groove *n.* 1 a channel or hollow.
2 a fixed routine. GROOVE *v.* to cut a groove.

grope *v.* to search (for) by feeling; to seek blindly.

gross *adj.* 1 fat; bulky. 2 coarse; vulgar.
GROSS *n.* 1 the whole; the total including everything. 2 twelve dozen (144).

ground *n.* 1 the surface of the Earth. 2 base, foundation or surface. 3 a special area of land.
4 belief; motive; reason.
GROUND *v.* 1 to run a ship ashore. 2 to keep an aircraft on the ground.

group *n.* a number of people or things gathered together; a cluster.
GROUP *v.* to place in groups.

grove *n.* a small wood or cluster of trees.

grow *v.* 1 to increase in size; to develop.
2 to cultivate. GROWER *n.*
GROWN *adj.* 1 enlarged. 2 fully mature.

growl *v.* to snarl; to murmur angrily.
GROWL *n.* a snarling sound.

growth *n.* 1 a development; progress.
2 what has grown or is growing.

grudge *v.* to be unwilling to give or allow (something to someone).
GRUDGE *n.* a feeling of resentment or ill will.

gruesome *adj.* horrible; repulsive; revolting.

gruff *adj.* rough and surly in manner; hoarse.

grumble *v.* to complain; to murmur.
GRUMBLE *n.* a complaint; a murmur; a protest.

grunt *n.* a sound made by a pig; a low gruff sound. GRUNT *v.* to make a gruff sound.

guarantee *v.* 1 to give one's word that something has happened or will happen. 2 to agree to be responsible for.
GUARANTEE *n.* an assurance; a pledge.

guard *v.* to defend against danger or attack; to protect. GUARD *n.* a defender; a protector.

guardian *n.* a person who protects or guards.

guerrilla, guerilla *n.* a person engaged in irregular warfare.

guess *v.* 1 to estimate without exact calculation. 2 to form an opinion without sufficient evidence. 3 to imagine; to suppose.
GUESS *n.* 1 a rough estimate. 2 an opinion formed without sufficient evidence.

guest *n.* 1 an invited visitor. 2 a person staying in a hotel.

guidance *n.* 1 leadership; management. 2 facts or advice which help a person to act properly.

guide *v.* to lead; to direct; to show the way.

guide *n.* a person who shows the way; a leader.

guilt *n.* the fact of having done wrong or having broken the law.

guilty *adj.* responsible for an offense or crime.

guitar *n.* a six-stringed musical instrument.

gulf *n.* 1 a large inlet of the sea. 2 a deep place. 3 a wide gap.

gull *n.* a white, long-winged, web-footed, fish-eating sea bird.

gully *n.* a channel worn by running water.

gulp *v.* to swallow hastily or greedily.
GULP *n.* the act of gulping.

gum *n.* 1 the flesh surrounding the teeth. 2 an adhesive.

gun *n.* a firearm; a weapon firing bullets, shells, etc.

gunpowder *n.* an explosive mixture in powder form.

gust *n.* a sudden blast of wind.

gutter *n.* a channel for carrying away rainwater.

gymnasium *n.* a room or hall for sports.

gymnast *n.* a person skilled in gymnastics.

gymnastics *n.* bodily exercises and activities.

H

habit *n.* something that is done regularly or by custom.

habitat *n.* the natural home of an animal or a plant.

habitation *n.* a home; a dwelling.

habitual *adj.* 1 formed by habit. 2 usual; regular.

haddock *n.* a seafish of the cod family.

hail *n.* frozen drops of rain.
HAIL *v.* 1 to fall as hail. 2 to greet; to welcome.

hair *n.* fine filaments growing from the skin of many mammals, including humans.

hale *adj.* healthy; robust; strong.

half *n.* one of two equal parts.
HALF *adj.* forming one of two equal parts. *pl.* HALVES.

hall *n.* 1 an entrance, passage or room. 2 a large room for public or private functions.

Hallowe'en *n.* the evening before All Saints' Day, October 31st.

halo *n.* a circle of light around the sun or moon or around the head of a sacred figure in a painting. *pl.* HALOES.

halt *v.* to stop; to hesitate.
HALT *n.* a stopping place.

halter *n.* a rope or strap for leading horses.

halve *v.* 1 to divide into two equal parts. 2 to reduce by half.

ham *n.* 1 the back of the thigh. 2 the salted and cured thigh of a pig; a gammon.

hammer *n.* a tool with a heavy steel head for driving in nails, etc.
HAMMER *v.* to beat or strike with a hammer; to beat as with a hammer.

hammock *n.* a bed of canvas or netting suspended by cords at each end.

hamper *v.* to hinder.

hand *n.* the part of the arm below the wrist.
HAND *v.* to pass by hand.

handicap *n.* 1 a disadvantage; a disability. 2 an allowance given to some competitors to enable all to start on equal terms.
HANDICAP *v.* to hinder.

handkerchief *n.* a square of material for wiping or blowing the nose.

handle *n.* the part by which an article is held.
HANDLE *v.* 1 to touch or feel with the hand. 2 to manage.

handsome *adj.* 1 good-looking. 2 generous.

hang *v.* to suspend; to drape; to droop.

hangar *n.* a building for housing aircraft.

hanger *n.* a hook or device on which something is hung.

haphazard *adj.* by chance or at random.

happen *v.* 1 to take place. 2 to occur by chance.

happening *n.* an event; an occurrence.

happily *adv.* 1 joyfully. 2 fortunately.

happiness *n.* joy; contentment.

happy *adj.* 1 feeling or showing joy.
2 contented; satisfied.

harbor *n.* a place of shelter for ships.
HARBOR *v.* to shelter.

hard *adj.* 1 firm; not easily broken. 2 difficult.
3 severe; harsh.

harden *v.* to make or become firm or solid.

hardly *adv.* only just; not quite.

hardship *n.* something hard to bear; severe
suffering.

hardy *adj.* 1 strong; able to bear suffering.
2 (of plants) that can grow in the open in a
temperate or cold climate.

hare *n.* a rodent like a large rabbit, with long
ears, short tail and long hind legs.

harm *v.* to injure; to damage.
HARM *n.* an injury; a wrong.

harmful *adj.* causing injury or damage.

harmless *adj.* doing no harm.

harmony *n.* 1 agreeable combination of musical
notes or of colors. 2 agreement; friendship.

harness *n.* the equipment of reins, bit, collar,
straps, etc., for harnessing a horse.
HARNESS *v.* 1 to put in harness. 2 to control and
use (natural energy) for power.

harp *n.* a triangular stringed musical instrument.
HARPIST *n.*

harpoon *n.* a barbed spear with rope attached for
catching whales, etc.

harsh *adj.* 1 rough to the touch, taste, eye or ear.
2 cruel; severe. HARSHLY *adv.*

harvest *n.* 1 the time of gathering in the ripened
crops. 2 the crops gathered in.
HARVEST *v.* to cut and gather the crops.

haste *n.* speed; rapidity; urgency; hurry.

hasten *v.* to hurry; to accelerate.

hasty *adj.* 1 hurried; done without thinking.
2 quick-tempered.

hat *n.* a covering for the head.

hatch *v.* 1 to incubate (eggs); to come out of
(an egg). 2 to think out a plan or scheme.
HATCH *n.* 1 an opening in deck or floor.
2 a half-door.

hate *v.* to dislike very much; to detest; to loathe.
HATE *n.* a great dislike.

hatred *n.* a bitter dislike of someone or
something.

haul *v.* to pull or drag with effort.
HAUL *n.* 1 a pull. 2 a rich find or catch.

haunt *v.* to visit a person or place often.
HAUNT *n.* a place visited frequently.

have *v.* 1 to possess; to own. 2 to contain.
3 to obtain.

haven *n.* a place of refuge or shelter; a harbor.

havoc *n.* a great destruction.

hawk *n.* a bird of prey in the eagle family.
HAWK *v.* 1 to hunt with hawks. 2 to sell (goods)
from door to door.

hay *n.* grass cut and dried as food for animals.

hazard *n.* 1 a risk; a danger; 2 an obstacle.
HAZARD *v.* 1 to risk; to place in danger.
2 to guess. HAZARDOUS *adj.*

haze *n.* a light mist.

hazy *adj.* 1 misty. 2 confused; vague.

he *pron.* a male person or animal already named.

head *n.* 1 that part of the body consisting of the
face, skull, brain, etc. 2 a chief part, place or
person.
HEAD *v.* 1 to be at the top or in front of.
2 to strike with the head.

headache *n.* a pain in the head.

heal *v.* to cure; to restore. HEALER *n.*
HEALING *adj.*

health *n.* 1 the condition of a person's body and
mind. 2 freedom from illness or disease.

healthy *adj.* 1 in good health. 2 wholesome.

heap *n.* a pile, mound or group of things.
HEAP *v.* to pile up.

hear *v.* to perceive the sound of; to listen to.

hearing *n.* 1 the sense by which sound is
perceived; the ability to hear. 2 a trial of a law
case.

hearse *n.* a funeral vehicle for carrying a coffin.

heart *n.* 1 the organ that pumps blood around
the body. 2 the center; the core.

hearth *n.* the floor or base of a fireplace.

hearty *adj.* 1 strong; healthy. 2 enthusiastic;
jovial.

heat *n.* 1 hotness; warmth. 2 anger.
HEAT *v.* to make hot. HEATED *adj.* angry.

heater *n.* an appliance for providing warmth or
heating water.

heathen *n.* a person who does not believe in
God.

heather *n.* a heath plant with small purple or
white flowers.

heaven *n.* 1 the dwelling place of God.
2 the sky.

heavens *n. pl.* the sky with all the stars and
planets.

heavy *adj.* having great weight, size, abundance, force, strength, etc.

Hebrew *n.* the language of the Jews.

hectare *n.* a metric measurement of area. 10,000 square meters (2,471 acres).

hectic *adj.* exciting; wildly active.

hedge *n.* a fence of growing shrubs, bushes or small trees.
HEDGE *v.* 1 to fence; to enclose. 2 to avoid making a decision or promise.

hedgehog *n.* a small animal covered with prickly spines.

heel *n.* the back part of the foot.

height *n.* 1 distance from top to bottom. 2 altitude. 3 a high place.

heir *n.* a person who inherits; a successor. *fem.* HEIRESS.

helicopter *n.* an aircraft able to take off and alight vertically, to fly and to hover.

helium *n.* a rare, light and colorless gas in the atmosphere.

hell *n.* 1 believed by some to be where the wicked go after death. 2 a place or state of misery or suffering.

helm *n.* the wheel or tiller by which a ship is steered. HELMSMAN *n.*

helmet *n.* a protective head cover worn by motorcyclists, soldiers, firefighters, etc.

help *v.* to aid; to assist.
HELP *n.* aid; assistance. HELPER *n.*

helpful *adj.* giving help; useful.

helpless *adj.* powerless; useless.

hem *n.* the edge of a garment, piece of material, etc., folded over and sewed down.
HEM *v.* to fold over and sew down.

hemisphere *n.* 1 half a sphere. 2 half the globe or half the world.

hen *n.* a female bird.

her *pron.* a female person or animal already named. HER *adj.* of, or belonging to, a female.

herald *n.* 1, an official who carries messages and makes public announcements. 2 an announcer; a messenger; a forerunner.
HERALD *v.* to proclaim; to announce.

herb *n.* a plant used to provide flavor in cooking, or as a medicine.

herd *n.* 1 a group of animals. 2 a crowd of people. HERD *v.* to collect together.
HERDSMAN *n.* a keeper of a herd.

here *adv.* in this place or to this place.

hereditary *adj.* handed down from one generation to the next.

heredity *n.* the passing on of characteristics from animals and plants to their offspring.

heritage *n.* something which is inherited or will be inherited; a right.

hermit *n.* a person who chooses to live alone.

hero *n.* a man admired for his brave deeds or courage. *fem.* HEROINE. *pl.* HEROES.

heroic *adj.* brave; courageous.

heroism *n.* great gallantry or courage.

hesitate *v.* to pause in doubt or indecision; to be reluctant.

hesitation *n.* doubt; indecision.

hexagon *n.* a six-sided plane figure with six angles. HEXAGONAL *adj.*

hibernate *v.* to pass the winter in sleep. HIBERNATION *n.*

hidden *adj.* 1 concealed. 2 kept secret.

hide *v.* 1 to put or to keep out of sight; to conceal. 2 to keep secret.
HIDE *n.* 1 a place of concealment. 2 the skin of an animal.

hideous *adj.* horribly ugly; frightful.

high *adj.* 1 reaching a long way upwards; elevated. 2 chief; important. 3 strong; shrill.

highway *n.* a public road.

hijack *v.* to take over control unlawfully of an aircraft, ship, train or vehicle by force.

hike *n.* a long walk.

hill *n.* a mass of high land; rising ground; a slope.

him *pron.* a male person or animal already named.

hinder *v.* to obstruct; to delay.

Hindu *n.* a person whose religion is Hinduism, ususally from northern India.

hinge *n.* the joint on which a door, gate or lid hangs and swings.
HINGE *v.* 1 to turn on a hinge. 2 to depend upon.

hint *n.* an indirect suggestion; a slight indication.
HINT *v.* to make an indirect suggestion.

hip *n.* 1 the upper part of the thigh. 2 the fruit of the wild rose.

hippopotamus *n.* a large African animal living in or near rivers.
pl. HIPPOPOTAMI, HIPPOPOTAMUSES.

hire *v.* to employ (a person) and pay wages.

his *pron.* belonging to him.
HIS *adj.* of or belonging to him.

history *n.* 1 the study of past events. 2 an account of what has happened in the past. *pl.* HISTORIES.

hit *v.* to strike; to collide (with).
HIT *n.* 1 a stroke or blow. 2 a great success.

hitch *v.* 1 to fasten loosely. 2 to move with a jerk.
HITCH *n.* 1 a fastening or tethering; a knot. 2 an unexpected difficulty or delay.

hive *n.* 1 a place where bees live. 2 a busy place.

hoard *n.* a hidden store of foods, treasure, etc.
HOARD *v.* to store or to collect. HOARDER *n.*

hoarse *adj.* rough and husky. HOARSELY *adv.*

hoax *n.* a practical joke.
HOAX *v.* to play a practical joke on; to deceive.

hobble *v.* 1 to limp or to walk lamely. 2 to restrict the movement of an animal by tying a rope between two of its legs.

hobby *n.* a favorite pastime or recreation. *pl.* HOBBIES.

hoe *n.* a long-handled tool used for loosening soil and removing weeds.

hog *n.* 1 a pig. 2 a greedy person.
HOG *v.* 1 to keep selfishly. 2 to take more than a fair share of.

hoist *v.* to lift up; to lift by means of a rope.
HOIST *n.* equipment used for hoisting; an elevator.

hold *v.* 1 to grasp; to grip. 2 to stop; to restrain. 3 to have; to keep.
HOLD *n.* 1 a grasp; a grip. 2 the cargo space in a ship.

hole *n.* an opening or hollow in something; a cavity.

holiday *n.* a day of rest or recreation.

hollow *adj.* 1 having an empty space inside; not solid; sunken. 2 insincere.
HOLLOW *n.* 1 a hole. 2 a small valley.
HOLLOW (OUT) *v.* to make hollow; to excavate.

holly *n.* an evergreen shrub or tree with glossy prickly leaves and red berries.

holy *adj.* to do with God or religion; sacred.

honest *adj.* fair; truthful; true. HONESTLY *adv.*

honey *n.* a sweet, thick fluid made by bees from the nectar of flowers.

honor *n.* 1 fame; a high reputation. 2 respect for truth, fairness and honesty.
HONOR *v.* 1 to respect. 2 to confer an honor upon.

hood *n.* 1 a covering for the head and neck. 2 anything of a hoodlike shape.

hoof *n.* a horny substance protecting the feet of certain mammals. *pl.* HOOFS, HOOVES.

hook *n.* a curved piece of metal or plastic for catching or supporting something.
HOOK *v.* to catch, support or hold with a hook.

hoot *n.* 1 the cry of an owl. 2 the sound of a horn or siren. HOOT *v.* to make a hooting sound.

hop *v.* to jump on one foot.
HOP *n.* 1 a short jump. 2 a climbing plant, the flowers of which are used in beermaking.

hope *v.* to expect and wish (that something will happen). HOPE *n.* expectation; belief.

horde *n.* 1 a wandering tribe. 2 a great number of people; a multitude.

horizon *n.* the distant line where the earth or sea seems to meet the sky.

horizontal *adj.* parallel to the horizon; flat.

horn *n.* 1 the hard, usually curved and pointed, growths on the heads of some cattle and other mammals. 2 a musical wind instrument; a device for sounding a warning signal.

hornet *n.* a wasplike insect with a painful sting.

horrible *adj.* causing horror; hideous; shocking.

horrify *v.* to fill with horror; to shock.

horse *n.* a hoofed mammal used for riding and pulling loads.

horticulture *n.* the art of garden cultivation.

hospitable *adj.* friendly and welcoming.

hospital *n.* a building where sick or injured people are given medical treatment.

hospitality *n.* the friendly welcome and treatment of a guest or visitor.

host *n.* 1 a person who entertains guests. *fem.* HOSTESS. 2 a great number of people.

hostage *n.* a person held prisoner until certain demands have been met.

hostile *adj.* unfriendly; threatening; warlike.

hostility *n.* warfare; enmity.

hot *adj.* 1 very warm. 2 spicy to the taste. 3 hasty; eager.

hotel *n.* a building where meals and accommodations are provided for visitors.

hound *n.* a dog used for hunting.
HOUND *v.* to pursue; to persecute.

hour *n.* 1 sixty minutes; the twenty-fourth part of a day. 2 the fixed or appointed time.

hourly *adj.* occurring every hour.
HOURLY *adv.* every hour.

house *n.* (pron. HOWS) a building in which people live; a building with a specified use.
HOUSE *v.* (pron. HOWZ) to provide shelter or room for.

household *n.* the family or people living together in one house.

hover *v.* 1 to hang in the air. 2 to hang about.

how *adv.* 1 in what manner or way. 2 to what extent. 3 for what price.
HOW *n.* the way a thing is done.

however *adv.* in whatever way; to whatever degree. HOWEVER *conj.* though; in spite of.

howl *n.* a long wailing cry. HOWL *v.* to wail.

hub *n.* 1 the central part of a wheel. 2 the central point of interest.

huddle *v.* to crowd together. HUDDLE *n.* a crowd of people or things.

hue *n.* 1 a color; a shade of color. 2 an outcry.

huff *n.* a fit of temper or sulking.

hug *v.* 1 to close within the arms or to embrace. 2 to keep close to. HUG *n.* a squeeze; an embrace.

huge *adj.* very large; enormous; gigantic.

hull *n.* the body or frame of a ship.

human *adj.* of man or mankind.

humane *adj.* kind; merciful; sympathetic.

humanity *n.* 1 all human beings. 2 kindness and mercy.

humble *adj.* modest, unassuming. HUMBLE *v.* to shame; to defeat.

humid *adj.* damp; moist.

humidity *n.* 1 dampness. 2 the amount of water in the air.

humiliate *v.* to make someone feel humble; to shame.

humility *n.* humbleness; meekness.

humor *n.* 1 the ability to see the funny side of things. 2 a state of mind. HUMOR *v.* to try to please (a person) by agreeing.

humorous *adj.* full of humor; funny. HUMOROUSLY *adv.*

hump *n.* a lump.

hundred *n.* ten times ten; the number 100.

hunger *n.* the need or desire for food. HUNGER *v.* 1 to feel hunger. 2 HUNGER FOR or AFTER to desire; to crave.

hunt *v.* 1 to pursue. 2 to pursue and kill wild animals. HUNT *n.* 1 a search. 2 a group of hunters.

hunter *n.* 1 a person who hunts. 2 a horse used in hunting.

hurdle *n.* 1 a movable fence. 2 an obstacle.

hurl *v.* to throw with force.

hurricane *n.* a severe storm with high winds.

hurried *adj.* done with haste; quick.

hurry *v.* to move or to act quickly. HURRY *n.* haste; urgency.

hurt *v.* 1 to cause injury or pain to. 2 to cause offense or distress to. HURT *n.* an injury; a pain.

husband *n.* a married man. HUSBAND *v.* to use or manage carefully.

hush *v.* to make silent or quiet. HUSH *n.* a stillness; silence. HUSHED *adj.*

husk *n.* the dry covering of some fruits and seeds.

husky *adj.* hoarse and dry. HUSKY *n.* an Eskimo sled-dog.

hustle *v.* 1 to push or jostle together. 2 to hurry.

hut *n.* a small building, generally of wood.

hydraulic *adj.* worked by fluid pressure.

hydrogen *n.* a gas which produces water when combined with oxygen; the lightest substance known.

hyena *n.* a wild, wolflike animal.

hygiene *n.* the science of health.

hymn *n.* a song of praise to God.

hyphen *n.* the mark (-) used to join words or divide a word into parts.

hyphenate *v.* to join with a hyphen.

hypnosis *n.* an artificially-induced sleep.

hypnotize *v.* to put a person into a state of hypnosis. HYPNOTIST *n.*

hypocrisy *n.* a pretense of being virtuous and respectable.

hypocrite *n.* a person who pretends to be good.

hypotenuse *n.* the longest side of a right-angled triangle, the side opposite the right angle.

hysterical *adj.* having hysterics; very easily excited.

hysterics *n.* an attack of uncontrollable laughing or weeping.

I

ice *n.* frozen water. ICE *v.* to cover with icing.

iceberg *n.* a large floating mass of ice in the ocean.

Iceland *n.* a large island in the North Atlantic Ocean between Norway and Greenland.

icicle *n.* a hanging spike of ice formed by the freezing of dripping water.

icing *n.* a sugary layer on the top or outside of a cake, tart, etc.

icy *adj.* 1 covered in ice; very cold. 2 unfriendly, cool.

idea *n.* 1 a thought, a fancy. 2 a plan or scheme.

ideal *n.* a perfect example; the highest standard. IDEAL *adj.* perfect.

identical *adj.* exactly alike in every detail. IDENTICALLY *adv.*

identify *v.* 1 to recognize; to establish the identity of. 2 to treat as identical.

identity *n.* 1 absolute sameness. 2 who a person is.

idiot *n.* a foolish or weak-minded person.

idle *adj.* 1 unoccupied; not working. 2 useless; lazy. IDLE *v.* to pass time idly.

idol *n.* 1 an image which is worshipped; a false god. 2 a greatly-loved person or thing; a hero.

igloo *n.* a dome-shaped snow hut built by Eskimos.

igneous *adj.* to do with fire.

ignite *v.* to set on fire; to catch fire.

ignition *n.* 1 a setting on fire. 2 the device for igniting the gasoline-air mixture in the cylinders of a gasoline engine.

ignorance *n.* lack of knowledge, information or awareness. IGNORANT *adj.* lacking knowledge; uninformed.

ignore *v.* to refuse to take notice of; to disregard.

ill *adj.* 1 sick; unwell. 2 evil; bad. 3 unfortunate; unlucky.

illegal *adj.* against the law; unlawful; not legal. ILLEGALLY *adv.*

illegible *adj.* not legible; unreadable.

illicit *adj.* unlawful; illegal; forbidden; prohibited. ILLICITLY *adv.*

illiterate *adj.* unable to read or write. ILLITERACY *n.*

illness *n.* poor health; sickness.

illogical *adj.* against the rules of reason; without logic. ILLOGICALLY *adv.*

illuminate *v.* 1 to light up; to throw light upon. 2 to decorate (a page or document) with gold, silver, colors, etc.

illusion *n.* something that deceives. ILLUSORY *adj.* deceptive.

illustrate *v.* 1 to make clear; to explain. 2 to explain by examples or by drawings and pictures.

illustration *n.* 1 an example which helps to make a matter clear. 2 a drawing or picture in a book, newspaper, etc. ILLUSTRATOR *n.*

image *n.* 1 a copy or close likeness; a statue. 2 a reflection seen in a mirror or camera lens.

imaginary *adj.* imagined; existing only in the mind; unreal.

imagination *n.* the ability to form ideas and images in the mind.

imagine *v.* to form a picture in the mind; to suppose.

imitate *v.* to copy; to mimic.

imitation *n.* a copy; a sham; a counterfeit. IMITATION *adj.* false.

immaculate *adj.* pure; faultless; spotless.

immaterial *adj.* not important; trivial.

immature *adj.* not fully developed; not mature.

immediate *adj.* 1 with nothing coming between; close. 2 happening at once; prompt. IMMEDIATELY *adv.*

immense *adj.* very large; vast. IMMENSELY *adv.*

immerse *v.* 1 to dip or plunge (something) into liquid. 2 IMMERSE ONESELF IN to give (one's) total attention to. IMMERSION *n.*

immigrant *n.* a person who settles in a country that is not his own.

immigrate *v.* to enter a country to settle there. IMMIGRATION *n.*

imminent *adj.* about to happen.

immoral *adj.* morally wrong; evil; wicked.

immune *adj.* free or safe from; exempt from.

immunity *n.* freedom from, esp. disease; exemption from.

impact *n.* 1 a blow or collision. 2 effect; influence.

impair *v.* to damage; to weaken.

impale *v.* to fix on a sharp stake or spear.

impartial *adj.* not favoring one more than another; fair. IMPARTIALITY *n.* fairness.

impatience *n.* restlessness; lack of patience.

impede *v.* to hinder; to obstruct. IMPEDIMENT *n.* obstruction.

impel *v.* 1 to drive forward; to urge. 2 to persuade.

impend *v.* 1 to be about to happen. 2 to threaten. IMPENDING *adj.*

imperfect *adj.* not perfect; faulty.

imperial *adj.* concerning an empire or emperor or empress; majestic.

imperil *v.* to place in peril; to put in danger.

imperishable *adj.* that cannot perish; everlasting.

impersonate *v.* 1 to pretend to be someone else. 2 to act the part of.

impertinent *adj.* insolent; saucy; rude.

impervious *adj.* 1 not allowing anything to pass through; impenetrable. 2 deaf to.

impetuous *adj.* acting hastily and on impulse.

impetus *n.* the force moving a thing along; encouragement.

implement *n.* a tool; an instrument. IMPLEMENT *v.* 1 to complete. 2 to carry out (a plan or instructions).

implicate *v.* to involve a person in an offense, crime, etc.; to entangle in.

implore v. to beg or request earnestly.

imply v. to suggest the meaning of; to hint.

import v. 1 to bring (goods) into the country from abroad. 2 to convey a meaning.
IMPORT n. the meaning; importance.
IMPORTS n. pl. goods brought into the country from abroad.

important adj. mattering very much; of great influence, authority or consequence.
IMPORTANCE n.

impose v. 1 to apply (esp. taxes, penalties).
2 to force (oneself on others).
3 IMPOSE UPON to take advantage of (someone).

imposing adj. grand; large, impressive.

impossible adj. not possible, that cannot be done. IMPOSSIBILITY n.

impostor n. a person who pretends to be somebody else in order to deceive.

impress v. 1 to influence; to affect strongly.
2 to mark by pressing or stamping.

impression n. 1 an influence or effect on the mind or feelings; a vague feeling. 2 a pressed or stamped mark.

impressive adj. having a great effect on the mind or senses; dramatic; imposing.

improbable adj. not likely to be true or to happen.

improper adj. 1 wrong; not suitable.
2 indecent.

improve v. to make or to become better.

improvise v. to speak, play or do without preparation.

impudent adj. disrespectful; rude; insolent.
IMPUDENCE n.

impulse n. 1 a sudden decision to do something without thinking. 2 a sudden surge.

impure adj. not pure; mixed with other things.
IMPURITY n.

inability n. lack of ability, power or means.

inaccessible adj. that cannot be reached; unapproachable.

inaccurate adj. not accurate; not correct; not exact. INACCURACY n.

inactive adj. not active; doing nothing.
INACTIVITY n.

inadequate adj. not adequate; not sufficient.
INADEQUACY n.

inarticulate adj. unable to speak clearly or distinctly.

inaudible adj. not able to be heard.

inaugurate v. to begin; to introduce; to make a formal opening or to admit someone at a ceremony. INAUGURATION n.

incapable adj. not capable; not able to act normally.

incendiary n. 1 a bomb or device for starting a fire. 2 a person who maliciously sets fire to property. 3 a person who stirs up trouble.

incense n. (pron. IN-sense) a mixture of spices which gives off fragrant sweet fumes when burned.
INCENSE v. (pron. in-SENSE) to enrage; to make angry.

incentive n. 1 something which encourages or incites to action. 2 an aim or urge.

incessant adj. continual; not ceasing.

inch n. a measure of length, one twelfth of a foot (2.54 centimeters).

incident n. an event; an occurrence; an episode.

incidental adj. happening as a result; casual.

incision n. a cut or gash; a cutting into something.

incite v. to urge on; to stir up.

inclement adj. severe, esp. of weather or climate.

inclination n. 1 a leaning; a slope; a slant.
2 a liking or affection for.

incline v. 1 INCLINE TOWARD to lean or to slope toward. 2 INCLINE TO to have a liking for.
INCLINE n. a slope; a slant. INCLINED adj.

include v. 1 to put among others as part of a whole. 2 to contain.

inclusive adj. counting everything in; including everything. INCLUSION n.

income n. money that is received regularly from wages, investments, etc.

incomparable adj. not to be compared with; matchless; unequaled.

incompetent adj. not competent; not qualified or not able to do something; incapable.

incomplete adj. not complete; unfinished; imperfect.

inconsiderate adj. not considerate; thoughtless, lacking in regard for others; selfish.

inconsistent adj. not consistent; unreasonable; variable.

inconvenient adj. not convenient; awkward; troublesome; not suitable.

incorporate v. to combine into one whole.

incorrect adj. not correct; wrong; inaccurate; untrue.

increase v. (pron. in-KREASE) to become or make greater; to grow in numbers.
INCREASE n. (pron. IN-krease) a gain; a growth.
INCREASED adj.

incredible adj. hard to believe; surprising; amazing.

incubate *v.* to hatch eggs.

incurable *adj.* unable to be cured.

indebted *adj.* owing money or gratitude.

indecent *adj.* offending against modesty or accepted good taste; obscene.

indecisive *adj.* undecided; unable to make a clear decision.

indeed *adv.* in fact; really.

indefinite *adj.* not definite; vague; uncertain; unlimited.

independence *n.* being independent; freedom of action and thought.

independent *adj.* not dependent on or controlled by other persons or things; self-governing; uncontrolled.

index *n.* 1 the forefinger. 2 a pointer on an instrument. 3 an alphabetical list showing the contents of a book. INDEX *v.* to make an index.

Indian *adj.* belonging to India or its people. INDIAN *n.* an inhabitant of India.

indicate *v.* to point out; to show; to make known. INDICATION *n.*

indifference *n.* lack of interest or attention.

indifferent *adj.* 1 not interested; not caring. 2 neither good nor bad; moderate.

indigestion *n.* difficulty in digesting food; pain due to poor digestion of food.

indignant *adj.* feeling anger, scorn or injured innocence. INDIGNATION *n.*

indignity *n.* unworthy treatment; an insult; a slight.

indirect *adj.* not direct; not going straight to the point. INDIRECTLY *adv.*

indiscreet *adj.* not discreet; thoughtless in speech or behavior; lacking in caution.

indiscriminate *adj.* confused; making no distinctions.

individual *adj.* concerning only one of a group; single; special. INDIVIDUAL *n.* one person, animal or thing.

indulge *v.* 1 to satisfy (desires). 2 to spoil or pamper.

industrial *adj.* of industry and manufacture.

industrious *adj.* hard-working; diligent.

industry *n.* 1 the business of trade or manufacturing. 2 diligence; hard work.

inedible *adj.* not fit to be eaten.

ineffective *adj.* not producing the desired effect; having no effect; not effective.

inefficient *adj.* not efficient; not able or qualified to do the task or work required. INEFFICIENCY *n.*

inevitable *adj.* unavoidable; sure to happen.

inexpensive *adj.* not expensive; cheap.

inexperience *n.* lack of skill, knowledge or practice.

infallible *adj.* not fallible; never making mistakes; unfailing.

infant *n.* a baby; a young child. INFANCY *n.*

infantry *n.* foot soldiers.

infect *v.* 1 to pass on (a disease) to. 2 to cause somebody to share one's feelings.

infection *n.* 1 the means by which disease is spread. 2 anything that spreads widely and affects other people.

infer *v.* to reach a conclusion from the known facts or reasoning; to hint at. INFERENCE *n.*

inferior *adj.* lower in any way; not of the best quality. INFERIORITY *n.*

infest *v.* to overrun; to swarm over.

infiltrate *v.* to pass into in small numbers or to penetrate gradually.

infirm *adj.* feeble, weak or frail in health or mind. INFIRMITY *n.*

inflame *v.* 1 to make hot. 2 to make sore. 3 to rouse passion or anger.

inflammable *adj.* easily set on fire. (see FLAMMABLE).

inflate *v.* 1 to fill with air or gas. 2 to puff up with pride. INFLATED *adj.*

inflation *n.* 1 the act of blowing up. 2 a drop in the value of money.

inflexible *adj.* 1 unbending; stubborn. 2 rigid; stiff.

inflict *v.* to impose suffering (pain, etc.) upon (someone). INFLICTION *n.*

influence *n.* the ability to affect others. INFLUENCE *v.* to have an effect on.

influential *adj.* having great influence.

inform *v.* to tell; to instruct.

informal *adj.* not according to form; free and easy; friendly.

informant *n.* a giver of information.

information *n.* knowledge; news; what is told.

infuriate *v.* to make angry; to fill with fury. INFURIATED *adj.*

ingenious *adv.* 1 clever; expert. 2 carefully planned. INGENUITY *n.*

ingredient *n.* one of the materials or parts in a mixture.

inhabit *v.* to live in; to occupy. INHABITED *adj.* INHABITANT *n.*

inhale *v.* to breathe in; to take into the lungs.

inherit *v.* 1 to receive property, money or title left in a will or as an heir. 2 to derive (qualities or character) from parents or ancestors.

inhuman *adj.* unlike a human; brutal; ruthless.

initial *adj.* occurring at the beginning.
INITIAL *n.* the first letter of a word.

initiative *n.* 1 the first step. 2 readiness to lead.

inject *v.* to drive or force into, esp. with a syringe. INJECTION *n.*

injure *v.* to harm; to damage. INJURED *adj.*

injury *n.* 1 harm; damage. 2 wrongful action or treatment. *pl.* INJURIES.

injustice *n.* a wrong; unfairness.

ink *n.* a colored liquid used in writing and printing.

inlet *n.* a narrow strip of water or small bay.

inmate *n.* an occupant of a hospital, prison, etc.

innocent *adj.* not guilty; free from guilt or blame. INNOCENCE *n.*

inoculate *v.* to give (a person) a mild form of a disease to safeguard against more serious attacks. INOCULATION *n.*

inquest *n.* a legal inquiry into the cause of a death, accident or other matters of fact.

inquire *v.* 1 INQUIRE OF to ask; to seek information. 2 INQUIRE INTO to investigate. 3 INQUIRE AFTER to ask about someone's well-being. INQUIRY *n.*

inquisitive *adj.* inquiring; curious; prying.

insane *adj.* not sane; mad; senseless; mentally ill. INSANITY *n.*

inscribe *v.* to write or engrave words, signs, etc., on stone, metal, paper, etc. INSCRIPTION *n.*

insect *n.* a small animal, such as a bee or fly, with six legs and three parts to its body-head, chest and abdomen.

insecure *adj.* 1 unsafe; liable to give way; not feeling secure. 2 lacking confidence.

insert *v.* to put (something) in; to add (something) to. INSERTION *n.*

inside *prep.* on the inner side of; within.
INSIDE *adj.* contained within; internal.
INSIDE *n.* inner side or surface; the interior.

insight *n.* the power to understand clearly.

insignificant *adj.* unimportant, negligible; little; of no consequence.

insincere *adj.* not sincere; not to be trusted.

insist *v.* to demand or maintain firmly; to urge strongly. INSISTENCE *n.*

insolent *adj.* impudent; insulting; rude.
INSOLENCE *n.*

inspect *v.* to examine carefully; to investigate. INSPECTION *n.*

inspiration *n.* 1 taking in air (see RESPIRATION). 2 originality; a sudden good idea.

inspire *v.* to encourage with noble thoughts and ideas. INSPIRED *adj.*

install *v.* 1 to fix in position. 2 to place (a person) in rank or office, esp. at a ceremony. INSTALLATION *n.*

instance *n.* an example; a particular case.

instant *n.* 1 a precise moment in time. 2 a moment.

instantly *adv.* at once; immediately.

instead *adv.* in place of; as a substitute or alternative for.

instep *n.* the upper part of the foot between the toes and the ankle.

instinct *n.* a natural ability, or knowledge, which animals have without being taught.

institute *v.* to start; to establish.
INSTITUTE *n.* 1 a society or an organization formed for a special purpose. 2 a meeting place for a society.

institution *n.* 1 institute; establishment. 2 a custom or practice.

instruct *v.* to teach; to order or command.

instruction *n.* 1 teaching. 2 direction; order. INSTRUCTOR *n.* teacher.

instrument *n.* 1 a tool, implement or piece of apparatus. 2 apparatus for producing musical sounds.

insulate *v.* 1 to isolate; to separate. 2 to prevent loss of heat or electricity by means of a covering. INSULATION *n.* INSULATOR *n.*

insult *v.* to offend; to affront.
INSULT *n.* an insulting speech or action; an affront. INSULTING *adj.*

insurance *n.* 1 the payment made to or by an insurance company. 2 a safeguard against loss, injury or damage.

insure *v.* 1 to guarantee. 2 to arrange to receive compensation in the event of loss by fire, burglary, injury, etc.

insurgent *adj.* riotous; rebellious.
INSURGENT *n.* a rioter; a rebel.

integral *adj.* whole; complete; essentially part of a whole.

integrity *n.* wholeness; soundness; honesty.

intellect *n.* the ability to think, reason and understand. INTELLECTUAL *adj.*

intelligence *n.* 1 mental ability. 2 intellectual skill. 3 news; knowledge.

intelligent *adj.* 1 having or showing a high degree of understanding. 2 quick of mind.

intend *v.* to plan; to mean. INTENDED *adj.*

intense *adj.* very great or strong; violent.
INTENSITY *n.*

intent *adj.* resolved; eager; earnest.
INTENT *n.* intention; purpose.

intercept *v.* to stop (something or somebody) on the way from place to place; to check.

interest *n.* 1 a sum paid for the loan of money. 2 importance; concern. 3 special attention.
INTEREST *v.* to gain and hold attention (of.)
INTERESTING *adj.*

interested *adj.* 1 having an interest or share in. 2 displaying interest.

interfere (with or **in)** *v.* to meddle; to get in the way (of). INTERFERENCE *n.* INTERFERING *adj.*

interior *n.* 1 the inside. 2 the inland part of a country.

intermediate *adj.* coming between two things in time, place or order.

internal *adj.* 1 inside; situated in. 2 concerning the domestic affairs of a country.

international *adj.* having to do with matters between nations.

interpret *v.* to explain the meaning of something said or written; to translate.

interrogate *v.* to question closely; to cross-examine.

interrupt *v.* to make a break; to break in upon a person who is speaking or working.

interruption *n.* a stoppage; a sudden break into talk or work.

intersect *v.* to divide by crossing or cutting.
INTERSECTION *n.* a point where lines or roads cross.

interview *v.* to conduct an interview with.
INTERVIEW *n.* 1 a meeting for the assessment of a candidate. 2 a discussion with a person, intended for broadcasting or publication.

intimate *adj.* extremely friendly; familiar; confidential. INTIMATE *n.* a close friend.

intimidate *v.* to fill with fear in order to influence.

intolerable *adj.* that cannot be endured.

intolerant *adj.* not tolerant of ideas or opinions of others. INTOLERANCE *n.*

intoxicate *v.* 1 to make drunk. 2 to excite.

intricate *adj.* complicated; difficult to understand.

intrigue *v.* to carry on an underhanded plot; to make secret plans.

introduce *v.* to bring something into use; to make (one person) known (to another).
INTRODUCTION *n.*

intrude (upon) *v.* 1 to enter uninvited. 2 to force oneself on the attention of others.
INTRUDER *n.*

invade *v.* to enter a country as an enemy; to crowd into. INVADER *n.*

invalid *adj.* (pron. in-VAL-id) without value; having no legal force.
INVALID *n.* (pron. IN-valid) a person disabled by illness or injury.

invaluable *adj.* priceless; of great value.

invariable *adj.* not variable; constant; unchangeable; always the same.

invasion *n.* an attack and entry into a country by an enemy; an encroachment.

invent *v.* 1 to make or create something new; to devise. 2 to make up in the imagination.

invention *n.* something invented.

invert *v.* to turn upside down.

invertebrate *adj.* not having a backbone.
INVERTEBRATE *n.* an animal with no backbone.

invest *v.* 1 to put money into a business. 2 to buy something. INVESTMENT *n.*

investigate *v.* to examine; to inquire into.

investigation *n.* an examination; an inquiry.
INVESTIGATOR *n.*

invisible *adj.* not visible; that cannot be seen.

invitation *n.* a written or spoken request to do something.

invite *v.* 1 to request to come; to ask for. 2 to attract. INVITING *adj.*

invoice *n.* a list of goods supplied, with their prices and total cost; a bill.
INVOICE *v.* to make a detailed account (of).

involve *v.* 1 to include; to complicate. 2 to mix (someone) up in (crime, etc.).

inward *adj.* situated within; directed toward the inside.

ion *n.* an atom with an excess or shortage of electrons.

irate *adj.* very angry; furious.

iris *n.* 1 the colored part of the eye. 2 a plant with tuberous roots. *pl.* IRISES.

iron *n.* 1 a hard, heavy, strong, silver-gray, common metal with many uses. 2 an appliance for smoothing clothes, etc. 3 a golf club with a metal head. IRON *v.* to smooth with an iron.

irrational *adj.* unreasonable; absurd; not logical.

irregular *adj.* 1 not regular; not according to rule. 2 uneven; variable.

irresponsible *adj.* not responsible for conduct; without sense of responsibility.

irrigate *v.* 1 to supply dry land with water. 2 to supply with a constant flow of liquid.

irrigation *n.* a system of supplying dry land with water to improve cultivation.

irritate *v.* 1 to annoy; to make angry. 2 to inflame; to cause discomfort. IRRITATION *n.*

Islam *n.* 1 the faith taught by the prophet Muhammad. 2 the Muslim world.

island *n.* a piece of land surrounded by water.

isolate *v.* to keep (someone, something) apart or alone. ISOLATED *adj.*

isotope *n.* one of two or more forms of an element differing from each other in nuclear properties but having the same chemical properties.

Israeli *n.* an inhabitant of the State of Israel.

issue *v.* 1 to flow (from); to come out (of). 2 to publish; to give out; to distribute. ISSUE *n.* 1 a flowing out. 2 a publication. 3 the consequence.

Italian *adj.* belonging to Italy or its people. ITALIAN *n.* the language or an inhabitant of Italy.

itch *n.* 1 an irritation of the skin. 2 a restless desire; a longing for. ITCH *v.* 1 to have a skin irritation. 2 to long (for).

item *n.* 1 a single one out of a number. 2 a piece of news or an article.

ivory *n.* a hard, white substance from the tusks of elephants, walruses, etc.

ivy *n.* an evergreen climbing plant that grows on trees and walls.

J

jab *v.* to poke suddenly. JAB *n.* a sharp stab.

jack *n.* a screw device for lifting heavy loads.

jacket *n.* 1 a short coat. 2 an outside covering.

jagged *adj.* having a sharp, rough edge.

jail *n.* a prison. JAILER *n.*

jam *v.* to squeeze; to block or wedge. JAM *n.* 1 a conserve of fruit boiled with sugar. 2 a blockage.

January *n.* the first month of the year.

Japanese *adj.* belonging to Japan or its people. JAPANESE *n.* the language or people of Japan.

jar *v.* 1 to jolt (nerves etc.). 2 JAR UPON or AGAINST to strike with a grating sound.

jar *n.* an earthenware or glass vessel.

jaw *n.* the bones of the mouth.

jealous *adj.* 1 envious of another person's good fortune or possessions. 2 suspicious.

jealousy *n.* envy; the feeling of being jealous.

jeer (at) *v.* to laugh or shout rudely at; to mock.

jerk *n.* a short, sudden pull; a twitch. JERK *v.* to pull suddenly; to twitch.

jest *v.* to joke or make fun. JEST *n.* a joke.

Jesus *n.* Jesus Christ, the founder of the Christian religion whose life and teachings are recorded in the New Testament.

jet *n.* 1 a stream of liquid or gas forced through a small opening under pressure. 2 an aircraft propelled by a jet engine. 3 a hard, black mineral used in making jewelry and ornaments. JET *adj.* deep, glossy black.

jettison *v.* to throw (goods or fuel) overboard from a ship, aircraft, balloon, etc., esp. to lessen load when in distress.

jewel *n.* 1 a precious stone; an ornament containing precious stones. 2 a precious thing or person.

jewelry *n.* precious stones; personal ornaments made of precious stones or metals. JEWELER *n.*

jig *n.* 1 a lively dance. 2 the music for such a dance.

job *n.* 1 a piece of work. 2 employment.

jockey *n.* a racehorse rider. JOCKEY (FOR) *v.* to try to gain a position of advantage.

jog *v.* 1 to push or nudge. 2 to remind. 3 to trot.

join *v.* 1 to fasten or put together. 2 to become a member of a club, team, society, etc. 3 to unite.

joint *n.* 1 the point at which two things are joined together. 2 the place where two bones join together. 3 a large piece of meat. JOINT *adj.* shared by two or more.

joke *n.* something said or done to make people laugh. JOKE *v.* to make a joke. JOKER *n.*

jolly *adj.* happy; merry.

jolt *v.* to jerk; to shake. JOLT *n.* a jerk; a shock.

jostle *v.* to knock or push against.

journalist *n.* a person who writes for a newspaper, magazine or journal.

journey *n.* distance traveled; an expedition; a voyage. JOURNEY *v.* to travel; to make a journey.

jovial *adj.* merry; cheerful.

joy *n.* a feeling of great happiness or pleasure. JOYFUL *adj.* JOYFULLY *adv.*

jubilant *adj.* shouting or singing for joy; triumphant.

judge *n.* 1 an official appointed to try accused persons in a court of law. 2 a person who decides the result of a competition or contest. 3 a person who decides on the merits of a matter. JUDGE *v.* 1 to try accused persons. 2 to be a judge or act as a judge. 3 to estimate something.

jug *n.* a container, with a handle and lip, for holding liquids.

juggle *v.* to perform tricks using plates, balls, etc. JUGGLER *n.*

juice *n.* liquid from fruit or vegetables.

July *n.* the seventh month of the year.

jumble *v.* to mix things up, to muddle. JUMBLE *n.* a confusion; a muddle. JUMBLED *adj.*

jump *v.* 1 to leap. 2 to spring upward or over something. 3 to give a sudden start. JUMP *n.* a leap; the act of jumping.

junction *n.* a place where roads or railroad lines join.

June *n.* the sixth month of the year.

jungle *n.* land thickly overgrown with trees and tangled vegetation.

junior *adj.* 1 younger in age or less experienced. 2 lower in position.

junk *n.* 1 worthless trash. 2 a Chinese sailboat.

jury *n.* a group of persons who listen to the evidence in a court of law and then give a verdict.

just *adj.* 1 fair, impartial. 2 well deserved; proper. JUST *adv.* 1 exactly. 2 recently. 3 barely, hardly. 4 only.

justice *n.* 1 fairness. 2 a magistrate.

justify *v.* to prove that something said or done is right or reasonable.

juvenile *adj.* to do with young people. JUVENILE *n.* a young person.

K

kale *n.* a green vegetable similar to cabbage.

kangaroo *n.* an Australian pouched mammal that jumps along.

keel *n.* the beam of metal or timber on which the framework of a boat or ship is built.

keep *v.* 1 to retain possession of (something). 2 to take care of. 3 to detain. KEEP *n.* the stronghold of a castle.

kennel *n.* a shelter for a dog.

kernel *n.* 1 the soft inner part of a nut or fruit stone. 2 the important part of something.

kettle *n.* a metal vessel with a spout, lid and handle, for boiling water.

key *n.* 1 an implement for operating a lock. 2 a lever on a piano, organ or typewriter. 3 a solution to, or explanation of, a problem. 4 a set of musical notes based on a particular note.

kick *v.* to strike with the foot. KICK *n.* the act of kicking.

kid *n.* a young goat.

kidnap *v.* to carry off a person unlawfully by force. KIPNAPPER *n.* a person who kidnaps.

kidney *n.* an organ in the body that removes waste matter from the blood.

kill *v.* to put to death; to cause the death of.

kiln *n.* a type of oven or furnace for firing pottery or baking bricks.

kilogram *n.* a metric unit of mass (weight), 1000 grams.

kilometer *n.* a metric unit of length, 1000 meters.

kilowatt *n.* a unit of electrical power, 1000 watts.

kilt *n.* a pleated skirt, of tartan cloth.

kimono *n.* a loose Japanese robe with wide sleeves, and tied with a sash.

kin *n.* a person's family and relations.

kind *n.* a sort; a type. KIND *adj.* gentle, friendly, considerate. KINDNESS *n.*

kindly *adj.* acting in a kind way; sympathetic. KINDLY *adv.* gently.

king *n.* 1 a male sovereign ruler. 2 the main piece in a game of chess.

kingdom *n.* a country ruled by a king or queen.

kink *n.* a twist or bend.

kiss *v.* to touch with the lips as a sign of affection. KISS *n.* a touch with the lips.

kitchen *n.* a room used for the preparation and cooking of food.

kite *n.* 1 a lightweight frame, covered with cloth or paper, flown at the end of a long string. 2 a bird of prey of the hawk family.

kitten *n.* a young cat.

knack *n.* the ability to do something cleverly and skillfully.

knee *n.* the joint between the lower and upper part of the leg.

kneel *v.* to go down on one or both knees.

knife *n.* a blade with a sharp edge for cutting, set in a handle. *pl.* KNIVES.

knight *n.* a man who has received the honor of knighthood, carrying the title of "Sir."

knit *v.* 1 to weave wool or yarn together by means of needles or a knitting machine. 2 to join closely together; to unite.

knock *v.* to strike; to hit (something).

knot *n.* 1 a tied loop or tangle in a string, rope, ribbon, etc. 2 a small group of people. 3 a dark, hard lump in wood. 4 the measure of a ship's speed: one knot = one nautical mile per hour.

know *v.* 1 to have information about (something). 2 to recognize. 3 to understand or have experience of (something).

knowing *adj.* cunning; shrewd.

knowledge *n.* understanding; information.

knuckle *n.* a joint in a finger.

Koran *n.* the Islamic holy book.

L

label *n.* a piece of paper, card or other material attached to something and indicating what it is, its destination or its owner.
LABEL *v.* to fix a label to (something); to write a label. LABELLED *adj.*

labor *n.* 1 hard work; effort. 2 the process of childbirth. LABOR *v.* to work hard.

laboratory *n.* a room or building equipped and used for scientific experiments and investigations. *pl.* LABORATORIES.

labyrinth *n.* a maze.

lace *n.* 1 a cord for fastening shoes and boots. 2 a fine openwork fabric.
LACE *v.* to fasten with laces.

lacerate *v.* to tear; to wound. LACERATION *n.*

lack *v.* to be without; to have too little of.
LACK *n.* the absence of something; a shortage.

lad *n.* a boy. *fem.* LASS.

ladder *n.* a climbing device made of wood, metal or rope, with rungs.

ladle *n.* a long-handled spoon for lifting liquids.
LADLE *v.* to serve or transfer with a ladle.

lady *n.* courteous word for a woman. *pl.* LADIES.

lag *v.* to fall behind; to dawdle.

lagoon *n.* a shallow stretch of water separated from the sea.

lair *n.* the den of a wild animal.

lake *n.* a large area of water enclosed by land.

lamb *n.* 1 a young sheep. 2 the meat from a young sheep.

lame *adj.* 1 crippled; unable to walk properly. 2 feeble; unconvincing.

lament *v.* to express grief or regret.
LAMENT *n.* a sorrowful song or poem.

lamp *n.* a device for giving artificial light.

lance *n.* a spear with a long shaft.
LANCE *v.* to pierce with a spear.

land *n.* 1 the solid part of the Earth's surface. 2 a country or territory.
LAND *v.* to alight on land from a boat or aircraft; to disembark.

landing *n.* 1 alighting on shore or ground; a disembarkation. 2 a level space at the top of a flight of stairs.

landlord *n.* the owner of land, houses or property to rent. *fem.* LANDLADY.

landmark *n.* a feature in a landscape which serves as a guide.

landscape *n.* a picture or view of the countryside.
LANDSCAPE *v.* to lay out a garden or park.

landslide *n.* the sliding down of a mass of earth, rocks, etc.

lane *n.* 1 a narrow country road. 2 a division of a road marked out to separate streams of traffic. 3 a sea or air route.

language *n.* words spoken or written by a particular person, nation or peoples.

lanky *adj.* tall and thin.

lantern *n.* a case with transparent sides, for containing a light.

lap *n.* 1 the part from waist to knees of a sitting person. 2 one circuit of a track.
LAP *v.* 1 to lick up a liquid with the tongue. 2 to overtake by a circuit on a track.

lapel *n.* the front part of a coat folded back toward the shoulder.

lapse *n.* 1 a small mistake or error. 2 passing of time.
LAPSE *v.* 1 to make a small mistake or error. 2 to pass gradually. 3 to come to an end.

larceny *n.* (legal term) theft.

larch *n.* a cone-bearing tree that is not an evergreen.

large *adj.* great in size; big.

largely *adv.* mainly; mostly.

lark *n.* 1 a small song-bird. 2 a prank or joke.

larva *n.* an insect in the grub or caterpillar stage.

larynx *n.* a cavity in the throat containing the vocal cords.

laser *n.* a device which strengthens an input of light, producing an extremely narrow and intense beam.

lash *n.* 1 a whip or a blow given with a whip. 2 an eyelash.
LASH *v.* 1 to whip. 2 to fasten or bind tightly.

lass *n.* a young girl. *masc.* LAD.

last *adj.* 1 coming after all others. 2 most recent.
LAST *v.* to continue; to remain in good condition.

lasting *adj.* continuing for a long time; permanent.

latch *n.* a fastening for a door, gate or window.

late *adj.* 1 after the proper or usual time. 2 near the end of the day or some stated time.

lately *adv.* recently; not long ago.

lathe *n.* a machine for turning wood, metal, etc., into circular and rounded shapes.

lather *n.* the froth made from soap and water.
LATHER *v.* to cover with lather.

Latin *n.* the language of the ancient Romans.

latitude *n.* 1 the distance north or south of the equator, measured in degrees. 2 a freedom from restraint.

latter *adj.* the second mentioned of two things or people.

laugh *n.* the sound a person makes when amused, happy or scornful.
LAUGH *v.* to make sounds expressing amusement, happiness or scorn.

laughter *n.* the act or sound of laughing.

launch *v.* 1 to set afloat. 2 to set in motion.
LAUNCH *n.* a motor boat.

launder *v.* to wash clothes.

laundry *n.* 1 a place where clothes are washed. 2 clothes etc. to be washed or clothes recently washed.

laurel *n.* a shiny-leaved evergreen shrub.

lava *n.* the molten matter that flows from a volcano and which cools and hardens into rock.

lavish *adj.* extremely generous; extravagant.
LAVISH *v.* to give generously or extravagantly.

law *n.* the rules made by a government according to which people are governed.

lawful *adj.* permitted by law; legal.

lawn *n.* an area of closely-mowed grass.

lawsuit *n.* a claim in a court of law.

lawyer *n.* a person skilled in law or legal work; a solicitor or barrister.

lax *adj.* careless; slack.

lay *v.* 1 LAY DOWN to put something down in a particular place or way. 2 LAY OUT to arrange. 3 to produce eggs.

layer *n.* a thickness of some material laid on another material.

lazy *adj.* not willing to work; idle. LAZILY *adv.* LAZINESS *n.*

lead *v.* (pron. LEED) 1 to guide or conduct someone. 2 to go first; to be in charge of something.

lead *n.* (pron. LED) 1 a heavy, soft bluish-gray metal. 2 the graphite used in pencils.

leader *n.* a person who leads.

leadership *n.* 1 command. 2 the ability to lead.

leading *adj.* 1 that which leads. 2 of most importance.

leaf *n.* a part of a plant growing from a stem or branch. *pl.* LEAVES.

league *n.* an association of sports teams that play games against each other.

leak *n.* 1 a crack or hole through which liquids or gases escape. 2 a disclosure of secret information.
LEAK *v.* to allow liquid to enter or escape.
LEAKING *adj.*

lean *v.* 1 to rest against. 2 to be in a sloping position. LEANING *adj.* in a sloping position.

lean *adj.* 1 thin. 2 without fat.

leap *v.* to jump; to bound.
LEAP *n.* a jump; a bound.

learn *v.* to gain knowledge or skill by study, experience or practice. LEARNER *n.*
LEARNING *n.* knowledge.

lease *n.* an agreement to let land or property for rent.

least *adj.* smallest.
LEAST *adv.* in the smallest amount.
LEAST *n.* the smallest degree.

leather *n.* the skin of an animal, prepared by tanning, used for making shoes, harnesses, etc.

leave *v.* 1 to go away. 2 to allow something to remain. LEAVE *n.* permission.

lecture *n.* 1 a talk on a particular subject given to an audience. 2 a reprimand. LECTURE *v.*

ledge *n.* a narrow shelf; a ridge.

lee *n.* the sheltered side.

leeward *adj. & adv.* on the sheltered side.

left *adj.* on or belonging to the same side of the body as the heart; on the side opposite to right.
LEFT *n. & adv.*

leg *n.* 1 a limb used in standing, walking and running. 2 a support of a table, chair, etc.

legacy *n.* property or money left to a person in a will.

legal *adj.* of the law; allowed by law.

legend *n.* an ancient story handed down from generation to generation.

legendary *adj.* 1 existing only in legend. 2 like a legend.

legible *adj.* clearly written; easy to read.

legitimate *adj.* lawful; genuine.

leisure *n.* free time.

lemon *n.* a pale yellow citrus fruit.

lend *v.* to give for temporary use.

length *n.* 1 the measurement from one end to another. 2 a space of time.

lengthen *v.* to increase the length of.

lenient *adj.* not severe; merciful; tolerant.
LENIENCY *n.*

lens *n.* a piece of glass with a curved surface used in eyeglasses, magnifying glasses and cameras to concentrate or disperse light.
pl. LENSES.

Lent *n.* the forty days before Easter, in memory of Christ's fasting in the wilderness.

leopard *n.* a spotted wild animal in the cat family. *fem.* LEOPARDESS.

leotard *n.* a close-fitting garment worn by acrobats, dancers and gymnasts, etc.

less *adj.* of smaller quantity; not so much of. LESS *n.* a smaller number or size.

lessen *v.* to make or become smaller.

lesson *n.* 1 something learned or taught; a set amount of teaching given at one time.
2 an example.

let *v.* 1 to allow (something to happen); to permit. 2 to grant the use of land, premises, etc., for rent.

lethal *adj.* causing death.

letter *n.* 1 a symbol or character representing a sound. 2 a written message.

lettuce *n.* a green garden plant used in salads.

level *n.* 1 a flat, smooth surface. 2 an instrument for testing the flatness of a surface.
LEVEL *v.* 1 to make flat. 2 to make equal.

lever *n.* 1 a bar or similar tool used to help raise a heavy load or to pry something open.
2 a handle for operating a machine.

levy *v.* 1 to collect a tax. 2 to raise an army.
LEVY *n.* 1 the tax collected. 2 people raised for an army. *pl.* LEVIES.

liable *adj.* 1 LIABLE FOR legally responsible for.
2 LIABLE TO likely to.

liar *n.* a person who tells lies.

libel *n.* a false written statement considered damaging to a person's reputation.
LIBEL *v.* to publish a falsehood about a person.

liberal *adj.* generous; open-minded.

liberate *v.* to set free; to release.
LIBERATION *n.*

liberty *n.* freedom; permission.

librarian *n.* a person who looks after a library.

library *n.* 1 a building or room containing a collection of books. 2 a collection of books.

license *n.* 1 an official permit to keep, use or do something.

lichen *n.* a mosslike plant which grows on rocks and trees.

lick *v.* to pass the tongue over (something) in order to taste, moisten or clean.
LICK *n.* a stroke with the tongue.

lid *n.* the cover for the top of a container.

lie *v.* 1 to be in a flat position. 2 to make a false statement.
LIE *n.* an untruth. LYING *v.* in a flat position.
LYING *n.* the telling of lies.

life *n.* 1 the state of being alive and able to breathe, feed, grow and move as animals and plants do. 2 the period between birth and death. 3 activity; vitality.

lift *v.* to raise (something) to a higher position; to rise; to go higher.

light *n.* 1 brightness which makes it possible to see things. 2 a source of light.
LIGHT *v.* 1 to cause something to burn or shine. 2 to give light to.

light *adj.* 1 having little weight; not heavy. 2 pale in color. 3 gentle.

lighten *v.* 1 to light up. 2 to make less heavy.

lightness *n.* lack of weight.

lightning *n.* a sudden flash of natural electricity usually produced during a thunderstorm.

like *v.* to be fond of or pleased with.
LIKE *adj.* resembling; similar to.
LIKENESS, LIKE *n.* something which is similar or equal to another thing.

likely *adj.* probable; suitable.
LIKELY *adv.* probably.

likeness *n.* a similarity; a resemblance.

liking *n.* a fondness.

lilac *n.* 1 a shrub with purple or white flowers. 2 a pale purple color.

limb *n.* 1 an arm or leg. 2 a branch of a tree.

lime *n.* 1 a white powder prepared from limestone and used in making cement.
2 a kind of tree. 3 a fruit rather like a lemon.

limit *n.* 1 a boundary. 2 a point not to be passed.
LIMIT *v.* to keep (something) within bounds; to restrict.

limited *adj.* narrow; restricted.

limp *adj.* soft; hanging loosely.
LIMP *v.* to walk lamely.

line *n.* 1 a long, thin mark. 2 a row of people or things.

liner *n.* a large passenger ship or aircraft.

linger *v.* to delay; to remain somewhere for a long time.

link *n.* 1 one ring in a chain. 2 a connection.
LINK *v.* to join; to connect. LINKED *adj.*

lion *n.* a large and powerful wild animal of the cat family. *fem.* LIONESS.

lip *n.* 1 one of the fleshy edges of the mouth. 2 the edge or rim of anything hollow.

liquid *n.* any substance that can flow.
LIQUID *adj.* flowing.

lisp *v.* to be unable to pronounce certain sounds correctly, e.g. to say *th* for *s*.

list *n.* 1 a number of items written down one after another. 2 a catalog.
LIST *v.* 1 to make a list. 2 to lean to one side.

listen *v.* 1 to hear or try to hear. 2 to follow the advice of.

liter *n.* a metric unit of capacity, 1000 milliliters

literacy *n.* ability to read and write.

literary *adj.* having to do with authors, books and literature.

literature *n.* 1 written or printed books, plays, poetry, etc. 2 all that has been written on a subject.

litter *n.* 1 trash left lying about. 2 a number of animals born to the same mother at one time. LITTER *v.* to scatter things untidily.

little *adj.* 1 small in size or amount. 2 short in time or distance. LITTLE *n.* a small quantity. LITTLE *adv.* not much; slightly.

lively *adj.* full of life and high spirits; exciting.

liver *n.* an organ of the body which produces bile and purifies the blood.

livid *adj.* 1 black and blue in color. 2 very angry.

living *adj.* having life. LIVING *n.* 1 the means of living. 2 all that are alive.

lizard *n.* a small four-legged reptile with a long body and tail.

load *n.* 1 a burden. 2 an amount carried; a cargo. LOAD *v.* 1 to put a load on. 2 to fill or charge. LOADED *adj.*

loaf *n.* a shaped mass of baked bread. *pl.* LOAVES. LOAF *v.* to waste time; to loiter.

loan *n.* anything lent. LOAN *v.* to lend.

loathe *v.* to hate; to detest.

lobby *n.* an entrance hall.

lobe *n.* the soft lower part of the ear.

lobster *n.* a large, edible shellfish with powerful claws and a long tail.

local *adj.* of a particular place or area. LOCALLY *adv.*

locate *v.* to find the exact position of.

location *n.* the place where something is situated.

lock *n.* 1 a device to fasten doors with a bolt turned by a key. 2 a section of canal where boats are raised or lowered to different levels. 3 a curl of hair. LOCK *v.* to fasten with a lock.

locomotive *n.* a railroad engine.

locust *n.* an insect, similar to a grasshopper, that destroys crops and other plants.

lodge *n.* a small house used by sportsmen. LODGER *n.* a paying guest.

log *n.* 1 a piece of a tree that has been felled. 2 a book for recording an aircraft's flight or a ship's voyage; a diary.

logic *n.* sound reasoning. LOGICAL *adj.*

loiter *v.* to hang around; to dawdle.

lone *adj.* alone; solitary. LONELY *adj.* LONELINESS *n.*

long *adj.* lengthy; lasting for a long time.

long *v.* to want (something) very much; to yearn for.

longing *n.* a great desire for something.

longitude *n.* distance east or west of Greenwich, England (see MERIDIAN).

look *v.* 1 to turn the eyes of attention toward something. 2 to seem or appear. 3 to search. LOOK *n.* the act of looking; appearance.

loom *n.* a machine for weaving cloth. LOOM *v.* to appear in a menacing way.

loop *n.* the doubled-over part in a piece of string, rope, etc. LOOP *v.* to make a loop.

loose *adj.* 1 slack; not fixed. 2 not in captivity.

loosen *v.* to make or become loose.

loot *n.* property taken by thieves. LOOT *v.* to plunder and steal.

lop *v.* to trim or cut off a part of.

lord *n.* 1 a master; a ruler. 2 a nobleman.

lose *v.* 1 to fail to keep. 2 to be defeated. 3 to misplace. LOSER *n.*

loss *n.* 1 the act of losing. 2 anything lost.

lost *adj.* 1 that cannot be found. 2 destroyed.

lot *n.* 1 a large number or amount. 2 the total amount. 3 an item for sale at an auction. 4 that which is drawn in a lottery (see LOTTERY).

lotion *n.* a liquid for healing or soothing the skin.

lottery *n.* a competition in which prizes are awarded by drawing lots.

loud *adj.* 1 noisy; making a great sound. 2 showy; gaudy. LOUDLY *adv.*

love *n.* fondness and affection. LOVE *v.* to feel fondness and affection for.

lovely *adj.* beautiful; pleasing; enjoyable.

loving *adj.* full of love; affectionate.

low *adj.* 1 the opposite of high; not reaching far up. 2 coarse and vulgar. LOW *n.* the sound made by cattle.

lower *v.* 1 to let or bring something down. 2 to reduce.

lowly *adj.* humble; meek.

loyal *adj.* true and faithful. LOYALTY *n.*

lubricate *v.* to apply oil or grease to reduce friction.

lucid *adj.* clear, easily understood. LUCIDLY *adv.*

luck *n.* good or bad fortune; chance.

lucky *adj.* having or bringing good luck.

luggage *n.* a traveler's bags, suitcases and trunks.

lukewarm *adj.* 1 neither hot nor cold; tepid. 2 indifferent.

lull *v.* to soothe or calm.
LULL *n.* 1 a pause in a storm. 2 a peaceful interval.

lullaby *n.* a soothing song to lull a child to sleep.

lumber *n.* rough timber.
LUMBER *v.* to move heavily.

luminous *adj.* 1 giving out light. 2 bright and shiny.

lump *n.* a shapeless mass; a swelling.

lunar *adj.* concerning the moon.

lunatic *n.* an insane person.

lunch *n.* the midday meal.

lung *n.* one of the two breathing organs in the chest.

lunge *n.* a sudden thrust or movement forward.
LUNGE *v.* to thrust forward suddenly.

lurch *v.* to roll or pitch to one side.
LURCH *n.* a sudden roll or stagger.

lure *v.* to tempt or entice.
LURE *n.* something used to entice or bait.

lurk *v.* to lie in wait; to stay hidden.

luscious *adj.* delicious to taste or smell.

lush *adj.* fresh and juicy; growing abundantly.

luxury *n.* something enjoyed but not really necessary.

lynch *v.* to put (someone) to death without a lawful trial.

lyric *n.* the words for a song.

M

macaroni *n.* a food of flour paste made into long thin tubes and dried.

machine *n.* a mechanism; a device for applying mechanical power.

machinery *n.* 1 machines. 2 the parts of machines.

mad *adj.* 1 mentally ill; insane. 2 very angry.
MADLY *adv.*

madam *n.* a respectful title given to a lady.

magazine *n.* 1 a periodical publication containing various articles. 2 a store for rifles, ammunition and explosives.

maggot *n.* the larva of certain types of fly.

magic *n.* 1 the supposed art of influencing events with the help of spirits or by witchcraft. 2 the art of doing conjuring tricks. MAGICIAN *n.*

magistrate *n.* a person with the authority to administer the law.

magnet *n.* a piece of iron or steel which has the power to attract other pieces of iron or steel. MAGNETIC *adj.*

magnetism *n.* the power of a magnet; the ability to attract.

magnificent *adj.* splendid; grand; beautiful.

magnify *v.* 1 to make something appear larger than it is. 2 to exaggerate. MAGNIFIED *adj.*

maid *n.* 1 a young unmarried girl. 2 a female servant.

mail *n.* 1 letters and parcels sent by the post office. 2 armor made of metal plates, chains or rings. MAIL *v.* to send by the post office.

main *adj.* most important; principal.
MAINLY *adv.*

maintain *v.* to continue; to keep in good condition. MAINTENANCE *n.*

majesty *n.* 1 greatness of manner; dignity. 2 a title of a king or queen.

major *adj.* greater; more important.
MAJOR *n.* a military officer, in rank between captain and lieutenant colonel.

majority *n.* the greater number; the larger part.

make *v.* 1 to construct or shape something. 2 to compel. 3 to add up to. 4 to bring about.

malaria *n.* a fever caused by mosquito bites.

male *n.* 1 a man or boy. 2 an animal or plant of the male sex.

malice *n.* spite; bad feeling. MALICIOUS *adj.*

malinger *v.* to pretend to be ill in order to avoid work. MALINGERER *n.*

mallet *n.* a wooden hammer.

mammal *n.* an animal that produces milk with which it feeds its young.

mammoth *n.* a large elephant, now extinct.
MAMMOTH *adj.* huge; gigantic.

man *n.* 1 a human being; mankind. 2 an adult male person.

manage *v.* 1 to be in charge of or to control. 2 to succeed in doing.

manager *n.* the person in charge of a business.

mane *n.* the long hair on the neck of a horse, a lion and some other animals.

maneuver *n.* 1 a planned movement or rehearsal by armed forces. 2 a clever plan or movement. MANEUVER *v.* to carry out such a movement.

manger *n.* a feeding-trough for horses and cattle.

mangle *v.* to tear or crush to pieces.

maniac *n.* a mad person.

manicure *n.* care of the hands and nails.

manifest *adj.* easily seen or understood; obvious.
MANIFEST *v.* to show clearly.

manipulate *v.* to control, manage or work (something) skillfully.

manner *n.* 1 the way a thing is done. 2 the way in which a person behaves.

mannerism *n.* an unusual or characteristic way of speaking or behaving.

manor *n.* 1 the land belonging to a lord or squire. 2 a large house in the country.

mansion *n.* a large house.

manslaughter *n.* killing a person unlawfully but without the intention of doing so.

mantel *n.* the shelf over a fireplace.

manual *adj.* done with the hands.
MANUAL *n.* a book of instructions or information; a handbook.

manufacture *v.* to make by machinery.
MANUFACTURE *n.* the making of articles or material in large quantities.

manure *n.* any substance that enriches and fertilizes the land.

manuscript *n.* a book or paper written by hand.
MANUSCRIPT *adj.* written by hand.

many *adj.* a large number; numerous.
MANY *n.* a large number.

map *n.* a drawing showing the shape and features of a continent, country or area, usually indicating rivers, roads, hills, etc.
MAP *v.* to make a map or plan of.

maple *n.* a tree similar to the sycamore, some kinds of which produce a syrup.

marble *n.* 1 a fine limestone that polishes brightly and is used for buildings and statues.
2 a small stone or glass ball used in various games.

March *n.* the third month of the year.

march *v.* 1 to walk with a regular step.
MARCH *n.* 1 the act of marching or the distance marched. 2 a piece of music for marching.

mare *n.* a female horse. *masc.* STALLION.

margarine *n.* a substance resembling butter and made from animal or vegetable fats.

margin *n.* 1 an edge; a border; the brink.
2 an amount to spare.

marine *adj.* to do with the sea.

mariner *n.* a sailor; a seaman.

maritime *adj.* having to do with the sea or ships.

mark *n.* 1 a stain, spot or pattern on something.
2 a target; a thing aimed at.
3 a number or symbol given as an award.
MARK *v.* 1 to make a mark on something.
2 to observe. 3 to give marks.

market *n.* 1 a public place for buying and selling.
2 the demand for a certain class of goods.
MARKET *v.* to buy and sell in a market.

maroon *n.* a brownish-red color.
MAROON *v.* to abandon (a person) in a deserted place.

marriage *n.* 1 the life together of a husband and wife. 2 a wedding ceremony.

married *adj.* joined together as man and wife.

marry *v.* 1 to take a person as husband or wife.
2 to perform the marriage ceremony.

Mars *n.* 1 a planet lying between Earth and Jupiter. 2 the Roman god of war.

marsh *n.* wet, low-lying ground.
MARSHY *adj.*

martyr *n.* a person who suffers because of his or her beliefs or cause.

marvel *v.* to be filled with wonder or astonishment.
MARVEL *n.* a wonderful or astonishing thing.

marvelous *adj.* extraordinary, astonishing.
MARVELOUSLY *adv.*

mascot *n.* an object or person believed to bring good luck.

masculine *adj.* opposite of feminine; belonging to men; concerning men.

mask *n.* 1 a covering to disguise the face.
2 a model of a face.
MASK *v.* to cover with a mask; to conceal.

mason *n.* a worker in stone.

masquerade *v.* to be in disguise.
MASQUERADE *n.* a masked ball.

mass *n.* 1 a lump, piece or large quantity.
2 the main body. 3 a crowd.
MASS *v.* to form into a mass.

massacre *n.* a great slaughter.
MASSACRE *v.* to slaughter many.

massage *n.* the rubbing and kneading of parts of the body to remove pain or stiffness.
MASSAGE *v.* to rub and knead parts of the body to remove pain or stiffness.

massive *adv.* large and heavy.

mast *n.* a wooden or metal pole supporting a ship's sails or a flag; a radio or television aerial.

master *n.* 1 an employer. 2 a male teacher.
fem. MISTRESS. 3 the captain of a ship.
4 an expert.

mat *n.* a thin pad to protect a surface.
MAT *v.* to twist and tangle. MATTED *adj.*

match *n.* 1 anything which agrees with or suits another thing. 2 an equal. 3 a game or contest.
4 a marriage. 5 a small piece of wood tipped with a substance which burns easily when rubbed. MATCH *v.* to be equal or similar to.

mate *n.* 1 a friend; a husband or wife. 2 one of a mated pair of animals or birds.
MATE *v.* to marry; to pair for breeding.

material *n.* any substance from which something can be made.
MATERIAL *adj.* 1 essential; important. 2 real; actual.

maternal *adj.* motherly; having to do with a mother.

maternity *n.* motherhood.

mathematics *n.* the science which deals with numbers and measurements.
MATHEMATICAL *adj.* MATHEMATICIAN *n.*

matrimony *n.* marriage.

matter *n.* 1 the material; the substance a thing is made of. 2 a subject written or spoken about.
MATTER *v.* to be important.

mattress *n.* a large, flat, oblong cushion for sleeping on.

mature *adj.* fully grown; ripe.
MATURE *v.* to ripen.

maul *v.* to hurt by handling roughly.

maximum *n.* the greatest number or quantity.
MAXIMUM *adj.* greatest.

May *n.* the fifth month of the year.

may *v.* am/is/are able (to do something); can (possibly).

maybe *adv.* perhaps; possibly.

mayor *n.* the chief elected official of a town or city.

maze *n.* an intricate and puzzling network of lines and paths; a labyrinth.

meadow *n.* a field of grass.

meal *n.* 1 food taken at one time; the food that is eaten. 2 grain ground to powder.

mean *v.* 1 to intend, to plan. 2 to be a sign of, to show. MEAN *n.* the middle, average.

meaning *n.* what is meant; an explanation.

means *n.* 1 method; way of doing something. 2 a person's money and possessions.

measles *n.* an infectious disease that causes red spots on the body.

measure *n.* 1 an amount, quantity or size.
MEASURE *v.* to find the amount, quantity or size (of something).

measurement *n.* the amount, quantity or size of anything.

meat *n.* animal flesh used as food.

mechanic *n.* a person skilled in the making, repairing or use of machinery.

mechanical *adj.* 1 concerned with machinery. 2 automatic; done without thinking.

medal *n.* a piece of metal shaped like a disc, cross or star awarded for bravery, merit, or to commemorate a special event.

meddle *v.* to interfere.

mediate *v.* to act as a peacemaker; to try to help settle disputes.

medical *adj.* concerning healing and doctors.

medicine *n.* 1 a liquid or tablet intended to cure or heal. 2 the science of healing.

medieval *adj.* of the Middle Ages.

medium *adj.* mid-way; average; moderate.
MEDIUM *n.* the means by which something is done. *pl.* MEDIA.

meek *adj.* mild and gentle.
MEEKLY *adv.* MEEKNESS *n.*

meet *v.* 1 to come face to face (with). 2 to assemble. 3 to satisfy.

meeting *n.* 1 a gathering; an assembly. 2 an encounter.

mellow *adj.* 1 soft and ripe. 2 pleasant; mature.
MELLOW *v.* to ripen; to mature.

melody *n.* an arrangement of musical notes; a tune.

melon *n.* a large, juicy fruit.

melt *v.* 1 to change a substance from solid to liquid. 2 to soften.

member *n.* 1 a person who belongs to a family, club, society, group, etc. 2 a limb of the body.

memento *n.* an object kept as a keepsake or souvenir.

memoir *n.* a record of events, a written personal account of what has happened.

memorable *adj.* worthy of being remembered.

memorial *n.* something which reminds people of a person or an event; a monument.

memory *n.* the ability to remember; something remembered.

menace *v.* to threaten.
MENACE *n.* a threat or danger. MENACING *adj.*

menagerie *n.* a collection of wild animals.

mend *v.* to repair something; to put back into good order.

mental *adj.* to do with the mind.
MENTALLY *adv.*

mention *v.* to speak of or refer to.
MENTION *n.* a remark about or a reference to.

menu *n.* a list of the food to be served at a meal or available in a hotel or restaurant.

mercantile *adj.* to do with buying, selling and trade.

mercenary *n.* a soldier hired to fight for a foreign country.
MERCENARY *adj.* working only for money.

merciful *adj.* showing mercy; lenient.

merciless *adj.* without mercy; unforgiving.

mercury *n.* 1 a heavy, silvery liquid metal. 2 Mercury *n.* the planet nearest to the sun.

mercy *n.* compassion; forgiveness; leniency, unwillingness to hurt.

merely *adv.* simply; only.

merge *v.* 1 to be joined together. 2 to become part of; to mingle.

merger *n.* a joining together into one.

meridian *n.* 1 an imaginary line passing through the North and South poles and cutting the equator at right angles.
2 the highest point in the sun's path.

merit *n.* excellence; worth.

mermaid *n.* an imaginary creature with the upper body of a woman and the tail of a fish.

merry *adj.* happy; cheerful; full of fun.

mesh *n.* the space between the threads of a net.
MESH *v.* to interlock; to engage.

mess *n.* 1 disorder; confusion. 2 a meal taken with others. MESS *v.* to make a mess of.

message *n.* news or information sent from one person to another.

messenger *n.* a person who carries a message.

Messiah *n.* the promised deliverer of the Jews whom Christians believe to be Christ.

metal *n.* a substance such as gold, silver, iron, tin, copper, lead, etc.

meteorology *n.* the study of the Earth's weather and atmosphere. METEOROLOGIST *n.*

meter *n.* 1 the main unit of length in the metric system, 1 meter = 100 cm = 1000 mm (39.37 inches). 2 the regular arrangement of syllables in a verse. 3 an instrument for measuring the amount of electricity, gas or water used.

method *n.* a way or means of doing something.

methodical *adj.* orderly; done according to a plan or system.

metric *adj.* to do with the decimal system of measurement.

metropolis *n.* a large city.

microbe *n.* a very tiny living thing; a germ.

microphone *n.* an instrument which enables sounds to be made louder, broadcast or recorded.

microscope *n.* an instrument for magnifying small objects. MICROSCOPIC *adj.*

mid *adj.* middle. MID *prep.* amid; among.

middle *n.* a point at equal distance from each end or side; the central point.
MIDDLE *adj.* in the middle; mid; central.

midnight *n.* the middle of the night; 12 o'clock at night.

might *n.* great power or strength.

mighty *adj.* strong; very great.

migrant *n.* a migrating animal, bird or person.

migrate *v.* to move from one place to another, esp. from one part of the world to another.
MIGRATION *n.*

mild *adj.* gentle; not severe or harsh.
MILDLY *adv.*

mile *n.* a measure of distance, 1,760 yards (1.61 kilometers).

mileage *n.* the distance in miles.

militant *adj.* aggressive; ready to fight.

military *adj.* having to do with soldiers or with warfare. MILITARY *n.* armed forces.

milk *n.* a white fluid produced by female mammals to feed their young.
MILK *v.* to obtain milk from a cow or other animal.

mill *n.* 1 a machine for grinding or crushing. 2 a building which contains machines for grinding and crushing, spinning and weaving, sawing, etc.

milligram *n.* a metric unit of mass (weight), one thousandth part of a gram.

milliliter *n.* a metric unit of capacity, one thousandth part of a liter.

millimeter *n.* a metric unit of length, one thousandth part of a meter.

million *n.* a thousand thousands, the number 1,000,000.

mime *n.* a play in which actions or dancing take the place of speaking.
MIME *v.* to act without speaking.

mimic *v.* to imitate, esp. in a mocking way.
MIMIC *n.* a person who imitates or copies.

mind *n.* 1 the mental powers by which a person thinks, feels and understands. 2 an opinion. 3 memory.
MIND *v.* 1 to look after something.
2 to watch out for. 3 to object to.

mine *n.* 1 a place where coal or other minerals are dug from the ground. 2 an explosive hidden under ground or water.
MINE *v.* 1 to dig for coal or minerals.
2 to place explosives under ground or water.

mine *pron.* belonging to me.

miner *n.* a worker in a mine.

mineral *n.* any substance obtained by mining, such as rocks, coal, iron, etc. MINERAL *adj.*

mingle *v.* to mix together.

miniature *adj.* very small; made on a small scale.

minimum *n.* the smallest possible quantity.
MINIMUM *adj.* smallest; least.
MINIMAL *adj.* very minute or slight.

minister *adj.* a clergyman.

minor *adj.* smaller; less important.
MINOR *n.* a person under 18 years of age.

mint *n.* 1 a place where coins are made.
2 a plant whose leaves are used for flavoring.
MINT *v.* to make coins.
MINT *adj.* in new condition.

minus *adj.* less than nothing; negative.
MINUS *n.* the sign (–) for subtraction.

minute *n.* (pron. MINIT) 1 a unit of time, 1/60 of
an hour. 2 a unit of angle measurement, 1/60 of
a degree.
MINUTE *adj.* (pron. my-NUTE) very small; very
exact.

miracle *n.* a wonderful happening beyond human
power; a wonderful event.

mirage *n.* an optical illusion which causes distant
objects to be seen in the air.

mirror *n.* a looking glass. MIRROR *v.* to reflect.

mirth *n.* merriment; laughter.

miscalculate *v.* to calculate wrongly.

miscellaneous *adj.* mixed, made up of several
kinds; various.

mischief *n.* 1 harm or injury done intentionally.
2 childish pranks.

mischievous *adj.* harmful; annoying; fond of
playing pranks.

miser *n.* a person who saves money and spends
as little as possible because of greed.

miserable *adj.* wretched and unhappy.

misery *n.* great unhappiness; suffering.

misfortune *n.* bad luck.

misgiving *n.* a feeling of fear or doubt.

misjudge *v.* to judge (someone or something)
wrongly.

mislead *v.* to deceive.

misplace *v.* to put in the wrong place.

miss *n.* a young girl; an unmarried woman.
MISS *v.* 1 to fail to hit, reach, meet or catch.
2 to regret the absence of (someone or
something).

missile *n.* a weapon thrown, fired or launched
by a rocket.

missing *adj.* lost; absent.

mission *n.* 1 an expedition or journey with a
special purpose. 2 a task or duty undertaken.
3 a place where missionaries work.

missionary *n.* a person sent to preach a religion.

mist *n.* a cloud of very fine water drops seen in
the air. MIST *v.* to turn misty; to cloud.

mistake *n.* an error; a misunderstanding.
MISTAKE *v.* to make a mistake about; to
misunderstand.

mistress *n.* a woman in charge or control.

mistrust *v.* not to trust (someone or something).
MISTRUST *n.* doubt; suspicion.

misty *adj.* hazy; covered with mist.

misunderstand *v.* to misinterpret words or
actions.

mix *v.* 1 to combine or blend two or more things.
2 to meet and mingle with other people. 3 to stir
or shake things together.

mixture *n.* a number of things or substances
combined together.

moan *n.* a low sound of pain or grief.
MOAN *v.* to utter a low sound of pain or grief.

moat *n.* a deep defensive ditch around a castle.

mob *n.* an unruly and disorderly crowd.
MOB *v.* to crowd around.

mobile *adj.* able to move freely; changing
quickly.

mock *v.* to make fun of (someone or something).
MOCK *adj.* imitation; not real.

model *n.* 1 an example or pattern. 2 a small copy
or version of something. 3 a person who poses
for an artist or photographer or who displays
clothing.
MODEL *v.* 1 to make a copy of. 2 to work as a
model.

moderate *v.* to make less violent or severe.
MODERATE *adj.* avoiding extremes; reasonable.

modern *adj.* belonging to the present time.

modest *adj.* humble, not boastful.

modify *v.* to change or vary (something).

moist *adj.* damp, slightly wet.

moisture *n.* dampness.

molar *n.* a back tooth.

mold *n.* 1 a hollow pattern which gives its shape
to whatever is poured or pressed into it.
2 a plant growth found in damp places.
MOLD *v.* to shape and model.

mole *n.* 1 a dark spot on the skin. 2 a small furry
burrowing animal.

molecule *n.* the smallest possible part of a
substance; a small particle.

mollusk *n.* a soft-bodied invertebrate animal—
clam, snail, oyster, octopus, etc.

molten *adj.* melted; liquefied by heat.

moment *n.* 1 a very short period of time.
2 importance or value.

monarch *n.* a king, queen, emperor or empress.

monastery *n.* a building where monks live or
lived. *pl.* MONASTERIES.

Monday *n.* the second day of the week.

monetary *adj.* having to do with money.

money *n.* coins and notes used for making
payment; wealth.

monk *n.* a man who takes religious vows and is a member of a community living in a monastery.

monkey *n.* an animal resembling man; a small ape.

monotonous *adj.* 1 tedious; with no variation. 2 boring; dull.

monsoon *n.* a wind that blows in the Indian Ocean bringing heavy rain in summer and dry weather in winter.

monster *n.* a large, frightening creature.
MONSTER *adj.* very large.

month *n.* 1 any of the twelve parts into which the year is divided. 2 the period in which the moon makes a complete revolution and a complete rotation.

monument *n.* a memorial erected in memory of a person or event.

mood *n.* a state of mind or feeling.

moon *n.* the heavenly body which travels around the Earth once each month and reflects light from the sun.

moor *v.* to secure (a boat) to a buoy or dock.

moral *adj.* 1 concerned with right and wrong behavior. 2 good; virtuous.
MORAL *n.* the lesson taught by a story or fable.

more *adj.* greater in number.
MORE *adv.* to a greater extent.

morning *n.* the first part of the day; the time before noon.

Morse *n.* a code of signals made up of dots and dashes.

mortar *n.* 1 the mixture of cement, sand and water used for laying bricks. 2 a short gun that fires shells at a high angle. 3 a basin in which substances are finely ground.

mortgage *n.* an agreement for borrowing money to buy a structure or land.

mortuary *n.* a building where dead bodies are kept before burial.

mosaic *n.* a design made with small pieces of glass or stone.

mosque *n.* an Islamic place of worship.

mosquito *n.* a bloodsucking insect that carries malaria. *pl.* MOSQUITOES.

moss *n.* a small plant found in damp places.

most *n.* the greatest quantity, extent or number.
MOST *adv.* in the greatest or highest degree.
MOST *adj.* greatest.

motel *n.* a hotel for motorists.

moth *n.* a winged insect usually seen at night.

mother *n.* a female parent.
MOTHER *v.* to act like a mother to.

motion *n.* 1 movement. 2 a plan put before a meeting.

motive *n.* a reason for doing something.

motor *n.* an engine that provides power.

motto *n.* a wise saying.

mound *n.* a bank of earth or stones; small hill.

mount *n.* 1 a mountain or hill. 2 an animal on which a person rides.
MOUNT *v.* 1 to climb; to get on to. 2 to rise or increase. 3 to prepare something for display.
MOUNTED *adj.*

mountain *n.* a high hill. MOUNTAINOUS *adj.*

mountaineer *n.* a person who climbs mountains.

mourn *v.* to grieve; to be sorrowful.

mouse *n.* a small mammal with a long tail. *pl.* MICE.

moustache *n.* hair grown on the upper lip.

mouth *n.* 1 the opening in the head containing the teeth and the tongue. 2 an opening or entrance.

move *v.* 1 to change from one position to another. 2 to set in motion.
MOVE *n.* the act of moving.

movement *n.* 1 moving; motion. 2 mechanism of a watch or clock. 3 a group of people who support a particular cause.

moving *adj.* 1 causing movement; in motion. 2 affecting the emotions.

mow *v.* to cut down.

much *n.* a great quantity or amount.
MUCH *adj.* great in quantity or amount.
MUCH *adv.* to a large extent.

mud *n.* a soft mixture of earth and water.
MUDDY *adj.*

mule *n.* 1 a cross between a horse and a donkey. 2 an obstinate person. 3 a type of spinning machine.

multiple *adj.* having many parts.
MULTIPLE *n.* a number or quantity which contains another an exact number of times, e.g. 100 is a multiple of 10.

multiply *v.* to increase; to increase a number a given number of times.

multiracial *adj.* of many races or people.

multitude *n.* a crowd; a great number.

mumble *v.* to speak indistinctly.

mumps *n.* a disease that causes the glands of the neck to swell.

municipal *adj.* having to do with a city or town.

munitions *n. pl.* military weapons, ammunition and supplies.

mural *adj.* to do with a wall.
MURAL *n.* a wall painting.

murder *n.* the unlawful and intentional killing of a human being.
MURDER *v.* to kill a human being unlawfully and intentionally.

murmur *n.* a low continuous sound; a mutter.
MURMUR *v.* 1 to speak in a low voice. 2 to make a low continuous sound; to mutter.

muscle *n.* fibers in the body which produce movement.

museum *n.* a building in which old, interesting and valuable objects are displayed.

mushroom *n.* a fungus which can be eaten.
MUSHROOM *v.* to grow quickly.

music *n.* an arrangement of pleasing sounds made by singing or by playing musical instruments.

musician *n.* a person skilled in composing or playing music.

Muslim *n.* a follower of Muhammad.

mussel *n.* a small, edible shellfish.

must *v.* am/are/is obliged to do (something).

mustard *n.* a plant whose seeds are ground and used as a spicy flavoring for food.

muster *v.* to assemble; to gather together.
MUSTER *n.* an assembly; a rally.

mute *adj.* unable to speak; silent.
MUTE *n.* a person unable to speak.

mutilate *v.* to damage (something) by tearing, breaking or cutting; to disfigure.

mutiny *n.* a revolt, in the armed forces, against authority.
MUTINY *v.* to revolt against authority.

mutter *v.* to murmur or speak in a low voice.

mutual *adj.* shared (feelings or actions); done by each to the other.

mysterious *adj.* puzzling; difficult to explain.

mystery *n.* a secret; something which cannot be explained.

mystify *v.* to bewilder; to puzzle.

myth *n.* a story handed down from ancient times; a legend.

N

nag *v.* to find fault (with) or scold continually.

nail *n.* 1 the hard covering on the tips of fingers and toes. 2 a sharp metal spike driven in with a hammer to join pieces of wood, etc.
NAIL *v.* to fasten with nails.

naive *adj.* simple in manner, thought or speech; immature.

naked *adj.* unclothed; uncovered; nude.
NAKEDNESS *n.*

name *n.* 1 the word by which a person, place or thing is known or called. 2 a person's reputation.
NAME *v.* 1 to give a name to (someone or something). 2 to mention by name.

nap *n.* a short sleep.
NAP *v.* to have a short sleep.

narrate *v.* to tell or relate a story.

narrative *n.* a spoken or written account of what happened.

narrow *adj.* 1 of small width compared to length. 2 selfish and unsympathetic towards another person's point of view.
NARROW *v.* to make or become less in breadth.

nasal *adj.* 1 relating to the nose. 2 sounded through the nose. NASALLY *adv.*

nasty *adj.* 1 unpleasant to the taste or smell. 2 difficult to deal with. NASTILY *adv.*
NASTINESS *n.*

nation *n.* 1 all the people of one country. 2 a tribe or large group of people who have the same customs, history, language, etc.

national *adj.* belonging to a nation or race.

nationality *n.* one's nation; a membership of a particular nation.

nationally *adv.* throughout a nation.

native *adj.* natural; possessed from birth.
NATIVE *n.* a person born in a particular place; a local inhabitant.

nativity *n.* birth, esp. the birth of Jesus Christ.

natural *adj.* 1 found in nature. 2 usual and normal. 3 simple and unaffected.

naturally *adv.* 1 simply and normally. 2 of course.

nature *n.* 1 the world of plants, trees, animals, land and sea, weather, etc. 2 the qualities and character of a person or thing.

nautical *adj.* to do with ships and sailors.

naval *adj.* to do with the navy.

nave *n.* the middle, or main, part of a church.

navel *n.* the small hollow in the center of a person's abdomen.

navigable *adj.* suitable for ships to sail through.

navigate *v.* to control and direct the course of an aircraft, ship or spacecraft. NAVIGATION *n.*

navigator *n.* a person who navigates.

navy *n.* a fleet of ships and the people who sail in them. *pl.* NAVIES.

near *adj.* 1 not far away in place or time. 2 closely related.

nearly *adv.* almost; closely.

neat *adj.* 1 smart and tidy. 2 cleverly done.

necessary *adj.* that cannot be done without; essential; unavoidable.
NECESSARY *n.* something that cannot be done without.

necessity *n.* something that cannot be done without; a great need.

neck *n.* 1 the part of the body joining the head to the shoulders. 2 the narrow top of a bottle, vase, etc.

necklace *n.* a string of beads, etc. worn around the neck.

need *v.* to be in want of; to require.
NEED *n.* 1 a want or a requirement. 2 poverty; distress.

needle *n.* 1 a thin, pointed instrument used in sewing and knitting. 2 the pointer in a compass or on a dial.

needy *adj.* very poor; in need.

negative *adj.* meaning or saying "no."
NEGATIVE *n.* 1 the words *no* and *not*.
2 in mathematics, a sign denoting quantities to be subtracted. 3 a photographic film on which light and dark areas are reversed.

neglect *v.* to fail to give proper attention or care to; to disregard.
NEGLECT *n.* a failure in attention or care; disregard.

negligence *n.* carelessness.

negligent *adj.* careless. NEGLIGENTLY *adv.*

negotiate *v.* 1 to discuss and try to come to an agreement about (something). 2 to get by or over (something).

neighbor *n.* a person who lives near to another.
NEIGHBORING *adj.* nearby; adjoining.

neighborhood *n.* the surrounding district.

neither *adv.* not either.
NEITHER *adj. & pron.* not one nor the other.

neolithic *adj.* of the later Stone Age.

nephew *n.* the son of one's brother or sister.

nerve *n.* 1 a fiber which carries feeling between the brain and all parts of the body. 2 courage; boldness.

nervous *adj.* 1 timid; fearful. 2 of the nerves.

nest *n.* the place where birds lay their eggs and rear their young; the home of certain animals and insects.
NEST *v.* to build a nest; to make a home in a certain place.

net *n.* 1 a mesh of cord, wire or nylon for catching birds, butterflies, fish, etc. 2 a piece of this material for enclosing a goal or dividing a court. NET *v.* to catch in a net.

neutral *adj.* 1 not taking sides in a quarrel or war. 2 not distinctly marked or colored.
NEUTRAL *n.* a person or nation taking no part in a dispute or war.

neutron *n.* a neutral part of an atom, that is, one that is electrically uncharged.

never *adv.* not ever; at no time.

new *adj.* recently bought or made; different; novel; changed; unused. NEWNESS *n.*

newly *adv.* recently.

news *n.* a report or information about recent events.

newspaper *n.* a daily or weekly printed publication containing news, notices and advertisements.

newt *n.* a small amphibian, lizard-like in appearance, but in the frog family, which lives in water but can survive on land.

next *adj.* nearest; immediately after or following.
NEXT *n.* the nearest one; the one after or following. NEXT *adv.* near; nearest.

nice *adj.* 1 pleasing; kind; friendly.
2 careful and exact. NICELY *adv.*

niece *n.* the daughter of one's brother or sister.

night *n.* the period of darkness between sunset and sunrise.

nimble *adj.* light and quick in movement; skillful.

nine *n.* the number one more than eight; the symbol 9.

nip *v.* to pinch or bite sharply.
NIP *n.* a small pinch or bite.

nitrogen *n.* a colorless, tasteless, odorless gas which makes up four-fifths of the air.

no *adj.* not any; not one.
NO *adv.* not at all.
NO *n.* a negative, denial or refusal.

noble *n.* a person of high rank, birth or title.
NOBLE *adj.* 1 of high rank, birth or title.
2 great and splendid; brave.

nobody *pron.* no person; no one.
NOBODY *n.* a person of no importance.

nocturnal *adj.* of or in the night.
NOCTURNALLY *adv.*

nod *v.* to bend the head forward in agreement or greeting.
NOD *n.* a forward movement of the head.

noise *n.* 1 any kind of sound. 2 a loud or harsh sound.
NOISE *v.* NOISE ABROAD to make public; to make known widely.

noisy *adj.* making a lot of noise. NOISILY *adv.*

nomad *n.* a member of a wandering group or tribe; a wanderer. NOMADIC *adj.*

nominate v. to appoint; to propose a person for a position or election.

none pron. no one; nothing.
NONE adj. not one; not any.
NONE adv. by no amount; not at all.

nonsense n. words and behavior which do not mean anything, or make sense.

noon n. midday; twelve o'clock in the middle of the day.

noose n. in a rope, a running loop which tightens when pulled.

nor conj. and not; and no more.

norm n. a standard or typical example to compare other things with.

normal adj. ordinary; typical; usual.

north n. in the Northern Hemisphere, the direction opposite to the Sun at midday; in the Southern Hemisphere, the direction of the sun at midday. NORTH adj. in or from the north. NORTH adv. towards the north. NORTHERN adj.

Norwegian adj. belonging to Norway or its people.
NORWEGIAN n. the language or one of the people of Norway.

nose n. 1 the part of the face containing the nostrils; the organ of smell. 2 the front end of anything.
NOSE v. to detect by smell; to search and pry.

nostril n. one of the two openings in the nose.

not adv. a word expressing denial or refusal.

notable adj. remarkable; famous; worth taking note of.

note n. 1 a short letter. 2 a single sound in music. 3 something written down as a reminder. 4 a piece of paper money. 5 fame or renown.
NOTE v. 1 to notice. 2 to set down in writing; to make a note.

nothing n. 1 not anything. 2 a thing of no importance. NOTHING adv. not at all.

notice v. to observe something; to note.
NOTICE n. 1 a written or printed announcement. 2 a warning. 3 attention.

notify v. to make something known to (someone); to give notice to.

notion n. an idea or opinion.

notorious adj. well known for bad reasons.

noun n. a word naming a person or thing.

nourish v. to help keep well by feeding; to care for.

nourishment n. food; nutrition.

novel adj. new and original.
NOVEL n. a long fiction story, usually filling a whole book. NOVELIST n.

novelty n. a new or unusual item.

November n. the eleventh month of the year.

novice n. a beginner or learner.

now adv. at the present time; immediately.

nuclear adj. concerning atomic energy; of the energy released when the nuclei of atoms are split or combined.

nucleus n. 1 the center around which a number of persons or things collect; a core. 2 the central point of an atom. pl. NUCLEI.

nugget n. a small rough lump of gold.

nuisance n. a person or thing that annoys.

numb adj. without the power to feel.

number n. 1 a word or figure showing how many. 2 a crowd; a quantity or amount. 3 one issue of a magazine or newspaper. NUMBER v. 1 to count. 2 to amount to.

numeral n. a figure; a number; a digit.

numerator n. the number above the line in a fraction.

numerous adj. many; great in number.

nun n. a woman having taken religious vows and living in a convent.

nurse n. 1 a person trained to look after sick or injured people. 2 a woman specially trained to care for young children.
NURSE v. 1 to look after a baby. 2 to look after sick or injured people.

nut n. 1 a fruit consisting of a seed within a hard shell. 2 a small block of metal for screwing onto a bolt.

nutritious adj. nourishing; efficient as wholesome food.

O

oak n. a large hardwood tree bearing acorns.

oar n. a pole with a flat blade used for rowing boats.

oasis n. a fertile place in the desert where water is found.

oath n. 1 a solemn promise to speak the truth. 2 a swear word.

oats n. pl. a cereal grown as food.

obedience n. doing, or being ready and willing to do, as told. OBEDIENT adj. OBEDIENTLY adv.

obey v. to do as told (by); to submit to.

obituary n. a notice of someone's death.

object n. (pron. OB-ject) 1 a thing that can be seen or touched. 2 an aim or purpose. OBJECT v. (pron. ob-JECT) to protest; to disapprove. OBJECTION n.

objective *n.* a thing which a person aims to do; a place which a person is trying to reach. OBJECTIVE *adj.* real, actual.

oblige *v.* 1 to do (someone) a favor; to help. 2 to force or compel.

oblique *adj.* 1 slanting. 2 greater or less than a right angle.

oblong *n.* a rectangle; a four-sided, right-angled figure greater in length than breadth.

oboe *n.* a wood-wind instrument.

obscene *adj.* indecent; disgusting. OBSCENITY *n.*

obscure *adj.* 1 dark; unclear; hidden. 2 not easily understood; unknown. OBSCURE *v.* to darken; to make less clear. OBSCURITY *n.*

observation *n.* 1 noticing or being noticed. 2 a remark or comment.

observe *v.* 1 to see; to watch carefully. 2 to obey. 3 to comment.

obsession *n.* a thought or intention which occupies the mind continually.

obsolete *adj.* out of date; no longer in use.

obstacle *n.* anything that gets in the way and hinders or stops progress.

obstinate *adj.* stubborn; not easily overcome. OBSTINATELY *adv.*

obstruct *v.* to get in the way; to block. OBSTRUCTION *n.*

obtain *v.* to buy or acquire. OBTAINABLE *adj.*

obvious *adj.* plain to see or understand; unmistakable. OBVIOUSLY *adv.*

occasion *n.* 1 a particular time. 2 a special time or event.

occasional *adj.* happening now and then; not regular or frequent. OCCASIONALLY *adv.*

occupation *n.* 1 an activity. 2 a person's business or work; a job.

occupy *v.* 1 to live in (house, etc.). 2 to take up space or time. 3 OCCUPY ONESELF WITH to keep busy.

occur *v.* 1 to happen. 2 to be found. 3 to come into the mind. OCCURRENCE *n.*

ocean *n.* 1 the water surrounding the land of the globe. 2 a great area of sea.

octagon *n.* an eight-sided figure. OCTAGONAL *adj.*

octave *n.* 1 a span of eight musical notes. 2 the interval between a note and the eighth above or below it.

October *n.* the tenth month of the year.

octopus *n.* a mollusk with eight arms.

odd *adj.* 1 not even; not divisible by two. 2 strange; unusual. ·

odor *n.* a smell. ODORLESS *adj.* without smell.

offend *v.* 1 to commit an offense; to break a law or rule. 2 to hurt a person's feelings. OFFENDER *n.*

offense *n.* 1 an unlawful act; the breaking of a law or rule. 2 hurting of the feelings.

offensive *adj.* 1 disgusting; causing hurt feelings. 2 used for attack, as of weapons. OFFENSIVE *n.* an attack.

offer *v.* 1 to hold out or put forward for acceptance or refusal. 2 to suggest a price. OFFER *n.* 1 an expression of readiness to do or give something. 2 the thing which is offered.

offering *n.* 1 something offered or given. 2 the act of offering.

office *n.* 1 a room or building used as a place of business. 2 an official position.

officer *n.* 1 a person in a position of command in the military, police, etc. 2 the holder of a public appointment; the president, chairman, treasurer, etc., of a club, society, etc.

official *n.* a person who holds a position of responsibility and authority. OFFICIAL *adj.* done or said with authority.

offspring *n.* descendant(s); person's child or children; animal's young.

often *adv.* many times; frequently.

oil *n.* a greasy liquid used for cooking, fuel, lubrication, etc. OIL *v.* to apply oil to make something run smoothly; to lubricate.

ointment *n.* a greasy substance for healing cuts and sores.

old *adj.* 1 having lived for a long time; elderly. 2 not new; worn; made a long time ago.

olive *n.* an evergreen tree; one of its small, oily berries. OLIVE *adj.* yellowish-green.

Olympic *adj.* 1 of or at Olympia in Greece, and the games once held there every four years. 2 about similar international games held in the present day.

ombudsman *n.* an official appointed to consider the grievances of individuals.

omelette, omelet *n.* beaten eggs, fried and folded, often flavored with herbs, cheese, ham, etc.

omission *n.* 1 something left out or not done. 2 neglect.

omit *v.* to leave out or leave undone.

once *adv.* for one time; on one occassion. AT ONCE *adv.* immediately. ONCE *conj.* as soon as. ONCE *n.* one time.

one *n. & pron.* a single thing or person. ONE *adj.* single.

onion *n.* an edible bulb with a strong smell and flavor.

onlooker *n.* a spectator.

only *adj.* alone; by itself. ONLY *adv.* not more than; singly. ONLY *conj.* but then.

onslaught *n.* a fierce attack.

onward *adj.* forward. ONWARD *adv.* further on.

open *adj.* 1 not closed; not covered. 2 not enclosed. 3 frank; clear. OPEN *v.* 1 to make (a thing) open; to unfasten. 2 to begin; to start.

opening *n.* 1 a gap; a space. 2 a beginning; an opportunity.

openly *adv.* not secretly; in full view.

opera *n.* a musical drama where the words are sung.

operate *v.* 1 to work; to cause (something) to work. 2 to perform an operation.

operation *n.* 1 the process or method of working. 2 a military campaign. 3 surgical treatment.

opinion *n.* a view or judgment; a person's belief.

opponent *n.* a rival; an adversary; someone on the opposite side.

opportunity *n.* a good chance or occasion to do something.

oppose *v.* 1 to fight or play against. 2 to be against (something); to resist.

opposite *adj.* 1 facing. 2 entirely different. OPPOSITE *n.* one of two things as different as possible.

opposition *n.* 1 resistance. 2 those who resist or oppose.

oppress *v.* to treat cruelly or to govern harshly.

optical *adj.* to do with the eyes or sight.

optimist *n.* a person who takes a hopeful and cheerful view of things. OPTIMISTIC *adj.*

option *n.* 1 a choice. 2 a right to choose. OPTIONAL *adj.*

oral *adj.* 1 spoken; verbal. 2 by or for the mouth.

orange *n.* a round, juicy fruit with a thick, golden-colored skin. ORANGE *adj.* a reddish-yellow color.

orbit *n.* the path in which a planet, satellite or spacecraft moves around another body.

orchard *n.* a piece of ground where fruit trees are grown.

orchestra *n.* a group of musicians who play together.

ordeal *n.* a severe test of courage, character or endurance.

order *n.* 1 a command. 2 a request for the supply of something. 3 the manner in which things are arranged in relation to one another.

orderly *adj.* 1 well arranged; methodical. 2 well behaved.

ordinary *adj.* 1 usual; normal. 2 plain; uninteresting.

ore *n.* a rock or solid mineral from which metals or other valuable substances may be extracted.

organ *n.* 1 a part of the body with particular work to do. 2 a large musical wind instrument.

organism *n.* an animal or plant.

organize *v.* to arrange (something); to plan. ORGANIZER *n.*

oriental *adj.* of the Far East. ORIENTAL *n.* a person from a Far Eastern country.

origin *n.* the beginning; the point where something began.

original *adj.* earliest; first; not copied; not imitation. ORIGINAL *n.* 1 a model from which others are made. 2 a genuine work of art.

originality *n.* inventiveness; freshness.

ornament *n.* an object or decoration that adds beauty to something.

ornate *adj.* elaborately or richly decorated.

ornithology *n.* the study of birds. ORNITHOLOGIST *n.* an expert in ornithology.

orphan *n.* a child who has lost one or both parents through death.

ostrich *n.* a large, fast-running African bird that cannot fly.

other *adj.* not the same (as already mentioned); different.

otter *n.* a fish-eating mammal that lives by a river or stream.

ought *v.* should; must.

ounce *n.* a measure of weight, one sixteenth of a pound (28.3 grams).

our *adj.* belonging to us.

out *adv.* 1 away from a place or not in it. 2 in the open air. OUT *prep.* out of.

outbreak *n.* a sudden beginning or breaking out.

outburst *n.* a sudden bursting out of something, esp. sound or feelings.

outcome *n.* the result or consequence of something.

outcry *n.* 1 a loud wail of anger. 2 a protest.

outfit *n.* the clothes and equipment needed for a special purpose.

outlet *n.* a way out; an exit.

outlook *n.* 1 a view. 2 what seems likely to happen; a forecast.

output *n.* the quantity of things produced.

outrage *n.* a violent or cruel action. OUTRAGE *v.* to shock; to offend.

outside *n.* the outer part or surface of something.

outspoken *adj.* frank and bold in speech.

outstanding *adj.* prominent; superior; excellent; easily seen.

outward *adj.* 1 on the outside. 2 on the way out.

oval *adj.* shaped like an egg.

ovation *n.* cheering and applause; an enthusiastic reception.

oven *n.* a heated box for baking or roasting things, esp. food.

over *prep.* 1 covering all or part of. 2 across; from side to side. 3 higher than, in position, authority, value, etc. OVER *adv.* 1 on the opposite side; across. 2 more than required. 3 ended; finished. OVER *adj.* upper; outer.

overboard *adv.* over the side of a boat.

overdue *adj.* beyond the stated time of arrival of payment, etc.; late.

overhaul *v.* 1 to examine and repair thoroughly. 2 to overtake.

overlap *v.* partly to cover another thing; to overhang. OVERLAP *n.* the overhanging part.

overture *n.* 1 a piece of orchestral music performed at the beginning of a concert or opera. 2 an offer or proposal.

overturn *v.* 1 to turn over; to upset. 2 to overthrow.

overwhelm *v.* 1 to overcome completely. 2 to flood or sweep away.

owe *v.* to be in debt.

owl *n.* a night-flying bird of prey.

own *v.* 1 to possess. 2 OWN UP to admit; to confess. OWN *adj.* belonging to a certain person.

oxygen *n.* a gas without color, taste or smell, forming part of the air and without which plants and animals would die.

oyster *n.* an edible shellfish in the snail family.

P

pace *n.* 1 a single step in walking. 2 speed of walking or moving. PACE *v.* to walk with regular steps.

pacifist *n.* a person who is opposed to war.

pacify *v.* to make calm and peaceful.

pack *n.* 1 a bag or bundle of things wrapped together for carrying. 2 a group of animals herding or hunting together. 3 a set of playing cards. PACK *v.* 1 to gather together in a box, bag or case. 2 to crowd together.

package *n.* a bundle or parcel.

pact *n.* an agreement or treaty.

pad *n.* 1 soft material used as a protection against damage or injury. 2 sheets of paper fastened together at one edge. 3 the sole of the foot in some quadrupeds. 4 a guard for parts of the body when playing games. PAD *v.* 1 to fill or cover with padding. 2 to walk with a soft tread.

paddle *n.* a short oar with a broad blade. PADDLE *v.* to propel with a paddle.

padlock *n.* a detachable lock with a hinged loop. PADLOCK *v.* to secure with a padlock.

pagan *n.* a heathen. PAGAN *adj.*

page *n.* one side of a sheet, or leaf, of paper in a book.

pageant *n.* 1 an outdoor performance based on people and events from history. 2 a colorful parade or show. PAGEANTRY *n.*

pail *n.* a bucket.

pain *n.* mental or physical suffering.

painful *adj.* of pain or suffering. PAINLESS *adj.*

paint *n.* a coloring substance. PAINT *v.* 1 to cover with paint. 2 to make a picture in paint. PAINTER *n.*

painting *n.* a painted picture.

pair *n.* two things of the same kind; a couple; a set of two. PAIR *v.* to form pairs.

Pakistani *adj.* belonging to Pakistan or its people. PAKISTANI *n.* one of the people of Pakistan.

palace *n.* the official residence of the ruler of a country, a bishop, or a person of high rank.

palate *n.* 1 the roof of the mouth. 2 the sense of taste.

palatial *adj.* splendid; like a palace.

pale *adj.* whitish and having little color. PALE *v.* to turn white. PALELY *adv.*

palette *n.* a board on which an artist mixes colors.

palm *n.* 1 a tropical tree with broad, spreading leaves. 2 the flat of the hand. PALM *v.* to conceal in the palm of the hand.

pamper *v.* to indulge; to spoil with too much kindness. PAMPERED *adj.*

pamphlet *n.* a small booklet.

pan *n.* a container used in cooking.

pandemonium *n.* a scene of confusion and uproar.

pane *n.* a sheet of glass in a window.

panel *n.* 1 a flat piece of wood, metal or other material forming part of a door, wall, etc. 2 a group of people answering questions.

panic *n.* a sudden and great fear sometimes affecting a number of people.

panorama *n.* a wide and complete view of a landscape.

pant *v.* to take short, quick gasps of breath.

paper *n.* 1 a material made from woodpulp, rags, etc., and used for wrapping, for writing and for printing on. 2 a newspaper.
PAPER *adj.* made of paper.

parable *n.* a story which teaches a lesson.

parachute *n.* an umbrella-shaped apparatus, made of nylon, which enables a person or object to descend safely from an aircraft in flight.
PARACHUTE *v.* to descend by parachute.
PARACHUTIST *n.*

parade *n.* 1 a procession or display moving past spectators. 2 a military display or inspection.
PARADE *v.* to assemble for a parade; to march in a procession.

paradise *n.* 1 the Garden of Eden; heaven. 2 a place or state of complete happiness.

paragraph *n.* 1 a distinct passage or section in a book or piece of writing. 2 a separate item in a newspaper.
PARAGRAPH *v.* to divide into paragraphs.

parallel *adj.* 1 alike; similar. 2 continuously the same distance apart.
PARALLEL *n.* 1 a line marking latitude. 2 a comparison or similarity.

parallelogram *n.* a four-sided figure with its opposite sides parallel and equal.

paralysis *n.* a state of being unable to move or feel anything.

paralyze *v.* to affect with paralysis; to make helpless or powerless.

paramount *adj.* supreme; above all others.

parasite *n.* an animal or plant that grows and lives on another.

parcel *n.* a small bundle or package.

pardon *v.* to forgive; to excuse.
PARDON *n.* forgiveness.

pare *v.* to trim or reduce by cutting away the edge or surface of.

parent *n.* a father or mother. PARENTAL *adj.*

parliament *n.* a body of people responsible for making the laws of their country.
PARLIAMENTARY *adj.*

parrot *n.* a bird with brilliant feathers and a hooked bill, often able to imitate the human voice.

part *n.* 1 a portion or share; some, but not all. 2 a piece of something. 3 a character in a play.
PART *v.* to separate or divide. PARTLY *adv.*

partial *adj.* incomplete; forming only a part of.

partial (to) *adj.* favoring; fond of.

participate *v.* to take part or have a share in.
PARTICIPATION *n.*

particle *n.* a very small amount; the smallest possible amount.

particular *adj.* 1 having to do with one person or thing. 2 special; important.

partisan *n.* a guerrilla; a member of a resistance movement.

partition *v.* 1 to divide into parts. 2 to separate by means of a partition.
PARTITION *n.* a dividing wall or screen.

partly *adj.* to some extent; not completely.

partner *n.* 1 one of two people who share or do things together. 2 a person who shares in a business. 3 a husband or wife.
PARTNER *v.* to associate with another person as a partner. PARTNERSHIP *n.*

partridge *n.* a game bird.

party *n.* 1 a group of people with the same ideas or interests. 2 a social gathering of people usually celebrating a special occasion.
pl. PARTIES.

pass *v.* 1 to go past; to travel. 2 to succeed. 3 to disappear. 4 to declare something to be suitable.
PASS *n.* 1 the act of passing. 2 a narrow way over hills and mountains. 3 a permit.

passable *adj.* 1 fairly good; acceptable. 2 that can be crossed or traveled over.

passage *n.* 1 a narrow corridor. 2 a way through. 3 a short extract from a book, speech or piece of music.

passenger *n.* a person traveling in a train, bus, ship, aircraft, etc.; a person being driven in a car.

passion *n.* 1 a strong feeling of emotion or love. 2 an enthusiasm for something. PASSIONATE *adj.*

passport *n.* an official document showing identity and carried by a person traveling abroad.

past *adj.* gone by; previous. PAST *n.* time already gone. PAST *prep.* 1 beyond. 2 up to and beyond.

paste *n.* 1 a mixture for sticking together paper, card, etc. 2 any sticky mixture.
PASTE *v.* to stick with paste.

pastel *n.* 1 a colored chalk crayon. 2 a picture drawn with pastels.
PASTEL *adj.* pale in shade or color.

pastime *n.* a sport, recreation or hobby that helps to pass the time away.

pastry *n.* a mixture of flour, fat and water baked in an oven.

pasture *n.* grassland for grazing sheep or cattle.
PASTURE *v.* to put sheep or cattle out to graze.

pat *n.* a light tap with the hand or with a flat object. PAT *v.* to tap lightly.

patch *n.* 1 a piece of material used to repair clothing, etc. 2 a small area of ground. PATCH *v.* to mend or repair.

patent *adj.* obvious; easily seen.
PATENT *n.* a right given to an inventor to prevent anyone using his invention without payment. PATENT *v.* to obtain a patent for.

paternal *adj.* 1 fatherly. 2 related on the father's side.

path *n.* 1 a track to walk along. 2 a course or line along which a person or thing moves.

pathologist *n.* a specialist in the study of diseases.

patience *n.* enduring pain or inconvenience without complaint.

patient *adj.* having or showing patience.
PATIENT *n.* a person receiving medical attention. PATIENTLY *adv.*

patriot *n.* a person who loves and serves his/her own country. PATRIOTIC *adj.*

patrol *v.* to keep watch by marching or sailing to and fro.
PATROL *n.* a person, or persons, or ship or aircraft on patrol.

pattern *n.* 1 a model; an example to be copied. 2 a decorative design.

pause *n.* a short stop or interval.
PAUSE *v.* to stop for a short time.

pave *v.* to cover an area with material such as asphalt.

paw *n.* an animal's clawed foot.
PAW *v.* to scrape with a paw.

pay *v.* 1 to give money in return for goods bought, work done or services received. 2 to be profitable. 3 PAY FOR to be punished for; to suffer. PAY *n.* money earned, wages, salary.

payment *n.* 1 the act of paying. 2 the money paid.

pea *n.* a climbing plant with round seeds in pods; the seed of the pea plant.

peace *n.* 1 freedom from war, violence and disorder. 2 quietness and calm.

peaceful *adj.* calm; quiet; full of peace.

peach *n.* a tree with soft-skinned, fleshy fruit with a rough stone.

peacock *n.* a male bird with long, colorful, spreading tail feathers. *fem.* PEAHEN.

peak *n.* 1 the pointed top of a hill or mountain. 2 the highest level or point of something.

pear *n.* a soft, tapering fruit.

pearl *n.* a smooth, round, silvery-white granule formed in the shell of an oyster.

peasant *n.* in some countries, a person who works on the land.

pebble *n.* a small smooth stone.

peculiar *adj.* 1 odd; unusual. 2 particular; individual.

pedal *v.* to work with the foot; to use a pedal. PEDAL *n.* a lever worked by the foot.

peddle *v.* to go from place to place selling goods.

pedestal *n.* the base of a column or statue.

pedestrian *n.* a person who goes on foot; a walker.

pedigree *n.* a list of a person's or animal's ancestors. PEDIGREE *adj.* pure-bred.

peel *n.* the skin or rind of many fruits.
PEEL *v.* 1 to remove the skin or rind of. 2 to come off in flakes.

peep *v.* 1 to look through a narrow opening. 2 to glance quickly.

peer *n.* 1 a person's equal. 2 a nobleman.

peer *v.* to look at or closely into.

peg *n.* a pin for fastening or hanging things on.

pellet *n.* a small hard ball or pill.

pen *n.* 1 an instrument for writing with. 2 an enclosure for animals.

penal *n.* having to do with punishment.

penalty *n.* 1 a fine or other punishment. 2 a disadvantage imposed for breaking a rule in sports.

pencil *n.* an instrument containing graphite, for writing and drawing.

pendant *n.* an ornament hanging from a necklace or chain.

pending *adj.* awaiting a decision; undecided.

pendulum *n.* a freely-swinging weight, esp. in a clock.

penetrate *v.* 1 to make or find a way through. 2 to find out or see through. PENETRATION *n.*

penguin *n.* an Antarctic sea-bird that can swim under water but cannot fly.

penicillin *n.* a drug for preventing the growth of many disease-causing bacteria.

peninsula *n.* an area of land almost surrounded by water.

pension *n.* a regular payment of money to a retired person.

people *n.* 1 men, women and children. 2 the persons composing a community, country or nation.

pepper *n.* 1 a plant whose seeds are ground into a hot spice for flavoring. 2 a bright green or red vegetable.

perceive *v.* to see; to understand.

percentage *n.* the rate or portion per hundred.

perception *n.* the ability to see and understand.

perch *n.* 1 a freshwater fish. 2 a roosting place for a bird. PERCH *v.* to roost; to rest; to alight.

percussion *n.* the striking together of two objects and the sound produced.

perennial *adj.* 1 lasting for many years. 2 of plants that carry on growing year after year.

perfect *adj.* (pron. PER-fect) complete; without fault; excellent. PERFECT *v.* (pron. per-FECT) to make perfect.

perforate *v.* to pierce with a hole or holes. PERFORATED *adj.* PERFORATION *n.* a hole.

perform *v.* 1 to do (something); to carry out. 2 to entertain an audience.

performance *n.* 1 the carrying out of a duty, command, etc. 2 the presentation of a play, exhibition, demonstration, etc. PERFORMER *n.*

perfume *n.* 1 a sweet smell. 2 a liquid with a fragrant smell.

perhaps *adv.* possibly; it may be.

peril *n.* a great danger or risk. PERILOUS *adj.* very dangerous; risky.

perimeter *n.* 1 the line enclosing a plane figure; the circumference. 2 the boundary of something.

period *n.* 1 a length of time. 2 the time during which something takes place.

periodical *adj.* happening at regular intervals. PERIODICAL *n.* a magazine or journal which is published at regular intervals.

periscope *n.* a device with mirrors for viewing objects above the surface or above eye-level.

perish *v.* 1 to die. 2 to decay; to wither.

perjure *v.* to give false evidence under oath. PERJURY *n.*

permanent *adj.* 1 long lasting; intended to last for ever. 2 fixed; not to be moved. PERMANENTLY *adv.*

permission *n.* consent given.

permit *v.* (pron. per-MIT) to allow (something) to be done. PERMIT *n.* (pron. PER-mit) written permission to do something; a pass.

perpendicular *adj.* standing upright at right angles to the base; vertical.

perpetrate *v.* to commit (a blunder or crime).

perpetual *adj.* 1 unceasing, everlasting.

persecute *v.* to treat cruelly; to oppress or torment. PERSECUTED *adj.* PERSECUTION *n.*

perseverance *n.* a constant effort to achieve something. PERSEVERE *v.*

Persian *adj.* belonging to Persia or its people. PERSIAN *n.* the language or one of the people of Persia (now called Iran).

persist *v.* to persevere; to go on in spite of difficulties.

person *n.* an individual human being.

personal *adj.* 1 belonging to a particular person. 2 private. 3 referring to an individual.

personality *n.* 1 the qualities making up a person's character. 2 a well-known person.

personnel *n.pl.* the employees of a business or organization.

perspective *n.* the art of drawing scenes or objects as they appear to the eye.

perspire *v.* to sweat. PERSPIRATION *n.*

persuade *v.* to cause or influence (someone to do or believe something). PERSUASION *n.*

pervade *v.* to spread through or penetrate all parts of.

pessimist *n.* a person who always expects the worst to happen. PESSIMISTIC *adj.*

pest *n.* 1 a troublesome or destructive insect or animal. 2 a nuisance.

pester *v.* to annoy and worry (somebody) continually.

pet *n.* a tame animal kept and treated with fondness. PET *v.* to fondle.

petal *n.* one of the brightly-colored leaves in a flowerhead.

petition *n.* 1 an appeal. 2 a written request signed by many people.

petrify *v.* 1 to turn to stone. 2 to paralyze with fear and horror. PETRIFIED *adj.*

petroleum *n.* a mineral oil found in various parts of the world.

petty *adj.* unimportant; trivial.

pew *n.* a long wooden bench with a high back, used in churches.

phantom *n.* a ghost; an apparition.

pharmacist *n.* a person who prepares medicines.

phase *n.* a stage in the development of something.

pheasant *n.* a long-tailed game bird.

phenomenal *adj.* remarkable; uncommon.

philately *n.* the collection and study of postage stamps. PHILATELIC *adj.* PHILATELIST *n.*

philosophy *n.* the study of the meaning and understanding of life.

photograph *n.* a picture taken by means of a camera. PHOTOGRAPHER *n.* PHOTOGRAPHY *n.* the science and art of taking photographs.

phrase *n.* 1 a small group of words without a verb and forming part of a sentence.
2 a short sequence of musical notes.
PHRASE *v.* to say in words.

physical *adj.* 1 having to do with the body.
2 that can be touched and seen; to do with the laws of nature. PHYSICALLY *adv.*

physician *n.* a doctor; a person qualified to practice medicine.

physics *n. pl.* the scientific study of heat, light, sound, electricity, magnetism and mechanics.

pianist *n.* a person who plays the piano.

piano *n. abbrev.* pianoforte, a musical instrument played by striking keys with the fingers.

pick *v.* 1 to choose; to select. 2 to pull or pluck.
PICK *n.* 1 a choice; a selection. 2 a tool for breaking hard ground.

picket *n.* 1 a group of strikers who try to dissuade others from working.
PICKET *v.* 1 to position a group of people or soldiers as pickets. 2 to tether horses.

pickle *n.* food preserved in salt, vinegar, etc. esp. vegetables.
PICKLE *v.* to preserve in salt or vinegar.

picnic *n.* a meal eaten for pleasure out of doors.

picture *n.* 1 a drawing, painting or photograph.
2 a vivid description of something.
PICTURE *v.* to imagine.

picturesque *adj.* 1 like a picture. 2 charming or vivid in description.

pie *n.* fruit, meat, or fish covered with pastry and baked.

piece *n.* 1 a part or fragment of something.
2 a single item. 3 an instance or example.
PIECE *v.* to put parts together to make a whole.

pier *n.* 1 a structure built out into the sea as a protection, landing-stage or promenade.

pierce *v.* to bore a hole through something; to penetrate.

piercing *adj.* 1 penetrating. 2 shrill. 3 cold and bitter.

pig *n.* 1 a swine. 2 a block of metal cast in a mold.

pigeon *n.* a bird in the dove family.

pike *n.* 1 a large, fierce, freshwater fish.
2 a spear with a long shaft and a sharp head.

pile *n.* 1 a number of things on top of each other; a mound. 2 a post of concrete, steel or wood driven into the ground as a support for a building, bridge, etc.
PILE *v.* to make into a heap.

pilfer *v.* to steal (things) in small quantities.
PILFERER *n.*

pilgrim *n.* a person who makes a journey to a shrine or holy place.

pilgrimage *n.* a pilgrim's journey.

pill *n.* medicine made up into a tablet.

pillar *n.* 1 an upright column supporting a roof or an arch. 2 a monument or landmark.

pillow *n.* a cushion for the head.

pilot *n.* 1 the person who controls an aircraft during flight. 2 a person who steers ships in and out of a harbor. PILOT *v.* to act as a pilot.

pin *n.* a piece of thin, stiff wire with a point and a head, used for fastening papers or material together. PIN *v.* to fasten with a pin.

pinch *v.* 1 to squeeze with the finger and thumb.
PINCH *n.* 1 a sharp squeeze. 2 a small amount.

pine *n.* an evergreen, cone-bearing tree.
PINE *v.* 1 to waste away from sickness or grief.
2 PINE FOR or AFTER to long for.

pink *n.* 1 a pale red color. 2 excellent condition.

pint *n.* a measure for liquids, one eighth of a gallon (0.57 liter).

pioneer *n.* an original explorer or settler; a person who tries a new method, idea or enterprise.
PIONEER *v.* to be the first to do something.

pipe *n.* 1 a long hollow tube for conveying water, gas, etc. 2 a bowl with a hollow stem for smoking tobacco. 3 a musical wind instrument.
PIPE *v.* 1 to convey through a pipe. 2 to play music on a pipe.

piracy *n.* robbery at sea.

pirate *n.* a person who robs a ship at sea.

pistil *n.* the part of a flower which produces seeds.

pistol *n.* a small gun, held in one hand when firing.

piston *n.* 1 the part of an engine which moves inside the cylinder. 2 a valve on a musical instrument.

pit *n.* a deep hole in the ground.

pitch *v.* 1 to throw or fling something. 2 to rise and fall with the waves. 3 to erect (a tent).
PITCH *n.* the highness or lowness of a musical note.

pith *n.* the white spongy substance in the stems of plants or in fruit peel.

pitiful *adj.* 1 showing or arousing pity.
2 deserving contempt.

pitiless *adj.* showing no pity; merciless.

pity *n.* a feeling of sorrow and sympathy for the troubles and sufferings of others.
PITY *v.* to feel sorry for.

pivot *n.* a point or pin on which something turns.
PIVOT *v.* to rotate on a point or pin.

placard *n.* a poster or notice.

place *n.* 1 a particular spot, position, town, locality, etc. 2 a job; a position.
PLACE *v.* to put in a certain spot or position.

placid *adj.* calm; peaceful; not easily ruffled.
PLACIDLY *adv.*

plague *n.* a widespread deadly disease or affliction. PLAGUE *v.* to pester; to tease.

plaid *n.* (pron. PLAD) a length of tartan woolen cloth.

plain *adj.* 1 easily seen or understood; 2 simple; undecorated. 3 straightforward.
PLAIN *n.* a large area of flat country.
PLAINLY *adv.*

plan *n.* 1 a method for doing something. 2 a map, drawing or diagram of a building, street, town, etc.
PLAN *v.* 1 to think out and prepare a scheme or proposal. 2 to draw a plan.

plane *n.* 1 a level surface. 2 a tool for smoothing wood. 3 an aircraft.
PLANE *v.* 1 to smooth wood with a plane. 2 to glide; to skim over water.

planet *n.* a heavenly body which moves in orbit around the sun.

plank *n.* a long flat piece of timber.

plant *n.* 1 any living thing that is not an animal. 2 the machinery and equipment of a factory.
PLANT *v.* 1 to place plants and seeds in the soil so that they will grow. 2 to position firmly.

plantation *n.* 1 an area of land planted with trees. 2 an estate for growing cotton, rubber, sugar, tobacco, etc.

plaster *n.* 1 a mixture of lime, sand and water for spreading on walls and ceilings to form a smooth surface. 2 a dressing for a wound.
PLASTER *v.* to cover with plaster.

plastic *adj.* 1 easily molded into shape. 2 made of plastic.

plastic *n.* a synthetic substance made from chemicals.

plate *n.* 1 a round, shallow dish for holding food. 2 a flat sheet of metal. 3 articles of gold or silver.
PLATE *v.* to cover with a thin plating of metal.

plateau *n.* an area of high, level land.
pl. PLATEAUX, PLATEAUS.

platform *n.* 1 a stage or raised floor in a hall. 2 a raised surface for passengers at a railroad station.

platinum *n.* a heavy and very valuable grayish-white metal.

plausible *adj.* 1 apparently honest, probable and reasonable. 2 good at giving reasons.

play *v.* 1 to frisk or move about in a lively, happy manner. 2 to take part in a game. 3 to perform upon a musical instrument. 4 to act a part.
PLAY *n.* 1 a game; an amusement. 2 a story for acting.

playwright *n.* a person who writes plays; a dramatist.

plea *n.* 1 a request. 2 in a court of law, a defendant's answer to the charge against him. 3 an excuse.

plead *v.* 1 to answer a charge in a court of law. 2 to offer as an excuse.
3 PLEAD WITH to beg; to entreat.

pleasant *adj.* agreeable; giving pleasure; enjoyable. PLEASANTLY *adv.*

please *v.* 1 to give joy or pleasure to. 2 to choose; to be willing. 3 word used when making a polite request. PLEASING *adj.*

pleasure *n.* 1 a feeling of happiness or delight. 2 something that gives happiness.

pledge *n.* 1 a solemn promise; an agreement. 2 something given as security.
PLEDGE *v.* 1 to promise; to guarantee. 2 to give as security.

plenty *n.* as much as or more than is needed; a large number or quantity.
PLENTY *adv.* quite enough; in abundance.
PLENTIFUL *adj.*

pliable *adj.* 1 easily bent; flexible. 2 easily influenced.

pliers *n.pl.* a small tool for gripping things.

plod *v.* to travel slowly and steadily; to trudge.

plot *n.* 1 a small piece of ground. 2 a secret plan. 3 the main outline of a story or play.
PLOT *v.* to scheme; to draw up a plan.

plow *n.* 1 a farming implement for turning the soil. 2 a similar implement for moving snow.
PLOW *v.* to use a plow.

pluck *n.* bravery; courage.
PLUCK *v.* 1 to pick or gather (flowers or fruit). 2 to pull the feathers off a dead bird. 3 to snatch.

plug *n.* 1 a piece of material (rubber, plastic, etc.) used as a stopper. 2 a fitting to connect an appliance to the electrical supply.
PLUG *v.* to stop up a hole or gap.

plumage *n.* the feathers on a bird.

plumb *adj.* upright; vertical.
PLUMB *v.* 1 to test whether a wall or other object is vertical. 2 to find the depth of water.

plumber *n.* someone who installs and repairs water-pipes, faucets, etc.

plump *adj.* fat and rounded.

plunder *v.* to steal by force.
PLUNDER *n.* loot; booty.

plunge *v.* to thrust or dive into water.
PLUNGE *n.* a dive.

plural *adj.* more than one.

plus *n.* the sign (+), the symbol of addition.
PLUS *prep.* with the addition of.

plutonium *n.* a radioactive element made from uranium.

pneumatic *adj.* 1 filled with air. 2 operated by compressed air.

pneumonia *n.* inflammation of the lungs.

poach *v.* 1 to cook food gently in a liquid. 2 to catch game or fish illegally.

pocket *n.* a small bag or pouch sewn into a piece of clothing for carrying small articles.

pod *n.* a long seedcase on some plants.

poem *n.* a piece of rhythmic verse or poetry.

poet *n.* a person who writes poetry.

poetry *n.* a poet's thoughts and feelings usually arranged in lines and verses, often with a regular rhythm and pattern of lines.

point *n.* 1 the sharp end or tip of something. 2 an aim or purpose. 3 a place or position. 4 a headland or cape. 5 a mark in scoring.
POINT OUT to direct attention to.
2 POINT AT to aim at. POINTED *adj.*

poise *n.* balance, assurance, self-confidence.
POISE *v.* to balance or hover.

poison *n.* 1 a substance which can cause death or serious illness to living things. 2 a harmful influence.
POISON *v.* 1 to give poison to. 2 to corrupt or infect. POISONOUS *adj.*

poke *v.* to prod or thrust at, or into, with a finger, stick, etc. POKE *n.* a prod or thrust.

polar *adj.* concerning the North and South Poles.

pole *n.* 1 a long round piece of wood or metal; a tall post. 2 the North or South Pole. 3 each of the opposite ends of a magnet.

police *n.* the body of men and women appointed to enforce and maintain law and order.
POLICE *v.* to maintain law and order.

policy *n.* 1 a plan or course of action. 2 an insurance agreement.

polish *v.* to make something smooth by rubbing.
POLISH *n.* 1 a substance used for polishing. 2 smoothness; gloss. POLISHED *adj.*

Polish *adj.* belonging to Poland or its people.
POLE *n.* an inhabitant of Poland.
POLISH *n.* the language of Poland.

polite *adj.* courteous; having good manners.
POLITELY *adv.*

political *adj.* concerning politics, government or the state.

politician *n.* a person engaged in politics.

politics *n.pl.* the study and art of government.

poll *n.* 1 the counting of voters and votes at an election. 2 an estimation of public opinion.
POLL *v.* to receive votes at an election.

pollen *n.* the tiny yellow fertilizing grains found in flowers.

pollute *v.* to make (a thing) dirty or impure; to contaminate. POLLUTION *n.*

polo *n.* a game like hockey played on horseback.

polygamy *n.* the practice of having two or more wives or husbands at the same time.

polygon *n.* a figure with many angles and sides.

pompous *adj.* self-important; displaying exaggerated pride and dignity.

pond *n.* a pool of standing water; a small lake.

ponder *v.* to consider something; to think about.

pony *n.* a small horse.

pool *n.* a pond; a puddle; a deep place in a river.

poor *adj.* 1 having little or no money; having few possessions. 2 inferior; of low quality. 3 weak; feeble.

poorly *adj.* ill; in bad health.

Pope *n.* the head of the Roman Catholic Church.

poplar *n.* a tall, fast-growing tree.

poppy *n.* a wild or cultivated flower, usually red or scarlet in color. *pl.* POPPIES.

popular *adj.* well liked, favorite. POPULARITY *n.*

population *n.* the total number of people living in one place. POPULATED *adj.*

porcelain *n.* a fine kind of glazed china.

porch *n.* a covered entrance to a building.

pore *n.* the small opening of a sweat gland in the skin.

pork *n.* the flesh of a pig.

porous *adj.* having pores; not watertight.

port *n.* 1 a harbor. 2 a town with a harbor. 3 the lefthand side of a ship or aircraft.

portable *adj.* convenient for carrying; movable.

portion *n.* a part, share or helping of something.
PORTION *v.* to divide into parts or portions.

portrait *n.* a drawing, painting or photograph of a person; a vivid description.

portray *v.* to paint or draw a picture of; to describe in words.

Portuguese *adj.* belonging to Portugal or its people.

pose *n.* an assumed position or attitude.
POSE *v.* 1 to assume a certain position or attitude. 2 to behave in an unnatural way.

position *n*. 1 a place or spot where something is or should be. 2 a job or situation. 3 an attitude or posture.
POSITION *v*. to put in the proper position.

positive *adj*. 1 definite; certain. 2 in mathematics, greater than zero. 3 beyond doubt.

possess *v*. to have, to own, to control.
POSSESSOR *n*.

possession *n*. the act of possessing; something owned or occupied.

possibility *n*. something that may happen.

possible *adj*. that can happen; that can be done.

possibly *adv*. maybe; perhaps.

post *n*. an upright pole of wood, metal, concrete, etc.

postage *n*. the charge made for sending letters and parcels by mail.

poster *n*. a placard or advertisement displayed in a public place.

postpone *v*. to put (something) off until a later date; to defer.
POSTPONED *adj*. POSTPONEMENT *n*.

pot *n*. a bowl or jar for containing things.

pot *v*. to put in a pot; to plant in a pot.

potato *n*. a plant with tubers which are used for food. *pl*. POTATOES.

potential *adj*. possible at some future time.

pottery *n*. 1 articles made of baked clay. 2 the place where these things are made.

poultry *n*. chickens, hens, ducks, geese etc.

pounce (upon) *v*. to swoop and attack something; to leap upon.

pound *n*. a unit of weight, 16 ounces (454 grams).
POUND *v*. 1 to beat into powder or very small pieces. 2 to beat with heavy blows.

pour *v*. 1 to flow or to make something flow. 2 to rain heavily.

poverty *n*. the state of being poor; scarcity of.

powder *n*. very fine particles; anything crushed or ground into dust.
POWDER *v*. 1 to make into powder. 2 to sprinkle powder on.

power *n*. 1 the ability or authority to do something. 2 strength, force, energy.

powerful *adj*. strong, influential.

powerless *adj*. without power; weak, helpless.

practical *adj*. 1 skilled and efficient at doing or making things. 2 useful; workable.

practically *adv*. 1 in a practical way. 2 nearly; almost.

practice *n*. 1 a habit or custom. 2 an action done repeatedly. 3 action as opposed to theory. 4 the business of a doctor, a lawyer, etc.

practice *v*. 1 to do something regularly in order to become skillful. 2 to do something as a habit.

prairie *n*. a large treeless area of grassland.

praise *v*. 1 to speak highly of (a person or thing); to commend. 2 to worship.
PRAISE *n*. 1 the act of praising; approval. 2 worship.

pray *v*. 1 to ask earnestly. 2 to offer praise and prayer (to God). PRAYER *n*.

preach *v*. 1 to deliver a sermon. 2 to proclaim and make known. PREACHER *n*.

precarious *adj*. 1 doubtful, depending on chance. 2 uncertain; risky. PRECARIOUSLY *adv*.

precaution *n*. care or action taken beforehand.

precede *v*. to come or go before. PRECEDENCE *n*.

precedent *n*. a past action or pattern which may serve as an example or rule in the future.

precious *adj*. 1 of great price or worth; valuable. 2 loved; prized.

precipice *n*. the very steep face of a cliff or mountain.

precise *adj*. 1 clear in meaning; definite; exact. 2 very particular. PRECISELY *adv*. PRECISION *n*.

predator *n*. an animal that hunts prey.

predecessor *n*. 1 the former holder of an office or position.

predicament *n*. a difficult, an awkward or a dangerous situation.

predict *v*. to foretell; to forecast.

preen *v*. 1 to make the feathers clean with the beak. 2 to show pride in oneself.

prefabricate *v*. to manufacture sections and units in a factory for assembly elsewhere.

preface *n*. an introduction to a book.

prefer *v*. to like better; to choose (one thing) before others. PREFERABLE *adj*. PREFERENCE *n*.

prefix *n*.1 a syllable or another word placed at the beginning of a word to change its meaning. 2 a title placed before a name as Mr., Dr., etc. PREFIX *v*. to place at the beginning.

pregnant *adj*. 1 fruitful. 2 with child.

prehistoric *adj*. belonging to a time before history was recorded.

prejudice *n*. an opinion formed without full consideration of the facts; bias.
PREJUDICE *v*. to fill with prejudice.

preliminary *n*. the first or introductory stage.
PRELIMINARY *adj*. introductory; preparing for what follows.

premier *adj*. first in position, order or importance.

premium *n*. 1 an extra charge. 2 a regular payment on an insurance policy.

premonition *n.* a foreboding; a feeling that something is going to happen.

preparation *n.* things done to make ready.

preparatory *adj.* preliminary; introductory.

prepare *v.* to get ready, to make ready. PREPARED *adj.*

preposition *n.* a word placed before a noun or pronoun, and together with it forming a phrase: e.g. to, for, with, after, etc.

prescribe *v.* to order (someone) to use; to give directions; to lay down as a rule or guide.

prescription *n.* 1 the doctor's instructions for the dispensing of medicine. 2 the medicine prescribed.

presence *n.* being present; a personal appearance.

present *n.* (pron. PREZ-ent) a gift. PRESENT *adj.* now; being in a particular place.

present *v.* (pron. pre-ZENT) 1 to give, to offer. 2 to introduce.

preservation *n.* protection; a preserved condition.

preserve *v.* 1 to keep (something) safe. 2 to keep something in good condition.

preside *v.* to take control; to chair a meeting.

president *n.* a person who presides; the head of a state or republic.

press *v.* 1 to push; to crush; to urge. 2 to make (something) flat or smooth. PRESS *n.* 1 a device for pressing things. 2 a printing machine. 3 the newspapers.

pressure *n.* 1 a force which presses or pushes. 2 strong influence or persuasion.

presumably *adv.* as may be supposed; probably.

presume *v.* to take for granted; to suppose.

pretense *n.* pretending; a false claim.

pretend *v.* to sham; to claim falsely.

pretext *n.* an excuse; a false reason.

pretty *adj.* attractive to eye or ear. PRETTY *adv.* fairly; moderately.

prevail *v.* 1 to win. 2 PREVAIL UPON to persuade.

prevalent *adj.* common; usual; widespread.

prevent *v.* to stop; to hinder. PREVENTION *n.*

previous *adj.* earlier in time; former. PREVIOUSLY *adv.*

prey *n.* 1 an animal or bird that is hunted, killed and eaten by another. 2 a victim. PREY (UPON) *v.* to hunt; to plunder.

price *n.* the money asked or paid for anything sold; the cost. PRICE *v.* to fix the price of.

pride *n.* 1 a high opinion of oneself; arrogance. 2 something which gives a feeling of pleasure. 3 a group of lions.

priest *n.* 1 a clergyman. 2 a religious leader.

primary *adj.* first; most important; original.

prime *adj.* 1 first in importance, rank or time. 2 of highest quality. PRIME *n.* the time of greatest health and strength. PRIME *v.* 1 to prepare (something) for use by filling. 2 to apply first coat of paint.

primitive *adj.* 1 ancient; early. 2 rough; crude; simple.

prince *n.* the son of a king or queen; a ruler, *fem.* PRINCESS.

principal *adj.* chief; most important. PRINCIPAL *n.* the head of a school.

principally *adv.* chiefly; mainly.

principle *n.* a rule of conduct; a fixed rule or law.

print *v.* to make letters and pictures on paper by means of a printing press. PRINT *n.* 1 a mark made by pressure. 2 a photograph produced from a negative. 3 printed lettering. PRINTER *n.* PRINTING *n.*

prior *adj.* earlier, before. PRIOR *adv.* previously. PRIOR *n.* head of a monastery or convent.

priority *n.* the right to be first; the right to do something before others.

prison *n.* a place where criminals are detained.

prisoner *n.* a person kept in prison; a captive.

privacy *n.* seclusion; being private.

private *adj.* 1 concerning one person or group; personal. 2 hidden from view; secret. PRIVATE *n.* an ordinary soldier.

privilege *n.* a right or advantage enjoyed by a limited number of people.

prize *n.* a reward; an honor; an award for success. PRIZE *v.* to value something highly.

probable *adj.* likely to be; likely to happen.

probably *adv.* very likely.

probe *v.* 1 to investigate (something) deeply. 2 to examine with a probe. PROBE *n.* an instrument used for probing.

problem *n.* something hard to understand or deal with.

procedure *n.* the way in which something is usually done; the method.

proceed *v.* 1 to move forward; to continue.

process *n.* 1 the method of manufacture. 2 a series of events which bring about change and development.

procession *n.* a body of people, vehicles, etc., moving forward in order.

proclaim *v.* to make a public announcement, to declare openly. PROCLAMATION *n.* an official announcement.

produce v. (pron. pro-DUCE) 1 to bring forward.
2 to create or make. 3 to prepare
(a play) for performance.
PRODUCE n. (pron. PRO-duce) 1 the quantity.
2 goods.

producer n. 1 the person who produces anything.
2 the person supervising the presentation of a
stage, film or television performance.

product n. 1 something produced by a natural
process or by manufacture. 2 the number
obtained by multiplying two numbers together.

production n. 1 the act of producing.
2 the quantity or thing produced.

productive adj. fertile; able to produce.

productivity n. efficiency in production.

profession n. 1 an occupation with certain
educational requirements. 2 a declaration.

professional adj. 1 connected with a profession.
2 earning a living by skill etc.

professor n. a teacher of high rank, usually in a
college or university.

proficient adv. skilled; expert. PROFICIENTLY adv.

profile n. a side view; an outline of something.

profit n. financial gain; benefit.
PROFIT (BY OR FROM) v. to gain profit or benefit
from. PROFITABLE adj.

profuse adj. plentiful; abundant; extravagant.
PROFUSION n. plentifulness; great abundance.
PROFUSELY adv.

program n. 1 list of events which are to take
place; a plan. 2 details of an entertainment.
3 a broadcast on television or radio.

progress n. (pron. PRO-gress) 1 forward
movement. 2 an advance, improvement or
development.
PROGRESS v. (pron. pro-GRESS) to move
forward.

prohibit v. to forbid; to prevent.

prohibitive adj. too costly; intended to prevent.

project n. (pron. PRO-ject) a plan, scheme or
undertaking.
PROJECT v. (pron. pro-JECT) 1 to throw forward
2 to jut out. PROJECTING adj.

projectile n. something thrown or shot through
the air; a missile.

projector n. an apparatus for projecting slides or
films on to a screen.

prolific adj. producing abundantly; fruitful.

prolong v. to make longer; to cause to continue.
PROLONGED adj.

promenade n. a place set aside for walking.
PROMENADE v. to walk for pleasure or display.

prominent adj. 1 clearly seen; standing out.
2 famous, important. PROMINENCE n.

promise n. 1 an assurance that a person will do
or will not do something. 2 a sign of something
to come.
PROMISE v. to give an assurance (to do or not to
do something).

promising adj. full of promise; encouraging.

promontory n. a headland; a cape.

promote v. 1 to raise to a high rank or position.
2 to help, encourage, or support. PROMOTER n.

promotion n. a rise in rank or position; an
advancement.

prompt adj. acting quickly; without delay.
PROMPT v. 1 to encourage or cause (a person to
do something. 2 to help an actor or speaker who
has forgotten his words. PROMPTLY adv.

prone adj. 1 lying face downward. 2 inclined or
liable (to do something).

pronoun n. a word used instead of a noun:
e.g. I, you, he, this, etc.

pronounce v. 1 to utter; to speak (a word)
distinctly. 2 to make a public declaration.

pronunciation n. the way in which a word is
pronounced.

proof n. 1 test or trial. 2 evidence of the truth.
3 a printer's trial copy.

propaganda n. the spreading of ideas and
information (sometimes false) in an attempt to
persuade people.

propel v. to drive on or push forward.

propeller n. a revolving shaft with blades which
turns rapidly to propel a ship or aircraft.

proper adj. 1 right, correct, suitable.
2 respectable. PROPERLY adj.

property n. 1 something owned; possessions.
2 land or buildings. 3 a special quality or ability.

prophecy n. a prediction; something foretold.
pl. PROPHECIES.

prophesy v to make a prophecy; to foretell.

prophet n. 1 a person who foretells the future.
2 a person who interprets God's will.
fem. PROPHETESS.

proportion n. 1 a comparison of the quantity,
size or importance of one thing with that of
another. 2 a relative part or share.

proposal n. a suggestion, something put forward
for consideration; an offer.

propose v. to suggest, to offer. PROPOSER n.

proposition n. something proposed; a scheme; a
suggestion.

propulsion n. a driving foward; the force that
propels.

prose n. language as it is spoken or written and
not in verse.

prosecute *v.* to take legal action against. PROSECUTION *n.*

prospect *n.* (pron. PROS-pect) 1 something expected or hoped for. 2 a wide view. PROSPECT *v.* (pron. pros-PECT) to explore; to search for minerals.

prospector *n.* a person who searches for mineral deposits.

prosper *v.* to succeed; to flourish. PROSPERITY *n.* PROSPEROUS *adj.*

protect *v.* to defend from danger; to shield. PROTECTOR *n.* PROTECTION *n.*

protected *adj.* defended; guarded; fortified.

protein *n.* a substance found in eggs, meat, milk, etc. which is an essential part of the diet.

protest *v.* (pron. pro-TEST) to raise an objection; to express disapproval. PROTEST *n.* (pron. PRO-test) an objection; a complaint.

Protestant *n.* a member of any of the Christian bodies that broke away from the Church of Rome at the time of the Reformation.

proton *n.* an atomic charge of positive electricity.

protrude *v.* to stick out; to project.

proud *adj.* 1 having pride or dignity. 2 conceited; arrogant. PROUDLY *adv.*

prove *v.* 1 to test; to verify. 2 to show that something is true.

proverb *n.* a short, wise saying in general use.

provide *v.* 1 to supply; to give. 2 to get ready in advance.

province *n.* 1 a large division of a country. 2 the extent of a person's duty or authority.

provincial *adj.* belonging to a province.

provision *n.* 1 what is provided. 2 preparation for future need.

provisional *adj.* temporary; for the time being.

provisions *n. pl.* supplies of food and drink.

provocative *adj.* intentionally irritating; annoying.

provoke *v.* to make angry; to annoy.

prowl *v.* to go about stealthily. PROWLER *n.*

proximity *n.* nearness.

prune *v.* 1 to trim by cutting away unwanted branches, shoots, etc. 2 to cut out or get rid of unnecessary parts.

prune *n.* a dried plum.

pry (into) *v.* 1 to look and peer inquisitively. 2 to be over-curious about other people's affairs. PRYING *adj.*

psalm *n.* a sacred song; a hymn.

pseudonym *n.* an assumed name.

psychiatry *n.* the study and treatment of mental and nervous disorders. PSYCHIATRIST *n.*

psychology *n.* the study of the mind. PSYCHOLOGIST *n.*

public *adj.* 1 concerning the community as a whole; for general use. 2 open; well known. PUBLIC *n.* people in general; the community.

publication *n.* a published book, magazine, etc.

publicity *n.* advertising.

publicly *adv.* in public; openly.

publish *v.* 1 to make known generally. 2 to prepare and issue copies of a book, paper, magazine, etc., for sale. PUBLISHER *n.*

pudding *n.* a mixture of fat, sugar, eggs and flour baked or boiled.

puddle *n.* a small pool of water.

pull *v.* 1 draw or move towards. 2 to pluck; to tear. PULL *n.* the act of pulling; a strain; an effort.

pulley *n.* a wheel with a grooved rim in which runs a rope or chain for raising weights.

pulp *n.* a mass of soft, often juicy, substance.

pulpit *n.* a raised structure from which the preacher in a church or chapel gives the sermon.

pulsate *v.* to throb; to expand and contract rhythmically.

pulse *n.* 1 the regular beat or throb of the arteries as the blood is pumped through them. 2 a steady beat.

pump *n.* 1 a machine for pumping air or liquids through a pipe. 2 a soft, light shoe. PUMP *v.* to use a pump.

punch *n.* 1 a blow with the fist. 2 a tool for making holes. PUNCH *v.* 1 to hit with the fist. 2 to make a hole with a punch.

punctual *adj.* coming at the appointed time; in good time, not late. PUNCTUALLY *adv.*

punctuate *v.* to mark the pauses and emphasis in writing with periods, commas, exclamation marks, etc. PUNCTUATION *n.*

puncture *n.* a prick; a hole made by a sharp point. PUNCTURE *v.* to make a hole using a sharp point.

punish *v.* to make a person suffer for a crime or offense they have committed. PUNISHMENT *n.*

pupa *n.* the chrysalis stage in certain insects. *pl.* PUPAE. PUPAL *adj.*

pupil *n.* 1 a person who is being taught. 2 the round opening in the iris of the eye.

puppet *n.* 1 a doll or other figure with jointed limbs worked by strings. 2 a person whose actions are controlled by others.

purchase *v.* to buy. PURCHASE *n.* anything bought. PURCHASER *n.*

pure *adj.* 1 clean; unmixed with anything else. 2 free from faults. PURELY *adv.*

purify *v.* to make pure; to cleanse.

purity *n.* pureness; cleanness.

purple *adj.* a deep reddish-blue color made by mixing red and blue.

purpose *n.* an aim; a plan or intention. PURPOSELY *adv.*

purr *n.* the sound a cat makes when pleased. PURR *v.*

purse *n.* a small bag for carrying money.

pursue *v.* 1 to chase. 2 to continue discussing or going on with (something). PURSUER *n.*

pursuit *n.* 1 a chase or hunt. 2 a person's business or occupation.

push *v.* 1 to press against (something) in order to move it. 2 to urge on; to make an effort. PUSH *n.* 1 the act of pushing. 2 enterprise; drive.

put *v.* 1 to place (something) in a particular position. 2 to express in words.

putt *v.* 1 to tap a golfball toward a hole. PUTT *n.* the stroke made in golf. PUTTER *n.* a golfclub used in putting.

putty *n.* a paste used to fix glass into position.

puzzle *n.* 1 a problem or question which is difficult to solve. 2 a game to test a person's skill. PUZZLE *v.* 1 to bewilder (someone) 2 PUZZLE OVER to try to find the answer to a problem.

pygmy *adj.* small; dwarflike.

pyramid *n.* a solid figure with three or more equal triangular sides which meet at a point at the top.

pyrotechnics *n.pl.* the art of making and displaying fireworks.

python *n.* a large snake that kills its prey by coiling around it and crushing it.

Q

quadrangle *n.* 1 a figure with four sides, as a square or a rectangle. 2 a courtyard; a lawn with buildings around it.

quadrant *n.* 1 a quarter of a circle or its circumference. 2 an instrument used for measuring angles.

quadrilateral *n.* a four-sided figure. QUADRILATERAL *adj.* four-sided.

quadruped *n.* a four-footed animal.

quadruple *n.* an amount four times as great. QUADRUPLE *v.* to multiply by four.

quadruplet *n.* one of four children born of the same mother at the same birth.

quaint *adj.* odd; unusual; old-fashioned. QUAINTLY *adv.*

Quaker *n.* a member of the Society of Friends. a religious group.

qualification *n.* 1 proof of training or skill. 2 fitness; suitability.

qualified *adj.* 1 having the qualifications; authorized; licensed. 2 fitted; suitable.

qualify *v.* 1 to reach an acceptable standard. usually by examination, to follow a profession or trade. 2 to modify.

quality *n.* 1 the character or nature of anything. 2 the degree of goodness or badness. *pl.* QUALITIES.

quantity *n.* amount, measure or size. *pl.* QUANTITIES.

quarantine *n.* a period of isolation for animals, people or ships to prevent the spread of disease.

quarrel *n.* a dispute or angry argument. QUARREL *v.* to dispute or argue angrily.

quarry *n.* 1 a place where stone or slate is cut and dug. 2 a hunted animal. QUARRY *v.* to dig from a quarry. QUARRYING *n.*

quart *n.* a liquid measure equal to two pints (about 1.14 liters).

quarter *n.* 1 a fourth part. 2 a period of three months. 3 a district in a town or city. QUARTER *v.* to divide into four equal parts.

quarterly *adj.* once every three months. QUARTERLY *n.* a periodical published every three months.

quartet *n.* 1 a group of four musicians or singers. 2 a piece of music for four musicians or singers.

quartz *n.* a solid mineral containing silica.

quaver *v.* to shake, to tremble, esp. voice.

queen *n.* 1 a female ruler. 2 the wife of a king. 3 a piece in chess.

queer *adj.* strange; unusual.

quell *v.* to suppress; to crush.

quench *v.* 1 to extinguish; to put out a fire. 2 to satisfy a thirst.

query *n.* 1 a question. 2 a question mark. 3 an inquiry. QUERY *v.* 1 to ask a question. 2 to doubt.

quest *n.* a search.

question *v.* 1 to ask questions of. 2 to have doubts about. QUESTION *n.* 1 a sentence requesting information and requiring an answer. 2 a subject for discussion. QUESTIONER *n.*

questionable *adj.* doubtful; not reliable.

questionnaire *n.* a list of questions to be answered.

quick *adj.* 1 fast moving; rapid. 2 lively; alert.
3 hasty. QUICKLY *adv.* QUICKNESS *n.*

quicken *v.* to make or become quicker.

quiet *adv.* 1 without sound; silent.
2 without movement; calm. 3 kept secret.
QUIETLY *adv.* QUIETNESS *n.*

quilt *n.* a light, padded bedcover.
QUILT *v.* to stitch together pieces of material
with padding between.

quintet *n.* 1 a group of five musicians or singers.
2 a piece of music for five musicians or singers.

quit *v.* to go away; to leave.

quite *adv.* 1 completely; entirely. 2 to a certain
extent.

quiver *v.* to tremble; to shake.
QUIVER *n.* 1 tremble; a shudder. 2 a sheath to
hold arrows.

quiz *n.* a test of general knowledge.
QUIZ *v.* to question closely.

quota *n.* a share to be given to or received by
each member of a group; an allowance.

quotation *n.* 1 the repeating of something said or
written. 2 a price stated.

quote *v.* 1 to repeat something said or written by
another person. 2 to give or state a price.

quotient *n.* the number of times one number
divides into another.

R

rabbi *n.* a Jewish religious leader.

rabbit *n.* a small burrowing animal of the hare
family.

rabble *n.* a mob; a disorderly, noisy crowd.

race *n.* 1 a group of people or animals having the
same origin and characteristics.
2 a contest of speed.
RACE *v.* to run or move very fast.

racial *adj.* having to do with races and their
differences.

rack *n.* a framework for holding and supporting
articles.

racket *n.* 1 a stringed bat for playing tennis,
badminton, etc. 2 an uproar; a noise.

radar *n.* an electronic navigational device that
detects distant objects that come within its
range.

radiant *adj.* 1 giving out light or heat.
2 joyful; happy. RADIANCE *n.*

radiate *v.* 1 to send out rays of light and heat.
2 to spread out in all directions. RADIATION *n.*

radiator *n.* 1 an apparatus for radiating heat
using hot water, gas or electricity. 2 an
apparatus for keeping a gasoline engine cool.

radio *n.* the sending and receiving of sound
messages by means of electrical waves; an
apparatus for receiving radio broadcasts.
RADIO *v.* to send by means of radio waves.

radioactive *adj.* giving off radiant energy by the
breakdown of unstable atomic nuclei.
RADIOACTIVITY *n.*

radium *n.* a rare radioactive metal which gives
out rays that are used in the treatment of some
diseases.

radius *n.* the distance from the center to the
circumference of a circle. *pl.* RADII

raft *n.* a floating wooden platform.

rage *n.* violent anger.
RAGE *v.* to be furious or angry. RAGING *adj.*

raid *n.* a sudden attack.
RAID *v.* to make a sudden attack upon.
RAIDER *n.*

rail *n.* 1 a wooden or metal bar forming the top
part of a fence. 2 a steel bar forming part of a
railroad track.
RAIL *v.* to use angry language. RAILING *n.*

railroad *n.* 1 the track on which trains run.
2 a railroad system.

rain *n.* condensed moisture falling in drops from
the sky.
RAIN *v.* to fall in drops like rain. RAINY *adj.*

rainbow *n.* a colored arch formed in the sky by
the sun shining through raindrops.

raise *v.* 1 to lift up. 2 to construct. 3 to bring
up children or animals. 4 to collect (an army,
etc.).

raisin *n.* a dried grape.

rake *n.* a long-handled tool with several prongs
for smoothing or scraping soil.
RAKE *v.* to scrape or collect with a rake.

rally *v.* 1 to bring or come together again; to
reassemble 2 to recover partly; to revive.
RALLY *n.* 1 an assembly of people.
2 a recovery. 2 competition among motorists,
cyclists, etc.

ram *n.* 1 a male sheep. *fem.* EWE. 2 something
used for hammering with great force.
RAM *v.* to strike heavily with repeated blows.

ramp *n.* a slope joining two levels; an incline.

rampage *v.* to rush about in a violent manner.
RAMPAGE *n.* violent and unruly behavior.

rampart *n.* a defensive wall or mound.

ranch *n.* a large cattle farm. RANCHER *n.*

rancid *adj.* smelling or tasting stale or sour.

random *adj.* haphazard; without aim or purpose.

range *n.* 1 line; a row. 2 the choice or variety of anything. 3 the distance over which something can operate. 4 a piece of ground with targets for shooting.
RANGE *v.* 1 to set in a line. 2 to wander. 3 to vary between limits.

rank *n.* 1 a row or line. 2 a class or order of something. RANK *v.* to classify.

ransack *v.* to plunder; to search thoroughly.

ransom *n.* a sum of money paid or demanded for the release of a captive.
RANSOM *v.* to buy release or freedom.

rap *n.* a sharp, light blow.
RAP *v.* to strike a sharp, light blow.

rapid *adj.* quick, speedy, RAPIDLY *adv.*

rapids *n.pl.* a part of a river where the water flows rapidly over rocks.

rapture *n.* great delight, joy or ecstasy.
RAPTUROUS *adj.*

rare *adj.* scarce; uncommon; unusual.
RARELY *adj.* RARENESS *n.*

rarity *n.* a rare or an uncommon thing.
pl. RARITIES.

rascal *n.* 1 rogue. 2 a naughty or mischievous person.

rash *n.* an outbreak of spots on the skin.
RASH *adj.* hasty; reckless. RASHLY *adv.*

raspberry *n.* a small, soft, red fruit.
pl. RASPBERRIES.

rat *n.* a rodent, resembling a large mouse.

rate *n.* 1 a relative speed. 2 a local tax on property. 3 a fixed price.
RATE *v.* 1 to estimate the value of. 2 to value.

rather *adv.* more willingly; to a greater extent.

ratio *n.* the proportion of one thing to another.

ration *n.* a fixed allowance or share.
RATION *v.* to share something out in fixed quantities.

rational *adj.* reasonable; sensible.
RATIONALLY *adv.*

rattle *v.* to make a series of sharp sounds.
RATTLE *n.* 1 a series of sharp sounds. 2 a baby's plaything.

raucous *adj.* hoarse; harsh-sounding.
RAUCOUSLY *adv.*

ravage *v.* to plunder; to devastate.

rave *v.* 1 to talk wildly. 2 to talk enthusiastically.

ravenous *adj.* very hungry. RAVENOUSLY *adv.*

ravine *n.* a deep narrow valley.

raw *adj.* 1 not cooked. 2 not trained or experienced. 3 cold and damp. RAWNESS *n.*

ray *n.* a narrow beam of light or heat.

razor *n.* an instrument for shaving.

reach *v.* 1 to stretch. 2 to arrive at.
REACH *n.* 1 the distance a person can reach with the arm. 2 a straight stretch of river.

react *v.* 1 to act or behave in response to something said or done.

reaction *n.* a response caused by something.

read *v.* to look at and understand the meaning of printed or written words. READER *n.* READING *n.*

readily *adv.* 1 quickly; promptly. 2 willingly.
READINESS *n.*

ready *adj.* 1 prepared; prompt. 2 willing.

real *adj.* 1 actual; genuine, 2 actually existing.

realistic *adj.* like the real thing.
REALISTICALLY *adv.*

realize *v.* 1 to understand. 2 to sell for a price.

really *adv.* truly; without doubt.

realm *n.* a kingdom.

reap *v.* to cut and gather grain crops.

reappear *v.* to appear again.

rear *n.* the back of something; the point furthest from the front.
REAR *v.* 1 to bring up (young children or animals). 2 to rise up on the hind legs.

rearrange *v.* to arrange in a new order.
REARRANGEMENT *n.*

reason *n.* 1 an explanation or excuse. 2 a cause. 3 the capacity to understand.
REASON *v.* to think or talk over sensibly.
REASONING *n.*

reasonable *adj.* sensible; moderate; fair.

reassure *v.* to remove (someone's) doubts and fears; to encourage.
REASSURING *adj.* REASSURANCE *n.*

rebate *n.* a deduction or discount.

rebel *n.* (pron. REB-el) a person who resists authority or control.
REBEL (AGAINST) *v.* (pron. rib-EL) to resist; to oppose.

rebellion *n.* a revolt; open resistance to authority or control.

rebellious *adj.* taking part in a rebellion; defiant.

rebound *v.* (pron. ri-BOUND) to spring or bounce back; to recoil.
REBOUND *n.* (pron. RE-bound) a bounce back.

rebuke *v.* to reproach or criticize.
REBUKE *n.* a reproof

recall *v.* 1 to call back. 2 to remember.
RECALL *n.* 1 a call to return. 2 the ability to remember.

recede *v.* to go back or shrink back; to retreat
RECEDING *adj.*

receipt *n.* 1 the fact of receiving or being received. 2 a written acknowledgement that something has been received.

receive *v.* 1 to take or accept something that is offered. 2 to welcome (someone).

receiver *n.* 1 a person who receives. 2 the earpiece of a telephone. 3 a radio set.

recent *adj.* new; having happened a short time ago. RECENTLY *adv.*

receptacle *n.* a container for holding things.

reception *n.* 1 a welcome. 2 a formal meeting of welcome. 3 the quality of radio sound or television sound and picture.

recess *n.* 1 an alcove. 2 a break or interval in work; a holiday.

recipe *n.* 1 a list of the ingredients and directions for preparing a dish. 2 directions for doing something successfully.

recital *n.* 1 musical performance of playing or singing. 2 a detailed account of facts.

recite *v.* 1 to repeat aloud from memory. 2 to mention in order. RECITER *n.*

reckless *adj.* careless; not caring or thinking of the consequences. RECKLESSLY *adv.*

reclaim *v.* 1 to claim (something) back. 2 to recover; to improve. RECLAMATION *n.*

recline *v.* to lean or lie back; to rest.

recluse *n.* a person who lives alone and in solitude.

recognition *n.* the act of knowing or remembering what has been seen before.

recognize *v.* 1 to know again or remember. 2 to acknowledge; to admit.

recollect *v.* to remember. RECOLLECTION *n.*

recommend *v.* 1 to suggest; to advise. 2 to speak well of. RECOMMENDATION *n.*

reconcile *v.* 1 to make friendly again after a quarrel. 2 RECONCILE ONESELF TO to accept.

reconnaissance *n.* a preliminary inspection or survey before taking action.

reconnoiter *v.* to inspect or survey.

reconstruct *v.* 1 to build again. 2 to restore.

record *v.* (pron. re-KORD) 1 to write (something) down. 2 to make a reproduction of. RECORD *n.* (pron. RE-kord) 1 a written account. 2 a disk on which music or sound has been recorded. 3 an unbeaten performance.

recorder *n.* 1 a person who keeps a record of events. 2 a simple form of flute. 3 a (tape-recorder) an apparatus for recording sound on tape.

recount *v.* to tell; to describe in detail.

recover *v.* 1 to regain; to get back. 2 to return to normal health. RECOVERY *n.*

recreation *n.* games, sports, hobbies and other leisure interests.

recruit *n.* a person who has just joined the armed forces; a new member. RECRUIT *v.* to obtain recruits.

rectangle *n.* a figure with four straight sides and four right angles; a square or oblong. RECTANGULAR *adj.*

rectify *v.* to put right; to correct. RECTIFIED *adj.*

recuperate *v.* to recover from illness.

recur *v.* to happen again; to be repeated. RECURRENCE *n.*

red *adj.* a color ranging from crimson to orange.

redeem *v.* 1 to buy back. 2 to save; to rescue.

redirect *v.* to direct again; to readdress.

reduce *v.* 1 to make less or smaller. 2 to weaken. REDUCTION *n.*

redundant *adj.* more than is necessary, no longer useful or needed. REDUNDANCY *n.*

reed *n.* 1 tall plant that grows in or near water. 2 a vibrating strip in some wind instruments.

reef *n.* a ridge of rocks or sand just above or below the surface of the sea.

reek *v.* to give off an unpleasant smell.

reel *n.* 1 a cylinder, drum or bobbin on which wire, thread, cotton, paper, etc., is wound. REEL *v.* 1 to wind on a reel. 2 to stagger or walk unsteadily.

refer (to) *v.* 1 to go to (someone or something) for help, a decision or information. 2 to mention or speak about. 3 to indicate.

referee *n.* 1 a person who controls a game according to the rules. 2 person chosen to decide between opposing parties.

reference *n.* 1 the referring of a matter to someone for decision or settlement. 2 a book where information can be found. 3 a letter concerning the character or ability of a person; a testimonial.

refine *v.* to purify; to improve. REFINED *adj.*

refinery *n.* a place where materials are purified.

reflect *v.* 1 to throw back (light, heat, etc.). 2 to show an image as in a mirror. 3 to think matters over; to consider. REFLECTION *n.*

reflector *n.* a surface which throws back light, heat, radio signals, etc.

reform *v.* to change for the better; to improve. REFORM *n.* an improvement or amendment. REFORMED *adj.* REFORMER *n.*

refrain *v.* to hold back; to abstain from doing something. REFRAIN *n.* the chorus of a song; a tune.

refresh *v.* to freshen; to give new strength to. REFRESHING *adj.*

refreshment *n.* food and drink.

refrigerate *v.* to freeze or to chill (something).

refrigerator *n.* a device for keeping things chilled or frozen.

refuge *n.* a place of shelter.

refugee *n.* a person who seeks safety from disaster, danger or persecution.

refuse *v.* (pron. re-FUZE) to decline or to reject. REFUSE *n.* (pron. REF-use) trash; anything rejected as worthless.

regard *v.* 1 to look at. 2 to consider. 3 to respect.

regardless *adj.* not considering; without caring.

regards *n.pl.* kind wishes; friendly feelings.

regiment *n.* a military unit consisting of several companies or battalions.

region *n.* a district; an area; part of a country or of the world, REGIONAL *adj.*

register *n.* 1 an official record book. 2 the range between the highest and lowest notes of a voice or instrument. REGISTER *v.* to record official information.

regret *v.* to be sorry or sad about. REGRET *n.* sorrow.

regular *adj.* 1 normal; according to rule. 2 evenly spaced. REGULARLY *adv.*

regulate *v.* 1 to control. 2 to adjust. REGULATED *adj.* REGULATOR *n.*

regulation *n.* a rule or order.

rehearsal *n.* a practice.

rehearse *v.* to practice something to be performed. REHEARSED *adj.*

reign *n.* the period of time during which a king or queen rules. REIGN *v.* to rule.

rein *n.* a narrow strap for guiding and controlling a horse. REIN *v.* to guide; to control.

reindeer *n.* a kind of deer living in cold regions.

reinforce *v.* to strengthen; to supply further.

reinstate *v.* to replace in the position held before.

reject *v.* (pron. ri-JECT) to refuse; to discard. REJECT *n.* (pron. RE-ject) something discarded. REJECTED *adj.* REJECTION *n.*

rejoice *v.* 1 to feel joy or gladness. 2 to make joyful or glad. REJOICING *n.*

relapse *v.* to fall back. RELAPSE *n.* a return to a former condition or ways.

relate *v.* 1 to tell; to give an account of. 2 to join; to connect.

relation *n.* 1 any connection between persons or things. 2 a relative; a family member.

relative *n.* a relation. RELATIVE *adj.* having some relation; connected with.

relax *v.* 1 to become less tense or strict. 2 to rest.

relay *n.* a race involving successive runners. RELAY *v.* to pass on.

release *v.* to set free; to let go. RELEASE *n.* freedom; relief.

relent *v.* to become less severe; to yield.

relevant *adj.* to do with the matter being discussed. RELEVANCE *n.*

reliable *adj.* trustworthy; to be relied on; dependable. RELIABLY *adv.*

reliance *n.* trust, confidence. RELIANT *adj.*

relic *n.* something that has survived from a long time ago.

relief *n.* 1 help; assistance. 2 the easing of pain or worry. 3 a design which stands out from the surface. 4 a person who releases another from duty. RELIEVE *v.*

religion *n.* a particular set of beliefs and worship; the worship of God or of gods. RELIGIOUS *adj.*

relish *v.* to enjoy; to like the taste of. RELISH *n.* 1 enjoyment; a good taste. 2 a sauce.

reluctant *adj.* unwilling to do something.

rely (on or **upon)** *v.* to depend on; to trust.

remain *v.* 1 to stay; to continue. 2 to survive.

remainder *n.* the part left over or unused.

remark *v.* 1 to say; to comment. 2 to notice; to observe. REMARK *n.* a comment; something said.

remarkable *adj.* unusual; exceptional.

remedy *n.* a cure. REMEDY *v.* to cure or heal. REMEDIAL *adj.*

remember *v.* to recall to mind; to recollect.

remind *v.* to cause (someone) to remember.

remnant *n.* a small amount or piece left over.

remorse *n.* deep regret or repentance for a fault or wrongdoing.

remote *adj.* 1 far away; distant. 2 slight; faint. REMOTELY *adv.* REMOTENESS *n.*

removal *n.* 1 a dismissal. 2 a transfer; being removed. 3 an extraction.

remove *v.* 1 to take from one place to another; to transfer. 2 to take from its place. 3 to take off; to uncover. REMOVED *adj.*

rendezvous *n.* a meeting place. RENDEZVOUS *v.* to meet at a certain place.

renew *v.* 1 to make new. 2 to restore. RENEWAL *n.*

renounce *v.* to give up; to reject.

renovate *v.* to make something like new; to restore. RENOVATION *n.*

renown *n.* fame; glory; honor. RENOWNED *adj.*

rent *n.* 1 a payment made by a tenant to a landlord for the occupation of property. 2 a tear.

repair *v.* to mend; to restore.
REPAIR *n.* a mend; a restoration.

repatriate *v.* to send or bring a person back to his or her own country.

repay *v.* 1 to pay back. 2 to return a kindness.
REPAYMENT *n.*

repeat *v.* 1 to say or do again. 2 to recite.
REPEATEDLY *adv.*

repent *v.* to feel sorry for what has been done or left undone. REPENTANCE *n.*

repercussion *n.* 1 an echo. 2 the effect of something that has happened.

repetition *n.* repeating or being repeated.

replace *v.* 1 to put back in its place. 2 to take the place of (something or someone); to substitute. REPLACEMENT *n.*

replenish *v.* to fill again; to restock.

replica *n.* an exact copy; a duplicate.

reply *v.* to answer; to respond.
REPLY *n.* an answer; a response. *pl.* REPLIES.

report *v.* 1 to give an account of; to give information about. 2 to announce that one has arrived for duty. 3 to make a complaint.
REPORT *n.* 1 an account or statement. 2 the sound of an explosion.

reporter *n.* a person who collects news and information for a newspaper, radio or television.

represent *v.* 1 to show. 2 to describe. 3 to act for somebody. 4 to claim to be.
REPRESENTATION *n.* REPRESENTATIVE *n.*

repress *v.* to keep down; to restrain.

reprieve *v.* 1 to delay; to postpone. 2 to cancel or reduce punishment.
REPRIEVE *n.* a delay; a postponement.
REPRIEVED *adj.*

reprimand *n.* a rebuke.
REPRIMAND *v.* to rebuke; to censure.

reprisal *n.* an act of revenge or retaliation.

reproach *v.* to speak disapprovingly to; to blame.

reproduce *v.* 1 to produce again; to copy; to imitate. 2 to produce young. REPRODUCTION *n.*

reptile *n.* a crawling, vertebrate animal such as a snake, lizard, crocodile, etc.

republic *n.* a country which has an elected government but no king or queen.

repulsive *adj.* disgusting; loathsome.

reputable *adj.* worthy; well thought of.

reputation *n.* what is generally said or thought about a person's character.

request *v.* to ask; to require.
REQUEST *n.* something asked for.

require *v.* to want; to need. REQUIREMENT *n.*

rescue *v.* to free or save from attack, danger or captivity. RESCUE *n.* an act which saves from attack, danger or captivity. RESCUER *n.*

research *n.* a careful search or inquiry; a scientific study to discover new facts.

resemble *v.* to be like or similar to (someone or something). RESEMBLANCE *n.*

resent *v.* to feel or show bitterness or anger about something. RESENTFUL *adj.*
RESENTMENT *n.*

reserve *v.* to keep or store for a special purpose or person.
RESERVE *n.* 1 an emergency supply. 2 shyness. 3 an area of land set aside for certain animals or people to live in. RESERVED *adj.*

reservoir *n.* a place, often an artificial lake, where water is stored.

reside (at or **in)** *v.* to live in a place.

residence *n.* a house; a dwelling-place.

resident *n.* an occupant; a permanent inhabitant.
RESIDENTIAL *adj.*

resign *v.* to give up; to relinquish.

resilience *n.* elasticity; buoyancy. RESILIENT *adj.*

resist *v.* to oppose; to struggle against; to offer resistance. RESISTANCE *n.*

resistant *adj.* opposing; offering resistance.

resolute *adj.* firm; determined. RESOLUTELY *adv.*

resolution *n.* 1 firmness; determination. 2 a decision; a purpose.

resolve *v.* to make a decision; to intend.
RESOLVE *n.* a decision; an intention.
RESOLVED *adj.*

resort *n.* 1 place frequently visited. 2 something turned to for help.
RESORT (TO) *v.* 1 to visit frequently. 2 to turn to for help.

resource *n.* 1 a source of help; useful material. 2 enterprise; ingenuity. RESOURCEFUL *adj.*

respect *v.* to esteem; to show regard for.
RESPECT *n.* esteem; regard.

respectable *adj.* 1 deserving respect or honor. 2 decent. RESPECTABILITY *n.*

respectful *adj.* courteous; showing regard and esteem. RESPECTFULLY *adv.*

respective *adj.* individual; concerning each one.

respiration *n.* the intake of air; breathing.

respirator *n.* a mask worn over the mouth and nose to aid breathing or to purify the air breathed in.

respond *v.* 1 to answer; to reply. 2 to react.

response *n.* 1 an answer; a reply. 2 reaction.
RESPONSIVE *adj.*

responsible *adj.* 1 answerable or liable for.
2 trustworthy and reliable. RESPONSIBILITY *n.*

rest *n.* 1 a pause; a stop. 2 sleep.
3 the remainder.
REST *v.* 1 to pause or stop. 2 to sleep.

restaurant *n.* a place where meals may be bought and eaten.

restless *adj.* uneasy; impatient.

restoration *n.* a renewal; the act or process of restoring.

restore *v.* 1 to give back; to bring back.
2 to repair.

restrain *v.* to hold back; to keep under control.
RESTRAINT *n.*

restrict *v.* to keep within certain limits; to confine. RESTRICTION *n.*

result *n.* the outcome; the consequence.
RESULT *v.* to happen because of other actions or events. RESULTING *adj.*

resume *v.* to begin again.

resurrect *v.* to revive; to bring back to life.
RESURRECTION *n.*

retail *v.* 1 to sell in small quantities. 2 to sell to others. RETAILER *n.*

retain *v.* 1 to keep; to hold. 2 to employ.
RETAINING *adj.*

retaliate *v.* to repay in the same way.
RETALIATION *n.*

reticent *v.* cautious; reserved; saying little.
RETICENCE *n.*

retire *v.* 1 to withdraw. 2 to cease active employment. 3 to go to bed. RETIREMENT *n.*

retreat *v.* to move back; to retire.
RETREAT *n.* 1 a withdrawal or retirement.
2 a quiet, peaceful place.

retrieve *v.* 1 to recover anything lost. 2 to regain.

retriever *n.* a dog trained to find and bring in game that has been shot.

return *v.* 1 to come or go back. 2 to send or to give back.
RETURN *n.* 1 coming or going back.
2 a sending or giving back. 3 a profit.

reunion *n.* reuniting; a gathering of friends.

reunite *v.* to come together again.

reveal *v.* 1 to show what was hidden. 2 to make known; to disclose.

revenge *v.* to do harm to another person in return for harm done by him; to retaliate.
REVENGE *n.* a harmful repayment; a retaliation.
REVENGEFUL *adj.*

revenue *n.* income of an individual, business or nation.

reverse *v.* 1 to turn something the other way around or inside out. 2 to go backward.
3 to undo or to cancel (a decision).
REVERSE *n.* 1 the opposite; the other side of.
2 a defeat or failure.
REVERSE *adj.* opposite; backward.
REVERSIBLE *adj.*

review *v.* 1 to reexamine. 2 to inspect.
3 to give an opinion of.
REVIEW *n.* 1 reexamination. 2 an inspection.
3 criticism of a book, play, film, etc.

revise *v.* 1 to examine and correct faults and mistakes. 2 to study again. REVISED *adj.*
REVISION *n.*

revive *v.* to bring back to life or health.

revolt *v.* 1 to rebel. 2 to fill with disgust or horror. REVOLT *n.* a rebellion. REVOLTING *adj.*

revolution *n.* 1 a rebellion or uprising.
2 a turn or rotation. 3 a complete change in opinion, fashion, etc. REVOLUTIONARY *adj.*

revolve *v.* to turn around; to rotate.

revolver *n.* a pistol that will fire several shots without reloading.

revulsion *n.* disgust; a change of feeling.

reward *n.* something given or received for service or merit. REWARD *v.* to give a reward.

rheumatism *n.* a disease which causes pain and swollen joints.

rhyme *n.* a similarity of sound in endings of words or verse lines.
RHYME *v.* to use similar-sounding words.

rhythm *n.* a regular beat or accent in music or speech. RHYTHMIC *adj.*

rib *n.* one of the curved bones around the upper part of the body.

ribbon *n.* a long narrow strip of material.

rice *n.* 1 a cereal plant grown in marshy ground in warm climates. 2 the grain of the rice plant used as food.

rich *adj.* 1 wealthy; having much money or many possessions. 2 full of goodness or color.

rid *v.* to make free from; to remove something.

riddle *n.* a puzzling question.
RIDDLE *v.* to fill with holes.

ride *v.* 1 to be carried by an animal or vehicle.
2 to travel; to drive.
RIDE *n.* a journey on an animal or in a vehicle.
RIDER *n.*

ridge *n.* a mountain range.

ridicule *v.* to make fun of; to mock or laugh at.
RIDICULE *n.* mockery.

ridiculous *adj.* absurd; very silly.
RIDICULOUSLY *adv.*

rifle *n.* a gun having a long grooved barrel.
RIFLE *v.* to rob and plunder.

rift *n.*1 a crack or split. 2 a quarrel.

rig *v.* 1 to provide a ship with sails, ropes and gear. 2 to fit out with clothes or equipment. RIG *n.* the platform or equipment for drilling an oilwell.

right *n.* 1 that which is right. 2 something allowed by law or custom. 3 correctness. RIGHT *adj.* 1 just and true. 2 proper; correct. 3 the opposite of left.
RIGHT *adv.* correctly; exactly. RIGHTLY *adv.*

rigid *adj.* 1 stiff; unbending. 2 strict. RIGIDLY *adv.*

rigorous *adj.* very strict; severe; harsh. RIGOROUSLY *adv.*

rim *n.* the outer edge; the brim.

ring *n.* 1 a circle of gold, or other metal, worn on a finger. 2 any circular object. 3 an area where boxing matches are fought or where a circus performs. 4 a sound like a bell. RING *v.* 1 to encircle. 2 to make a sound like a bell.

rink *n.* a stretch of ice prepared for ice sports; an area used for roller-skating.

rinse *v.* to wash out; to remove soapy water.

riot *n.* a violent disturbance of the peace by a crowd. RIOT *v.* to join in a riot. RIOTER *n.* RIOTOUS *adj.*

rip *v.* to tear violently; to pull apart. RIP *n.* a tear.

ripe *adj.* mature; fully developed; ready for eating or heavesting. RIPEN *v.*

rise *v.* 1 to stand. 2 to go up; to ascend. 3 to swell; to increase. 4 to rebel. RISE *n.* 1 an upward slope. 2 an increase in pay or price.

risk *n.* a chance of loss, injury or danger. RISK *v.* to take a chance with. RISKY *adj.*

rite *n.* a religious or solemn ceremony.

rival *n.* an opponent; a competitor. RIVAL *v.* to oppose; to compete against. RIVALRY *n.*

river *n.* a large stream of water flowing into another river, a lake or the sea.

rivet *n.* a metal pin for fastening metal plates together. RIVET *v.* to join together with rivets.

road *n.* a highway for traffic.

roam *v.* to wander about. ROAMER *n.*

roar *n.* a loud, deep, hoarse sound. ROAR *v.* to make a loud, deep hoarse sound.

roast *v.* to cook in an oven or over a fire. ROAST *n.* a cut of meat for roasting.

rob *v.* 1 to steal from. 2 to plunder with violence. ROBBER *n.* ROBBERY *n.*

robe *n.* a long loose garment. ROBE *v.* to dress.

robin *n.* a small bird with a red breast.

robot *n.* a machine designed to work like a human.

robust *adj.* strong and healthy.

rock *n.* 1 a large piece of stone. 2 a hard sweet. ROCK *v.* to move backward and forward or from side to side.

rocket *n.* 1 a firework or signal which is fired high into the air. 2 a spacecraft or missile launcher.

rod *n.* a straight, slender stick or bar.

rodent *n.* an animal that gnaws, such as a rat, squirrel, etc.

rogue *n.* 1 a rascal; a scoundrel. 2 a mischievous person.

role *n.* 1 what a person has undertaken to do. 2 the part played by an actor.

roll *v.* 1 to turn over and over. 2 to flatten with a roller. 3 to rock and sway. ROLL *n.* 1 a turning over and over. 2 a bundle made by turning over and over. 3 a rocking and swaying movement. 4 a register. 5 the continued beat of a drum.

Roman *adj.* belonging to Rome or its people. ROMAN *n.* a resident of Rome.

romance *n.* 1 an imaginary story with happenings that have little to do with real life. 2 a love affair. ROMANCE *v.* to exaggerate or embroider the truth. ROMANTIC *adj.*

roof *n.* 1 the upper covering of a house or building. 2 the upper part of the mouth. ROOF *v.* to cover with a roof.

room *n.* 1 a part of a house or building enclosed by walls, floor and ceiling. 2 the space anything occupies.

roost *n.* a bird's resting place. ROOST *v.* to settle for sleep.

root *n.* 1 that part of the plant growing in the soil. 2 a base or source from which something grows. ROOT *v.* 1 to take root. 2 to fix firmly.

rope *n.* a thick cord made of twisted strands of hemp, nylon or wire. ROPE *v.* to tie with a rope.

rose *n.* a prickly shrub bearing beautiful and usually fragrant flowers.

rot *v.* to decay; to go bad. ROT *n.* 1 decay; badness. 2 nonsense; rubbish.

rotate *v.* to revolve; to turn like a wheel.

rotary *adj.* moving around like a wheel. ROTATION *n.*

rotten *adj.* bad; decayed; corrupt.

rough *adj.* 1 uneven; not smooth or level. 2 wild; stormy. 3 harsh; unpleasant. ROUGHNESS *n.*

round *adj.* shaped like a ball; circular; spherical. ROUND *n.* 1 a circle. 2 a bullet or cartridge. 3 a period in a boxing match, a game of golf, etc.

rout *n.* a complete and utter defeat. ROUT *v.* to put to flight.

route *n.* the course to be followed; the way traveled.

routine *n.* 1 a fixed and regular way of doing certain things. 2 a regular procedure or method.

row *n.* 1 a line of persons or things. 2 a trip in a row boat. ROW *v.* to move a boat by using oars.

row *n.* a noise; a noisy quarrel or disturbance.

rowdy *adj.* rough and noisy. ROWDYISM *n.*

royal *adj.* 1 having to do with a king or queen. 2 regal; splendid. ROYALTY *n.*

rub *v.* 1 to move one thing over the surface of another. 2 to clean or polish.

rubber *n.* a tough, elastic substance obtained from a tropical tree.

rubbish *n.* 1 trash; waste matter. 2 nonsense.

rubble *n.* waste fragments of brick, stone, concrete, etc.

rudder *n.* the device by which a boat or aircraft is steered.

rude *adj.* 1 impolite; insolent. 2 not decent; vulgar. 3 primitive; roughly made. RUDELY *adv.* RUDENESS *n.*

ruffle *v.* to disturb the smoothness of something; to annoy or irritate. RUFFLE *n.* a frill.

rug *n.* 1 a mat for the floor. 2 a thick blanket.

rugged *adj.* 1 rough; uneven. 2 robust; sturdy.

ruin *v.* 1 to spoil; to destroy. 2 to make poor. RUIN *n.* 1 the remains of an old or derelict building. 2 destruction; downfall. RUINED *adj.*

rule *n.* 1 a law, regulation or custom. 2 government. 3 a measuring device. RULE *v.* 1 to govern. 2 to make a decision. 3 to draw a straight line using a rule.

ruler *n.* 1 a person who rules or governs. 2 a drawing and measuring instrument.

ruling *n.* a decision; a judgment. RULING *adj.*

rumble *n.* a low rolling sound like thunder. RUMBLING *n.*

rumor *n.* general talk or gossip that may not be true.

run *v.* 1 to move on foot with quick steps. 2 to flow. 3 to travel; to go. 4 to manage (a business etc.). RUNNING *adj.* RUN *n.* 1 a race. 2 a journey; a voyage; a route. 3 a score made in cricket.

rung *n.* the step of a ladder.

rural *adj.* belonging to the countryside.

rush *v.* 1 to run or move forward violently or speedily. 2 to attack suddenly. RUSH *n.* 1 a violent or sudden forward movement. 2 a marsh plant.

Russian *adj.* belonging to Russia or its people. RUSSIAN *n.* the language or one of the people of Russia.

rust *n.* a yellowish-brown coating formed on iron by the action of moisture; corrosion. RUSTY *adj.*

rut *n.* 1 a groove made in the ground by a wheel; a furrow. 2 a fixed method or routine.

ruthless *adj.* without pity or mercy. RUTHLESSLY *adv.*

rye *n.* a cereal grain used for making flour or used as fodder.

S

sabbath *n.* a weekly day for rest and prayer: Saturday for Jews, Sunday for Christians.

sabotage *n.* damage done intentionally to equipment, machinery, etc. SABOTAGE *v.* to damage intentionally.

sack *n.* 1 a large bag made of coarse material. 2 the attack on and looting of a town.

sacred *adj.* holy; belonging to God or dedicated to some person or purpose.

sacrifice *n.* 1 something given up or a loss suffered for the sake of somebody or something else. 2 an offering to a god; the thing offered. SACRIFICE *v.* 1 to give up (something that is valued). 2 to offer something to a god.

sad *adj.* unhappy; full of sorrow. SADLY *adv.* SADDEN *v.* SADNESS *n.*

saddle *n.* a seat for the rider of a horse or bicycle. SADDLE *v.* 1 to put a saddle on. 2 SADDLE WITH to put a burden or load on (someone).

safari *n.* an expedition to see or to hunt big game.

safe *adj.* 1 secure from danger. 2 not dangerous. 3 careful; cautious. SAFE *n.* a steel chest for the storage of valuables. SAFELY *adv.*

safety *n.* security; freedom from danger or risks.

sag *v.* to sink or droop in the middle due to weight or pressure. SAGGING *n.*

sail *n.* 1 a canvas or nylon sheet which spreads to catch the wind and moves a boat forward. 2 the arm of a windmill. 3 a short voyage. SAIL *v.* 1 to be moved along by means of sails. 2 to commence a voyage. SAILING *n.*

sailor *n.* a seaman; a member of a ship's crew.

saint *n.* 1 a holy person. 2 a person officially given the title of saint after death.

salad *n.* a mixture of vegetables or fruit served raw.

salary *n.* a periodic payment in return for work.

sale *n.* 1 the exchange of goods for money. 2 time when goods are offered at reduced prices.

saliva *n.* fluid formed in the mouth.

salmon *n.* a large fish with pink flesh.

salt *n.* sodium chloride, a white crystalline substance used for flavoring and preserving food.

salute *n.* a gesture of respect, courtesy or friendship. SALUTE *v.* to make such a gesture.

salvage *v.* 1 to save (a wrecked or damaged ship). 2 to recover (goods or materials) from fire, flood, shipwreck or destruction. SALVAGED *adj.*

salvation *n.* a rescue from sin or danger.

same *adj.* alike; identical; unchanging.

sample *n.* a specimen; an example; a pattern. SAMPLE *v.* to test.

sanction *n.* 1 the approval or permission of someone. 2 a penalty imposed. SANCTION *v.* to approve or give permission for.

sanctuary *n.* 1 a holy place. 2 a place of refuge.

sand *n.* fine grains of rock. SAND *v.* 1 to sprinkle with sand. 2 to smooth with sandpaper.

sandal *n.* a sole strapped to the foot.

sandpaper *n.* a tough paper with a coating of sand for smoothing wood.

sandwich *n.* two slices of bread with a filling between them. *pl.* SANDWICHES. SANDWICH *v.* to put (something) between or among other things.

sane *adj.* of sound mind; sensible. SANITY *n.*

sanitary *adj.* free from dirt and infection; clean. SANITATION *n.*

sap *n.* the juice circulating in plants. SAP *v.* to drain of sap; to weaken.

sapling *n.* a young tree.

sarcasm *n.* a bitter, scornful and hurtful remark. SARCASTIC *adj.* SARCASTICALLY *adv.*

sardine *n.* a small fish of the herring kind, usually canned in oil.

sash *n.* 1 a strip of material worn over the shoulder or round the waist. 2 a window frame that slides up and down.

satellite *n.* 1 a body (usually a moon) which moves in orbit around a planet. 2 spacecraft or other man-made object sent traveling in orbit around a planet.

satin *n.* a silky material, shiny on one side.

satisfaction *n.* a feeling of pleasure or contentment

satisfactory *adj.* good enough; suitable; adequate.

satisfy *v.* 1 to please; to gratify. 2 to be enough for the needs of (someone or something). SATISFIED *adj.* SATISFACTORILY *adv.*

saturate *v.* to soak thoroughly; to fill with moisture. SATURATED *adj.* SATURATION *n.*

Saturday *n.* the seventh day of the week.

sauce *n.* 1 a liquid flavoring for food. 2 impertinence.

saucer *n.* a shallow dish to hold a cup.

sauna *n.* a steam bath.

saunter *v.* to stroll leisurely.

saunter *v.* to stroll leisurely. SAUNTER *n.* a leisurely stroll.

sausage *n.* minced and seasoned meat enclosed in a skin.

savage *adj.* wild; fierce and cruel. SAVAGE *n.* a person from a primitive tribe. SAVAGELY *adv.*

save *v.* 1 to rescue or preserve from harm or danger. 2 to keep for future use; to reserve. 3 to be economical. SAVE *prep.* except.

savings *n.pl.* money saved up.

savior *n.* 1 a person who rescues or saves. 2 THE SAVIOR Jesus Christ.

saw *n.* a tool with a toothed edge for cutting wood, metal, etc. SAW *v.* to cut with a saw.

say *v.* to speak; to express; to give an opinion.

saying *n.* a well-known remark or proverb.

scabbard *n.* a sheath for a bayonet, dagger or sword.

scaffold *n.* 1 framework of metal or wood supporting a platform on which workers can stand when a building is being built, repaired or painted. 2 a platform erected for carrying out an execution.

scald *v.* 1 to injure with hot liquid or steam. 2 to cook or clean in steam. SCALD *n.* an injury caused by hot liquid or steam. SCALDED *adj.*

scale *n.* 1 a series of graduated marks on a ruler, thermometer, map, etc. 2 a succession of musical notes. 3 a weighing instrument. 4 a thin flake of skin. SCALE *n.* 1 to climb. 2 to flake the scales off.

scalp *n.* the skin and hair on top of the head.

scan *v.* to examine carefully.

scandal *n.* 1 a shameful or disgraceful action. 2 malicious gossip. SCANDALOUS *adj.*

Scandinavian *adj.* belonging to Scandinavia. SCANDINAVIAN *n.* one of the people of Denmark, Norway or Sweden.

scar *n.* 1 the mark left by a healed wound. 2 a cliff; a crag. SCAR *v.* to mark with a scar.

scarce *adj.* not plentiful; in short supply. SCARCELY *adv.* hardly; not quite. SCARCITY *n.*

scare *v.* to frighten; to strike with terror. SCARE *n.* a state of fear; a fright.

scarf *n.* a length of material worn around the neck or shoulders.

scarlet *n.* a bright red color. SCARLET *adj.*

scatter *v.* to throw things in different directions; to disperse. SCATTERED *adj.*

scavenge *v.* to collect, or live on, refuse.

scene *n.* 1 the place where an action happens. 2 a view. 2 a part of a play; a stage set for a play. 4 a display of temper.

scenery *n.* 1 a view of the countryside. 2 painted scenes used for a stage play.

scent *v.* 1 to discover by the smell. 2 to suspect. SCENT *n.* 1 a smell; a perfume. 2 a trail or track. SCENTED *adj.*

schedule *n.* a list of details. SCHEDULE *v.* to make a list of details.

scheme *n.* a plot. SCHEME *v.* to plot. SCHEMING *n.*

scholar *n.* 1 a pupil or student. 2 a learned person. SCHOLARLY *adj.*

school *n.* 1 place for the education of children. 2 a shoal of fish or whales. SCHOOL *v.* to teach.

schooner *n.* a two-masted sailing ship.

science *n.* the knowledge of natural laws and truths based on observation, experiment, measurement and deduction. SCIENTIST *n.*

scientific *adj.* according to rules laid down by science. SCIENTIFICALLY *adv.*

scissors *n.* a cutting instrument with two blades.

scold *v.* to find fault with or blame noisily.

scoop *n.* 1 a bowl-shaped shovel or spoon. 2 special news printed by one newspaper before another. SCOOP *v.* 1 to move something with a scoop. 2 to obtain news before rivals do.

scope *n.* 1 the opportunity to do something. 2 range of plans and aims.

scorch *v.* to burn, dry up or singe a surface. SCORCHED *adj.* SCORCHING *adj.*

score *n.* 1 a scratch or cut. 2 points made in a game. 3 a copy of music showing vocal and instrumental parts. 4 twenty. SCORE *v.* 1 to scratch or cut. 2 to gain points in a game. 3 to arrange the parts in a piece of music.

scorn *n.* contempt. SCORN *v.* to show contempt for.

scoundrel *n.* a rogue; an unscrupulous person.

scout *n.* 1 a person sent out to spy or to obtain information. 2 a member of the Scout movement. SCOUT *v.* 1 to spy. 2 to explore.

scowl *v.* to frown; to look sullen. SCOWL *n.* a frown; a sullen look. SCOWLING *adj.*

scramble *v.* 1 to climb or crawl awkwardly. 2 to mix or jumble (something).

scrap *n.* 1 a small piece; a fragment. 2 waste material. SCRAP *v.* to discard or throw away.

scrape *v.* 1 to rub with something hard or sharp. 2 to injure or damage by scraping. 3 to manage with difficulty. SCRAPE *n.* 1 the act or sound of scraping. 2 damage caused by scraping. 3 an awkward or dangerous situation.

scratch *v.* 1 to mark (a surface) with something sharp. 2 to rub with the nails to relieve itching. 3 to withdraw from a race or competition. SCRATCH *n.* a mark or injury caused by scratching. SCRATCH *adj.* hurriedly gathered together.

scrawl *v.* to write hurriedly or hastily; to scribble. SCRAWL *n.* hurried, untidy writing.

scream *v.* to utter a loud sharp cry of pain or terror. SCREAM *n.* a loud cry or shriek.

screech *v.* to utter a harsh, shrill cry or sound. SCREECH *n.* a harsh, shrill cry or sound.

screen *n.* 1 a partition used to give protection from draughts, heat, light or view. 2 anything that conceals or gives protection or shelter. 3 a white or silver surface onto which slides or films may be projected. SCREEN *v.* 1 to protect, shelter or conceal from view. 2 to sieve. 3 to examine or pass through a test.

screw *n.* 1 a kind of nail with a spiral thread used for gripping wood or metal. 2 the propeller of a ship. SCREW *v.* 1 to fasten with a screw. 2 to twist.

scribble *v.* to write hurriedly and untidily; to scrawl.

script *n.* 1 handwriting. 2 the text of a film, play, radio or television program.

Scriptures *n.pl.* the Bible; sacred writings.

scroll *n.* a roll of parchment or paper.

scrub *v.* to rub hard or clean with a stiff brush. SCRUB *n.* 1 a good cleaning. 2 bushes or stunted trees.

scruple *n.* a feeling of doubt or hesitation about whether it is right to do something. SCRUPLE *v.* to doubt or hesitate (whether to do something).

scrutiny *n.* a close inspection or thorough examination of something.

sculptor *n.* a person who carves or models in wood, stone, metal, etc. SCULPT *v.*

sculpture *n.* the art of carving in wood, stone or metal; something so carved. SCULPTURED *adj.*

sea *n.* 1 the expanse of salt water that covers most of the Earth's surface. 2 an area of salt water. 3 a large area or quantity of something.

seal *n.* 1 a furry sea animal. 2 a design stamped on wax, lead, etc., and used for sealing a document, a packet, etc.
SEAL *v.* 1 to attach a seal. 2 to close and fasten something firmly. 3 to make a thing airtight.

seam *n.* 1 the line formed where two pieces of material are joined together. 2 a layer of coal, metal ore, etc. SEAM *v.* to join by a seam.

seamanship *n.* skill in sailing and navigating a ship.

search (for) *v.* 1 to look carefully for (something or someone). 2 to seek.
SEARCH *n.* 1 an attempt to find.
2 an investigation.
SEARCHER *n.* SEARCHING *adj.*

season *n.* 1 one of the four divisions of the year, spring, summer, autumn, winter.
2 a proper, suitable or favorable time for a particular activity.
SEASON *v.* 1 to bring into mature condition.
2 to flavor. SEASONING *n.*

seasonal *adj.* depending upon or changing with the seasons. SEASONABLE *adj.*

seat *n.* 1 something for sitting on. 2 the place where something is situated.
SEAT *v.* to provide seats for.

seclude *v.* to keep apart from others; to isolate. SECLUDED *adj.*

second *n.* 1 the next after the first in order, time, position, etc. 2 a helper for a fighter in a boxing match or duel. 3 a sixtieth part of a minute or of a degree.
SECOND *v.* to aid; to support.

secondary *adj.* coming second; of less importance.

secret *adj.* 1 kept hidden, not generally known. 2 secluded; quiet.
SECRET *n.* something hidden; something not to be generally known. SECRETLY *adv.*
SECRECY *n.*

secretary *n.* a person who deals with correspondence, records, arrangements, for an individual, company, organization or society, etc. SECRETARIAL *adj.*

secrete *v.* 1 to hide; to conceal. 2 to produce a juice or liquid.

section *n.* a part or division of something.
SECTIONAL *adj.*

sector *n.* 1 a part of a circle between two radii. 2 a particular area of activity.

secure *adj.* 1 safe; free from danger. 2 firmly fastened or established. SECURE *v.* 1 to succeed in getting. 2 to fasten firmly. SECURELY *adj.*

security *n.* 1 freedom from anxiety or danger. 2 a guarantee or assurance.

sediment *n.* solid matter that settles at the bottom of a liquid.

see *v.* 1 to perceive; to use the eyes to recognize. 2 to understand. 3 to examine: to look at. 4 to consult.

seed *n.* the grain or nut from which a new plant grows.

seek *v.* to look for; to try to find.

seem *v.* to appear to be; to look as if.
SEEMING *adj.*

segment *n.* a part cut off; a distinct part.
SEGMENTED *adj.*

seize *v.* 1 to grasp or grip suddenly. 2 to take by force. SEIZURE *n.*

seldom *adv.* rarely; not often.

select *v.* to pick; to choose carefully.
SELECT *adj.* carefully chosen; choice.
SELECTED *adj.* SELECTIVE *adj.*

selection *n.* a choice; whatever is selected.

self *n.* a person's own nature or character.

selfish *adj.* lacking in consideration for others; disregarding others.
SELFISHLY *adv.* SELFISHNESS *n.*

sell *v.* to exchange (goods or property) for money.

semi- prefix meaning "half; to some extent."

send *v.* to cause (something or somebody) to go or move somewhere.

senile *adj.* sick and feeble due to old age; having to do with old age.

senior *adj.* 1 older. 2 higher in rank or authority. SENIOR *n.* an older person; a person senior in rank or authority. SENIORITY *n.*

sensation *n.* 1 a feeling. 2 an event causing great excitement. SENSATIONAL. *adj.*

sense *n.* 1 the ability to hear, see, smell, taste and feel. 2 a feeling; an appreciation.
3 the meaning. SENSE *v.* to be aware of; to feel.

sensible *adj.* 1 having or showing good sense. 2 practical; useful. SENSIBLY *adv.*

sensitive *adj.* 1 having feelings and emotions that are easily affected. 2 easily upset.

sentence *n.* 1 a number of words which together form a complete statement.
2 the penalty imposed on a guilty person.
SENTENCE *v.* to pronounce sentence on.

sentry *n.* a guard.

separate *v.* to divide; to make or become separate. SEPARATE *adj.* SEPARATELY *adv.*

September *n.* the ninth month of the year.

sequel *n.* something that follows as the result of something else; a result.

sequence *n.* the arrangement in which things follow one another.

serene *adj.* calm; clear and peaceful.
SERENITY *n.*

sergeant *n.* a noncommissioned officer in the army, air force, and marines; police rank.

serial *adj.* forming a series; in successive parts or installments.

series *n.* a number of things arranged in order; a sequence.

serious *adj.* 1 thoughtful; earnest; responsible.
2 grave; dangerous. SERIOUSLY *adv.*

serpent *n.* a snake.

servant *n.* 1 a person who serves. 2 a person who carries out the orders of a particular person or organization.

serve *v.* 1 to work for. 2 to place food on the table for a meal. 3 to attend to customers in a shop. 4 to hit the ball into play at tennis.

service *n.* 1 working for others; acting as a servant. 2 an organization supplying some special need. 3 a form of worship.
4 a set of cups, saucers, etc.

session *n.* 1 the time spent at a particular activity. 2 a sitting of a meeting or conference.

set *v.* 1 to put; to place; to arrange.
2 to become solid. 3 to sink below the horizon.
SET *n.* 1 a group of people with the same interests. 2 a group of things of the same kind
3 a radio or television receiver.
SET *adj.* fixed; regular.

settle *v.* 1 to come to rest. 2 to sink to the bottom. 3 to agree upon. 4 to decide.
5 to make a home in one place.
SETTLED *adj.* SETTLEMENT *n.*

seven *n.* the number one more than six, the symbol 7.

sever *v.* to cut through; to separate.

several *adj.* 1 a few more than one or two; not very many. 2 separate; various.

severe *adj.* 1 strict; harsh. 2 serious; violent.
3 plain. SEVERELY *adv.* SEVERITY *n.*

sew *v.* to fasten together using a needle and thread; to stitch. SEWING *n.*

sewage *n.* water and waste matter carried away by a sewer.

sewer *n.* an underground drain for sewage.

sextant *n.* an instrument for measuring the angle between two distant objects used in navigation and surveying.

shabby *adj.* 1 worn; threadbare. 2 mean; unfair.
SHABBILY *adv.*

shade *v.* 1 to shield from strong light.
2 to change color gradually.
SHADE *n.* 1 an area shaded from bright light; something that shuts out bright light.
2 a slight difference of color.

shadow *n.* 1 an area of shade. 2 the shape of something obstructing the light.
SHADOW *v.* 1 to darken. 2 to watch; to follow.
SHADOWY *adj.*

shaft *n.* 1 a pole; a long handle. 2 the vertical opening to a mine; the space containing a lift.
3 a pillar or column. 4 a ray of light.
5 an arrow.

shake *v.* 1 to move something quickly to and fro or up and down. 2 to tremble; to shiver.
3 to wave; to brandish.
SHAKE *n.* a shudder, shock or jolt.

shale *n.* a rock formed from clay, which splits easily into thin layers or flakes.

shallow *adj.* 1 not deep. 2 superficial; trivial.
SHALLOWNESS *n.*

sham *v.* to pretend to be.
SHAM *n.* a pretense; a counterfeit.

shame *n.* a feeling of disgrace or guilt.
SHAME *v.* to disgrace.

shampoo *v.* to lather and wash the hair thoroughly.
SHAMPOO *n.* a lotion for washing the hair.

shape *n.* the form or outline of anything.
SHAPE *v.* to make (something) into a particular shape.

share *n.* one of the portions of something which is divided among several people or things.
SHARE *v.* 1 to divide among. 2 to use something jointly.

shareholder *n.* a person who holds shares in a business or company.

shark *n.* a large, sometimes ferocious sea fish.

sharp *adj.* 1 having a thin cutting edge or fine point. 2 quick at understanding.
3 painful; intense. 4 a semitone above the natural note in music.
SHARP *n.* the mark in music showing that a note is to be raised by a semitone. SHARPLY *adv.*

shatter *v.* to break suddenly and violently into pieces. SHATTERING *adj.*

shave v. 1 to remove hair with a razor.
2 to scrape or graze lightly.
SHAVE n. 1 shaving; being shaved. 2 a narrow miss or escape.

shears n.pl. a cutting tool with two movable blades.

sheath n. 1 a close-fitting cover. 2 a case, or scabbard, for a sword or dagger.

shed v. 1 to throw off. 2 to let something fall or flow. SHED n. a hut or small building.

sheep n. an animal raised for its wool and meat. pl. SHEEP.

sheer adj. 1 complete; thorough. 2 very steep.
3 very thin and transparent.
SHEER v. to turn aside; to go away.

sheet n. 1 a flat, thin piece of any material such as paper, glass, metal, ice. etc. 2 a flat area of anything. 3 a piece of linen or nylon used as a bed cover and to sleep under.

shelf n. 1 a board or ledge on a wall or in a cupboard for placing things on. 2 a ridge of rocks in the sea; a reef. pl. SHELVES.

shell n. 1 a hard outer covering or case; a pod or husk. 2 a metal case filled with explosive.
3 the outer walls of an unfinished or damaged building.
SHELL v. 1 to remove the shell from. 2 to fire shells at.

shellfish n. a sea creature with a hard outer shell. (e.g., oyster, clam).

shelter n. 1 a shield or protection against cold, wind, hardship, etc. 2 a building or shield that gives protection.
SHELTER v. to protect or shield.

shelve v. 1 to place on a shelf. 2 to set aside or postpone. 3 to slope.

shepherd n. a person who looks after sheep.
SHEPHERD v. to tend and look after; to direct and guide.

sheriff n. the chief law officer of an area, e.g., a city or county.

shield v. to protect; to shelter.
SHIELD n. 1 a piece of armor carried to protect the body. 2 a protection or safeguard.

shift v. to alter position; to move.
SHIFT n. 1 a change or alteration. 2 a relay or change of workers.

shimmer v. to shine with a quivering light; to gleam.

shin n. the front of the leg between the knee and the ankle. SHIN v. to climb.

shine v. 1 to give out or reflect light.
2 to polish. 3 to be bright and lively.
SHINE n. brightness; gloss; polish. SHINING adj.

ship n. a large boat or seagoing vessel.
SHIP v. to send by ship, SHIPPING n.

shipwreck n. the sinking or destruction of a ship.

shirt n. a thin garment worn on the upper part of the body.

shiver v. to shake or tremble from cold or fear.
SHIVER n. 1 a tremor. 2 a shudder caused by cold or fear.

shock n. 1 a fright or unpleasant surprise.
2 a violent knock or collision.
SHOCK v. 1 to cause fright or surprise. 2 to fill with disgust or horror.
SHOCKING adj. SHOCKINGLY adv.

shoe n. 1 an outer covering worn on the foot.
2 a metal rim nailed to a horse's hoof.
SHOE v. to fit a horse with shoes.

shoot v. 1 to fire a bullet, shell or missile. 2 to wound or kill by shooting. 3 to move very quickly. 4 to aim the ball at the goal in basketball, etc. 5 to sprout or grow.
SHOOT n. 1 a sprout or bud. 2 a shooting match.

shop n. a place where goods are sold.
SHOP v. to buy in shops. SHOPPING n.

shore n. 1 the coast; the beach, 2 a prop or support. SHORE (UP) v. to prop or to support.

short adj. 1 less than normal length or height.
2 not lasting very long. 3 brief; concise
4 insufficient. 5 curt; abrupt.

shortage n. a lack of; an insufficiency.

shorten v. to make or become shorter.

shortly adv. soon; briefly.

shot n. 1 the sound made by a gun.
2 lead pellets. 3 a marksman.

shoulder n. the part of the body between the neck and the upper arm.
SHOULDER v. 1 to push with the shoulder.
2 to accept responsibility.

shout v. to call loudly. SHOUTING n.
SHOUT n. a loud call. SHOUTING n.

shove v. to push roughly; to thrust.
SHOVE n. a push or thrust.

shovel n. a broad spade used for lifting coal and other loose materials. SHOVEL v. to use a shovel.

show v. 1 to cause or allow (something) to be seen. 2 to appear; to be visible. 3 to make something clear.
SHOW n. 1 a display; an entertainment; an exhibition. 2 a pretense.

shower n. a brief fall of hail, rain, snow, bullets, stones, arrows, etc.
SHOWER n. 1 to send or come down in a shower.
2 to give liberally.

shred v. to cut or tear into small pieces.
SHRED n. a thin piece or strip.

shrewd adj. 1 wise; clever. 2 cunning; astute.
SHREWDLY adv.

shriek *v.* to scream; to screech.
SHRIEK *n.* a scream; a screech.

shrill *adj.* having a piercing and high-pitched sound. SHRILLY *adv.*

shrink *v.* 1 to become or make smaller. 2 to move away quickly; to recoil.

shrivel *v.* to make or become dry and wrinkled.

shrub *n.* a small bush. SHRUBBERY *n.*

shrug *v.* to lift the shoulders slightly.
SHRUG *n.* a slight lift of the shoulders.

shudder *v.* to tremble; to shiver.
SHUDDER *n.* a tremble; a shiver.

shuffle *v.* 1 to move about dragging and scraping the feet. 2 to mix up.

shut *v.* to close (a door, window, lid, etc.).

shuttle *n.* a boat-shaped device which carries the weft thread through the warp on a weaving loom.
SHUTTLE *v.* to move backward and forward between two places.

shy *adj.* reserved; timid in company; bashful.
SHY *v.* 1 to throw; to hurl. 2 SHY AWAY FROM to take fright at something. SHYLY *adv.* SHYNESS *n.*

sibling *n.* a near relative, esp. a brother or sister.

sick *adj.* 1 ill; unwell. 2 wanting to vomit. 3 tired of; disgusted. SICKEN *v.* SICKENING *adj.*

sickness *n.* 1 an illness; a disease. 2 vomiting.

side *n.* 1 one of the flat surfaces of an object. 2 the part between the front and back of an object. 3 the part of the body between the hip and shoulder. 4 a team of players.

siege *n.* the surrounding of a town or fortress by troops in an attempt to make it surrender.

sieve *n.* a mesh used to separate the coarse parts of a liquid or solid.
SIEVE *v.* to sift through a sieve.

sift *v.* 1 to pass through a sieve. 2 to examine closely.

sigh *v.* to draw a deep breath showing sadness. weariness, relief. etc.
SIGH *n.* the act or sound or sighing. SIGHING *n.*

sight *n.* 1 the ability to see. 2 seeing or being seen. 3 something interesting or unusual to see. 4 the aiming device on a gun.
SIGHT *v.* 1 to see, to observe. 2 to aim a gun.

sign *n.* 1 a mark or object used to convey a meaning. 2 a gesture. 3 an indication or warning. 4 a board with a name or instruction on it.
SIGN *v.* 1 to make a sign. 2 to write a signature.

signal *n.* 1 a message sent by means of signs. 2 a set of lights or signs giving instructions. 3 a gesture; an indication.
SIGNAL *v.* to send a message by signs.

signature *n.* a person's name written by himself or herself.

significant *adj.* having meaning; important.
SIGNIFICANCE *n.* SIGNIFICANTLY *adv.*

silence *n.* 1 being silent. 2 quietness; absence of sound. SILENCE *v.* to quiet; to make soundless.

silent *adj.* making no sound. SILENTLY *adv.*

silhouette *n.* a shadow shape usually black on a white background.

silica *n.* a mineral substance in sand and quartz.

silk *n.* 1 a strong, fine thread spun by silkworms. 2. a fabric woven from silk thread.

silly *adj.* foolish; stupid. SILLINESS *n.*

silo *n.* a tower for storing grain or crops for use as fodder.

silt *n.* a sediment of fine soil or sand deposited by water. SILT (UP) *v.* to block or fill with silt.

silver *n.* 1 a soft, white precious metal. 2 articles and coins made from silver.
SILVER *adj.* made of silver or silver in color.

similar *adv.* like; of the same sort.
SIMILARLY *adv.*

similarity *n.* a likeness: a resemblance.

simile *n.* a reference to one thing to explain another like it; a comparison.

simmer *v.* 1 to boil gently. 2 to be in a state of suppressed anger or indignation.

simple *adj.* 1 plain; easy; not complicated. 2 easily deceived. SIMPLICITY *n.*

simplify *v.* to make easy and simple.
SIMPLIFICATION *n.*

simulate *v.* to pretend; to imitate.

simultaneous *adj.* happening at the same time.
SIMULTANEOUSLY *adv.*

since *adv.* 1 from then until now. 2 because.
SINCE *conj.* as; because. SINCE *prep.* after.

sincere *adj.* genuine; true; honest.
SINCERELY *adv.* SINCERITY *n.*

sing *v.* to make musical sounds with the voice.
SINGING *n.*

singer *n.* a person who sings.

single *adj.* 1 one only. 2 unmarried. 3 for the use of one person only.
SINGLE (OUT) *v.* to pick one at a time.
SINGLY *adv.*

singular *adj.* 1 one only. 2 odd; unusual; exceptional.

sinister *adj.* evil; threatening.

sink *v.* 1 to go under water; to submerge. 2 to move slowly downward. 3 to bore; to dig. 4 to lose strength.
SINK *n.* a basin with a drain to take away water.
SINKING *n.*

sip *v.* to drink in small quantities; to taste.
SIP *n.* a small drink; a taste.

sir *n.* 1 a title of respect given to men.
2 the title of a knight or baronet.

siren *n.* 1 a device which makes a hooting sound; a warning whistle. 2 a mythical creature, half woman, half bird, whose song lured sailors to destruction.

sister *n.* 1 of the daughters of the same parent. 2 a nun.

sit *v.* 1 to be seated (upon). 2 to cause to sit. 3 to hold a meeting. SITTING *n.*

site *n.* 1 a place chosen for some purpose. 2 the place where a town or building is or has been.

situation *n.* 1 a site; a position. 2 circumstances.

six *n.* the number one more than five, the symbol 6.

size *n.* 1. the largeness or smallness of something. 2 a particular measurement. 3 a weak glue.

skate *n.* 1 a steel blade fixed to a boot for gliding on ice. 2 a roller skate. 3 a kind of flat fish.
SKATE *v.* to move on skates. SKATER *n.*

skeleton *n.* 1 the bony framework of a body. 2 a framework or outline.

sketch *n.* 1 a quickly made drawing. 2. a short, comic play.
SKETCH *v.* to make a sketch.

ski *n.* a long, narrow strip of wood fastened to the foot for traveling over snow.
SKI *v.* to travel on skis. SKIER *n.* SKIING *n.*

skid *v.* to slip or slide accidentally.
SKID *n.* 1 a side-slip. 2 a piece of wood acting as a brake on a wheel.

skill *n.* the ability to do something well, expertly or efficiently. SKILLFUL *adj.*

skim *v.* 1 to remove something from the surface of a liquid. 2 to move quickly and lightly over a surface.

skin *n.* 1 the outer layer of the body of a person or animal. 2 the outer covering or layer.
SKIN *v.* to remove the skin from; to peel.

skip *v.* 1 to leap; to frisk. 2 to jump repeatedly over a turning rope. 3 to miss out pieces when reading.

skirmish *n.* a fight between small groups of people. SKIRMISH *v.* to take part in a skirmish.

skirt *n.* part of a woman's outer garment that hangs from the waist.
SKIRT *v.* to move along the edge of.

skull *n.* the bony framework of the head.

sky *n.* the cloud region surrounding the Earth.
pl. SKIES.

slab *n.* a thick, flat piece of wood, stone, etc.

slack *adj.* 1 not firmly held; loose, 2 slow; lazy.
SLACKEN *v.* SLACKNESS *n.*

slam *v.* to shut, or put down, violently.
SLAM *n.* the sound of slamming.

slander *n.* words spoken to harm a person's character.
SLANDER *v.* to make a false statement intended to harm someone. SLANDEROUS *adj.*

slang *n.* words and phrases in common use but not regarded as standard English.

slant *n.* a slope; a tilt.
SLANT *v.* to slope; to lean. SLANTING *adj.*

slap *v.* to smack with an open hand.
SLAP *n.* a smack.

slash *v.* 1 to make long cuts in; to slit. 2 to reduce drastically. SLASH *n.* a long cut.

slate *n.* a rock that splits easily into thin sheets and is used for roofing.

slaughter *v.* 1 to kill animals for food. 2 to kill or massacre many people or animals.
SLAUGHTER *n.* the killing of many animals or people.

Slav *n.* a member of an East European race speaking a Slavonic language—a Russian, a Pole, a Czech, etc. SLAVONIC *adj.*

slave *n.* a person who is the property of another and who is bound to obey and serve him.
SLAVE *v.* to work like a slave. SLAVERY *n.*

sleek *adj.* soft, smooth and glossy.

sleep *v.* to rest in a natural state of unconsciousness; to slumber.
SLEEP *n.* a natural state of unconsciousness; slumber; repose.

sleeper *n.* 1 a sleeping person. 2 a wooden beam supporting railway lines. 3 a berth in a railway sleeping carriage.

sleet *n.* a mixture of rain and hail or snow.

sleeve *n.* 1 the part of a garment covering the arm. 2 the outer cover for a record.

slender *adj.* 1 narrow; thin. 2 slim; slight.
SLENDERNESS *n.* SLENDERLY *adv.*

slice *n.* a thin piece cut off something.
SLICE *v.* to cut in slices.

slide *v.* to glide or move smoothly over a surface, esp. over snow or ice.
SLIDE *n.* 1 a smooth surface used for sliding. 2 a frame holding a photograph for use in a projector.

slight *adj.* 1 small; not important. 2 slender; slim. SLIGHT *n.* an insult; a snub.
SLIGHT *v.* to insult; to ignore.

slim *adj.* thin; slender.
SLIM *v.* to reduce weight by diet or exercise.

sling *n.* 1 a strap or device for hurling stones. 2 a support for an injured arm.
SLING *v.* 1 to throw something. 2 to lift with a sling.

slip *v.* 1 to slide accidentally; to fall. 2 to make a mistake. 3 to move quietly or stealthily; to escape.
SLIP *n.* 1 slide or fall. 2 mistake. 3 a piece of paper.

slipper *n.* a light shoe to wear indoors.

slit *n.* a long tear, cut or opening.
SLIT *v.* to cut open; to make a slit.

slogan *n.* a short, catchy phrase.

sloop *n.* a one-masted sailing ship.

slope *n.* an incline; a slant. SLOPING *adj.*

slot *n.* a narrow opening; a slit or groove.
SLOT (INTO) *v.* to put in place.

slow *adj.* 1 taking a long time. 2 behind time; late. 3 not quick to learn. SLOWLY *adv.* SLOWNESS *n.*

slum *n.* an area of a town where the houses are in a poor condition, overcrowded and unhealthy.

slump *v.* 1 to collapse. 2 to decrease suddenly.
SLUMP *n.* 1 a collapse. 2 a sudden or continuous fall in price, value, demand, etc.

slur *v.* 1 to speak indistinctly by running one's words together. 2 PUT A SLUR UPON to discredit (someone). 3 SLUR OVER to pass over lightly.
SLUR *n.* 1 the act of speaking indistinctly. 2 a discredit. SLURRED *adj.*

slush *n.* mud; thawing snow. SLUSHY *adj.*

sly *adj.* cunning; underhand. SLYLY *adv.*

smack *n.* 1 a sharp slap; a blow; the sound of a blow. 2 a small fishing boat.
SMACK *v.* to slap; to make a sound like a blow.

small *adj.* 1 little; not large. 2 not important.

smart *v.* to feel or cause a sharp pain; to sting.
SMART *adj.* 1 quick; sharp. 2 well-dressed; neat. SMARTEN *v.* SMARTNESS *n.*

smash *v.* 1 to break into pieces; to shatter. 2 SMASH INTO to collide (with).
SMASH *n.* a breakage; a collision.

smear *v.* 1 to spread with something sticky. 2 to slander.
SMEAR *n.* 1 a greasy mark; a daub. 2 a slander.

smell *n.* 1 the sense of smell. 2 an odor; a fragrance.
SMELL *v.* 1 to be aware of an odor. 2 to give off an odor or scent. SMELLY *adj.*

smile *v.* to express joy, pleasure, amusement, etc., by parting or drawing up the lips.
SMILE *n.* the act of smiling. SMILING *adj.*

smog *n.* a dense, smoky fog.

smoke *n.* the mixture of gas and carbon that rises from a fire.
SMOKE *v.* 1 to give off smoke. 2 to inhale tobacco smoke.

smooth *adj.* 1 having an even surface. 2 having no difficulties in the way. 3 without lumps. 4 pleasing; persuasive.
SMOOTHLY *adv.* SMOOTH *v.* to make smooth.

smother *v.* 1 to suffocate. 2 to cover thickly.

smuggle *v.* to take goods or persons illegally from one country to another. SMUGGLER *n.*

snack *n.* a quick, small meal.

snag *n.* 1 a jagged object. 2 a difficulty.
SNAG *v.* to damage by catching on something sharp.

snail *n.* a small, soft-bodied, crawling, invertebrate animal with a shell; a mollusk.

snake *n.* a long, legless, creeping reptile.

snap *v.* 1 to make a quick, sudden bite. 2 to break or crack. 3 to speak sharply.
SNAP *n.* 1 the act or sound of snapping. 2 a bite.

snarl *v.* 1 to growl and show the teeth. 2 to tangle up. SNARL *n.* a tangle. SNARLING *adj.*

snatch *v.* to grab something quickly.
SNATCH *n.* a quick grab.

sneak *v.* 1 to move quietly and furtively. 2 to behave or steal in a mean way.
SNEAK *n.* 1 a petty thief. 2 an underhand person.

sneer *v.* to show contempt and scorn.
SNEER *n.* an expression of contempt and scorn.

sneeze *n.* an uncontrollable burst of air from the mouth and nose. SNEEZE *v.* to emit a sneeze.

sniff *v.* to draw air in noisily through the nose; to smell. SNIFF *n.* the act or sound of sniffing.

snore *v.* to breathe noisily during sleep. SNORE *n.*

snow *n.* white flakes of frozen water vapor.
SNOW *v.* to fall as snow.

snub *v.* to treat with contempt.
SNUB *n.* an action showing contempt.

so *adv.* 1 in this or that manner. 2 to such an extent. 3 very.
SO *conj.* therefore; for that reason.

soak *v.* to drench; to wet through. SOAKING *n.*

soap *n.* a washing and cleansing material made from fats and oils.
SOAP *v.* to wash or rub with soap.

soar *v.* to rise in the air; to float in the sky.

sob *v.* to cry and gulp noisily.
SOB *n.* the sound of crying. SOBBING *n.*

sober *adj.* 1 not drunk. 2 calm; serious.

soccer *n.* a ball game in which the hands and arms may not be used except by the goalkeeper.

sociable *adj.* friendly; enjoying the company of other people. SOCIABLY *adj.* SOCIABILITY *n.*

social *adj.* 1 living in, or concerning, groups or societies. 2 in society. 3 friendly.
SOCIAL *n.* a gathering or party.

society *n.* 1 the system of living together in groups; a community. 2 a group of people with the same interests.

sock *n.* a short stocking.

socket *n.* a hole or hollow into which something fits.

soda *n.* a mineral substance used in baking, washing, and the manufacture of glass.

soft *adj.* 1 easily pressed into another shape. 2 not hard; yielding. 3 gentle; tender.
SOFTEN *v.* SOFTLY *adv.*

soil *n.* the ground; the top layer of the earth in which plants grow.
SOIL *v.* to make dirty; to stain. SOILED *adj.*

solar *adj.* concerning the sun.

soldier *n.* a member of a military force.

sole *n.* 1 the underside of a foot, boot or shoe. 2 a flat sea-fish.
SOLE *adj.* single, one and only. SOLELY *adv.*

solemn *adj.* 1 serious; thoughtful. 2 earnest; grave. SOLEMNLY *adv.*

solicit *v.* to ask for earnestly and repeatedly.

solid *adj.* 1 of substance throughout; not liquid or fluid. 2 rigid, hard and compact. 3 not hollow.
SOLID *n.* a substance which is hard right through.

solidify *v.* to make or become solid; to harden.

solitary *adj.* 1 alone or lonely. 2 without companions. 3 single.

solitude *n.* being solitary; isolation.

solo *n.* 1 a piece of music for one singer or player. 2 something undertaken by one person. SOLOIST *n.*

soluble *adj.* 1 that can be dissolved in a liquid. 2 that can be solved.

solution *n.* 1 a liquid having something dissolved in it. 2 the answer to a problem.

solve *v.* to find an answer to or explanation for.

solvent *n.* a liquid which will dissolve other substances. SOLVENT *adj.* able to pay all debts.

some *adj.* more or less; unspecified in number or quantity; about.
SOME *pron.* a little; a few; a certain number of persons or things.

somebody *n.* 1 an unspecified person. 2 an important person.

somersault *n.* a jump and a turn heels over head before landing on the feet.
SOMERSAULT *v.* to turn a somersault.

son *n.* a male child of a parent.

song *n.* 1 a piece of music for singing; something which is sung. 2 words set to music.

sonic *adj.* to do with sound or sound waves.

sonnet *n.* a poem containing fourteen lines of equal length.

soon *adv.* 1 in a short time. 2 early. 3 readily; willingly.

soothe *v.* 1 to make calm. 2 to reduce pain. SOOTHING *adj.*

soprano *n.* 1 the highest singing voice of a female or boy. 2 a person having such a voice.

sordid *adj.* dirty; mean; squalid.

sore *adj.* 1 painful, hurting when touched or used. 2 sad; annoyed.
SORE *n.* a painful or inflamed place on the skin. SORELY *adv.*

sorrow *n.* 1 sadness; grief. 2 regret; disappointment. SORROW *v.* to feel sorrow. SORROWFUL *adj.* SORROWFULLY *adv.*

sorry *adj.* feeling grief, pity or regret.

sort *v.* to arrange into groups or sets.

soul *n.* the part of a person that is believed to be immortal.

sound *adj.* 1 healthy; in good condition. 2 sensible; reliable. SOUNDLY *adv.*
SOUND *v.* 1 to make a sound. 2 to examine; to question.
SOUND *n.* 1 something that can be heard. 2 a strait; a channel.

soup *n.* a liquid food made from meat and vegetables.

sour *adj.* 1 having a sharp taste; bitter. 2 surly; bad-tempered.

source *n.* 1 the place or thing from which something starts; the origin. 2 a spring.

south *n.* a cardinal point of the compass opposite to north.
SOUTH *adj.* in or toward the south.
SOUTH *adv.* toward the south. SOUTHERN *adj.*

souvenir *n.* something given, bought or kept as a reminder of a person, place or event.

sovereign *n.* a monarch; a king or queen. SOVEREIGN *adj.* supreme; excellent.

sow *n.* (pron. like HOW) a female pig. *masc.* BOAR.

sow *v.* (pron. SO) to scatter or plant seed; to spread. SOWER *n.*

space *n.* 1 the distance between objects. 2 an empty gap or area. 3 the immeasurable expanse in which the planets and stars move. 4 a period of time.
SPACE *v.* to arrange at intervals, SPACED *adj.*

spacious *adj.* wide; roomy; extensive.

spade *n.* a tool with a broad flat blade and handle, used for digging.

span *n.* 1 the breadth of anything. 2 the part of a bridge between its supports. 3 a period of time. SPAN *v.* to stretch across from one side to the other.

Spaniard *n.* a native of Spain.

Spanish *adj.* belonging to Spain or its people.

spare *adj.* 1 extra; kept in reserve for use when needed. 2 thin; scanty. SPARE *v.* 1 to allow something to go unharmed. 2 to do without or use in small quantities. SPARING *adj.*

spark *n.* 1 a fiery particle. 2 a small flash of light or electricity. SPARK *v.* to make sparks.

sparkle *v.* to flash or glitter. SPARKLE *n.* brightness. SPARKLING *adj.*

sparrow *n.* a small, common, brownish bird.

sparse *adj.* scanty; thinly scattered. SPARSELY *adv.*

speak *v.* 1 to say in words; to talk. 2 to make a speech. SPEAKER *n.* SPEAKING *adj.*

spear *n.* a weapon with a sharp point on a long shaft. SPEAR *v.* to pierce with a spear.

special *adj.* 1 of a particular or rare kind. 2 reserved for a particular person, occasion or purpose. SPECIALLY *adv.*

specialist *n.* an expert in a particular subject.

species *n.* a group of plants or animals which have common characteristics.

specific *adj.* detailed; exact; precise. SPECIFICALLY *adv.*

specification *n.* a detailed and full description of something to be made or undertaken. SPECIFY *v.*

specimen *n.* an example or sample; a pattern.

spectacle *n.* an exciting or impressive display.

spectacles *n.pl.* a pair of lenses in a frame to correct faulty vision.

spectator *n.* a person who watches or looks on.

spectrum *n.* the band of colors seen in a rainbow or through a glass prism.

speech *n.* 1 the ability to speak; spoken words. 2 a language; a dialect. 3 a talk given to an audience.

speed *n.* 1 rapid movement; swiftness. 2 the rate at which something moves. SPEED *v.* to move rapidly.

spell *v.* to arrange letters in a particular order to form a word. SPELL *n.* 1 a short period of time; a continuous period. 2 a charm or influence.

spend *v.* 1 to pay out money. 2 to use up. 3 to pass time.

sphere *n.* 1 ball; a globe. 2 a solid having all points of its surface at an equal distance from the center. 3 a person's daily activity and influence. SPHERICAL *adj.*

sphinx *n.* 1 a fabled monster with the body of a lion and the head of a woman. 2 a person who is silent and secretive.

spice *n.* 1 a vegetable substance, such as nutmet, cloves or pepper, used to flavor food. 2 something that adds interest or excitement. SPICY *adj.*

spider *n.* a small invertebrate animal with eight legs that spins webs.

spike *n.* 1 a sharp, projecting point. 2 a long, pointed nail. 3 a cluster of flowers growing from a single stem. SPIKE *v.* to pierce with a spike. SPIKED *adj.* SPIKY *adj.*

spill *v.* 1 to fall or flow from a container. 2 to cause to fall or flow from a container. SPILL *n.* a fall or tumble.

spin *v.* 1 to twist (yarn, cotton, nylon, etc.). into a thread. 2 to turn around and around rapidly. SPIN *n.* a rapid, turning movement.

spine *n.* 1 the backbone. 2 a sharp, pointed thorn. SPINAL *adj.*

spiral *adj.* coiled around and around like a spring or the thread of a screw.

spire *n.* a tapering structure built on top of a tower; a steeple.

spirit *n.* 1 the soul; the personality. 2 a ghost. 3 courage; enthusiasm. 4 alcohol.

spit *n.* 1 a revolving rod on which meat is roasted. 2 a narrow piece of land projecting into the sea. SPIT *v.* to eject saliva, etc., from the mouth.

splash *v.* to bespatter with liquid. SPLASH *n.* the act or sound of splashing.

splendid *adj.* magnificent; excellent; glorious. SPLENDIDLY *adv.* SPLENDOR *n.*

splint *n.* a rigid piece of material used to keep a broken bone firmly in position.

splinter *n.* a small, sharp, broken fragment of wood, metal, glass, etc. SPLINTER *v.* to break into splinters.

split *v.* 1 to cut, break or come apart lengthways. 2 to divide into shares. SPLIT *n.* 1 the act or process of splitting. 2 a crack; a division; a separation.

spoil *v.* 1 to make or become damaged or useless. 2 to plunder. SPOIL *n.* plunder; loot.

spoke *n.* a radiating rod or bar joining the rim of a wheel to the hub.

sponge *n.* 1 a simple sea creature. 2 a light, porous, absorbent pad used in washing and cleaning. SPONGE *v.* to wash with a sponge. SPONGY *adj.*

sponsor *n.* a person who becomes responsible for another person.

spontaneous *adj.* happening or done naturally and freely.

spool *n.* a reel or small cylinder on which thread, film, ribbon, etc., is wound.

spoon *n.* a utensil with shallow bowl and a handle used in serving and eating food. SPOONFUL *n.*

sport *n.* 1 fun; amusement. 2 games and pastimes such as football, running, ice skating, fishing, etc.

spot *n.* 1 a small, round mark or stain. 2 a particular place. SPOT *v.* 1 to make a small mark or stain. 2 to notice or catch sight of.

sprain *v.* 1 to injure by twisting or spraining. 2 to twist or wrench a joint. SPRAIN *n.* an injury caused by a twist or wrench.

sprawl *v.* 1 to sit or lie with arms and legs spread out. 2 to spread out over a wide area. SPRAWL *n.* a sprawling attitude or movement. SPRAWLING *adj.*

spray *n.* 1 liquid carried through the air in small drops. 2 a device for spraying liquid. 3 a bunch of flowers. SPRAY *v.* to scatter liquid in small drops; to sprinkle.

spread *v.* 1 to stretch out; to extend. 2 to scatter; to distribute. 3 to make known. SPREAD *n.* 1 a covering. 2 an increase.

spring *n.* 1 a place where water flows from the ground. 2 a coil of metal or wire. 3 a leap or jump. 4 the season of the year between winter and summer. SPRING *v.* 1 to flow (from). 2 to recoil. 3 to leap or jump. 4 to come up; to sprout.

sprinkle *v.* to scatter or shower in small drops or particles. SPRINKLING *n.*

sprint *v.* to run a short distance at full speed. SPRINT *n.* a short, fast run or race. SPRINTER *n.*

sprout *v.* to begin to grow; to shoot. SPROUT *n.* a shoot; a new growth.

spur *n.* 1 a sharp instrument worn on a horse rider's heel. 2 a projecting ridge in a mountain range. SPUR *v.* to urge on.

spurt *v.* 1 to gush or spout out. 2 to speed up suddenly. SPURT *n.* 1 a sudden gush. 2 a short, sudden effort.

spy *n.* a person collecting and reporting secret information. SPY *v.* 1 to see. 2 to obtain secret information. 3 SPY OUT to observe or explore secretly.

squabble *v.* to bicker or quarrel noisily. SQUABBLE *n.* a petty quarrel.

squad *n.* a small group of trained people.

squall *n.* a sudden violent gust of wind. SQUALLY *adj.*

square *n.* 1 a figure having four equal sides and four right angles; anything shaped like this. 2 an open space with buildings on four sides. 3 the product of a number multiplied by itself. SQUARE *adj.* 1 square-shaped. 2 honest; fair.

squash *v.* 1 to crush; to squeeze. 2 to silence or repress.

squat *v.* 1 to sit on the heels. 2 to take possession of land or buildings without permission. SQUAT *adj.* short and stocky.

squeak *v.* to make a short, shrill cry. SQUEAK *n.* a short, shrill cry. SQUEAKY *adj.*

squeal *v.* to make a long, shrill cry. SQUEAL *n.* a long, shrill cry.

squeeze *v.* 1 to press tightly; to crush. 2 to pack tightly. SQUEEZE *n.* 1 a firm grip; an embrace. 2 a tight fit.

squirrel *n.* a small rodent, with a bushy tail, which lives in trees.

squirt *v.* to shoot out a jet of liquid.

stab *v.* to pierce, or thrust, with a short pointed weapon. STAB *n.* a wound caused by a thrust.

stability *n.* steadiness; firmness.

stable *n.* a building in which horses are kept. STABLE *v.* to keep or put a horse in a stable. STABLE *adj.* steady; firm; reliable.

stack *n.* a large pile; a heap. STACK *v.* to heap or pile (something) up.

stadium *n.* a sports arena.

staff *n.* 1 a stick or pole used as a support, weapon or symbol of office. 2 a group of persons employed in a business, school, etc. STAFF *v.* to provide (a business) with staff.

stage *n.* 1 a raised platform. 2 a regular stopping place. 3 a point or step in the development of something. STAGE *v.* to produce on the stage.

stagger *v.* 1 to reel; to walk or stand unsteadily. 2 to shock; to amaze. 3 to arrange in alternate order.

stagnate *v.* 1 to become motionless; to cease to flow. 2 to be dull and stale. STAGNANT *adj.* STAGNATION *n.*

stain *v.* 1 to discolor; to mark in patches. 2 to color. STAIN *n.* 1 a dirty mark or patch. 2 a paint or dye. 3 a blemish. STAINED *adj.*

stair *n.* a number of steps between the floors of a building; one of these steps.

stake *n.* 1 a strong, pointed post. 2 money risked in gambling.

stalactite *n.* a crystalline deposit hanging from the roof of a cave and formed by the dripping of water containing lime.

stalagmite *n.* a crystalline deposit rising from the floor of a cave and formed by the dripping of water containing lime.

stale *adj.* 1 not fresh; musty. 2 uninteresting; dull.

stalk *v.* to follow stealthily.
STALK *n.* the stem of a plant. STALKER *n.*

stall *n.* a division for one animal in a stable or barn. STALL *v.* 1 to stop; to halt. 2 to delay. 3 to lose flying speed in an aircraft and fall out of control.

stallion *n.* a male horse. *fem.* MARE.

stalwart *adj.* strong; reliable; determined.

stamen *n.* the part of a flower which produces the pollen.

stamina *n.* the power of endurance.

stammer *v.* to stutter and hesitate when speaking.

stamp *v.* 1 to put a foot down heavily on the ground. 2 to print a mark on (something). 3 to stick a postage stamp on (a letter or parcel) STAMP *n.* 1 a heavy tread. 2 something used to make a mark. 3 a postage stamp.

stampede *n.* a sudden flight of animals or people caused by fright, fear or panic.
STAMPEDE *v.* to run or cause to run in fear or panic.

stand *v.* 1 to be in an upright position. 2 to rise to the feet. 3 to endure.
STAND *n.* 1 the act of standing. 2 a stall. 3 a support.

standard *n.* 1 a flag or banner. 2 a measure. 3 average quality.
STANDARD *adj.* of the usual type; of the normal kind.

star *n.* 1 a tiny bright body seen in the sky at night. 2 a pattern with five or six points representing a star. 3 a famous or popular entertainer, athlete, etc.
STAR *v.* to play the leading part.

starboard *n.* the right-hand side of a ship or aircraft, etc.

stare *v.* to look continuously with a fixed gaze.
STARE *n.* a fixed gaze.

start *v.* 1 to begin; to commence; to make the first move. 2 to make a quick, sudden movement.
START *n.* 1 a beginning. 2 a quick, sudden movement. 3 an advantage.

startle *v.* to surprise or frighten (somebody or something). STARTLING *adj.*

starve *v.* to suffer or die from hunger.
STARVATION *n.*

state *n.* 1 the condition of someone or something. 2 a nation.
STATE *v.* to say; to declare. STATESMAN *n.*

stately *adj.* dignified; imposing; grand.

statement *n.* 1 something said or written. 2 an account.

static *adj.* at rest; not changing or moving.

station *n.* 1 a stopping place for trains and buses with buildings for passengers and staff 2 a headquarters for policemen, firemen or troops. STATION *v.* to place in position.

stationary *adj.* remaining in one place; not moving.

stationery *n.* writing materials.

statistics *n.pl.* facts and figures collected, classified and arranged to give information.
STATISTICAL *adj.*

statue *n.* a figure carved from stone or cast in metal.

status *n.* rank or social position.

stave *n.* 1 one of the narrow strips of wood forming the side of a barrel. 2 the lines on which notes of music are written.

stay *v.* 1 to remain. 2 to live in a place temporarily. STAY *n.* a prop; a support.

steady *adj.* 1 firm; not moving. 2 regular. 3 constant and reliable. STEADILY *adv.*
STEADINESS *n.*

steal *v.* 1 to take (something) dishonestly. 2 to move stealthily. STEALING *n.*

stealth *n.* secrecy; a furtive and secret manner.
STEALTHILY *adj.*

steam *n.* the vapor produced by boiling water.
STEAM *v.* 1 to give off steam. 2 to use steam power. 3 to cook in steam.

steel *n.* a hard metal made from iron, carbon, and other minerals.

steep *adj.* sloping sharply.
STEEP *v.* to soak in a liquid. STEEPNESS *n.*

steeple *n.* a spire built on a tower.

steer *v.* to guide; to direct.
STEER *n.* a bullock; a young ox.

stem *n.* 1 the stalk of a plant. 2 the forepart of a ship.
STEM *v.* to stop or hold in check; to dam up.

stencil *n.* 1 a sheet of metal or card with a pattern cut out. 2 a wax-covered skin used for duplicating copies.

sterilize *v.* to free from germs. STERILIZER *n.*

stern *adj.* strict; severe; grim; harsh.
STERN *n.* the rear part of a ship. STERNLY *adv.*

stew *v.* to cook by slow boiling.
STEW *n.* meat and vegetables that have been cooked gently.

stick *n.* 1 a straight, thin branch cut from a tree. 2 a slender piece of wood cut for a particular purpose. 3 a piece of celery, chalk, etc.
STICK *v.* 1 to pierce; to thrust into. 2 to glue (one thing to another).

stiff *adj.* 1 hard to bend, stir or move. 2 difficult. 3 strong; rigid. STIFFEN *v.*

stifle *v.* 1 to smother; to suffocate. 2 to keep back; to suppress.

still *adj.* 1 calm; without movement. 2 silent; quiet.
STILL *adv.* 1 up to and including the present time. 2 nevertheless.

stimulant *n.* something which increases physical or mental activity.

stimulate *v.* to arouse thought, action, interest or excitement.

stimulus *n.* something that rouses activity or energy.

sting *v.* to feel or cause acute pain.

stipulate *v.* to make conditions; to insist upon.
STIPULATION *n.*

stir *v.* 1 to start or keep moving. 2 to excite; to arouse. STIR *n.* a slight movement or activity. STIRRING *adj.*

stirrups *n.pl.* supports, hanging from a saddle, for the horse-rider's feet.

stitch *n.* 1 a loop of thread made in sewing or knitting. 2 a single, complete movement in sewing or knitting. 3 a sudden pain in the side. STITCH *v.* to sew with a needle and thread.

stock *n.* 1 a supply or store of goods for sale or use. 2 the animals on a farm; livestock. 3 family or ancestry.
STOCK *v.* 1 to store goods for sale. 2 to supply or obtain animals for a farm.

stocking *n.* a close-fitting covering for the foot and leg.

stole *n.* 1 a narrow band of silk worn around the neck and shoulders by a priest. 2 a woman's shoulder wrap.

stomach *n.* the organ of the body that receives and digests food.

stone *n.* 1 a small piece of rock; a piece of building stone. 2 the hard seed of fruits, such as the plum, apricot, etc.
STONE *v.* to throw stones at.
STONE *adj.* made of stone.

stool *n.* a low seat without a back.

stoop *v.* to bend forward and downward.
STOOP *n.* a forward bending of the body.

stop *v.* 1 to cease; to bring to an end. 2 to prevent; to hinder. 3 to come to rest; to halt. 4 to remain.
STOP *n.* 1 a halt; stopping or being stopped. 2 a short stay. 3 a punctuation mark. 4 a mechanism in a musical instrument which regulates its sounds.

storage *n.* the placing of goods in store; the charge for storing goods.

store *n.* 1 a stock of something kept for future use. 2 a place where goods are kept. 3 a large shop selling a variety of goods.
STORE *v.* 1 to put aside for future use. 2 to place in a warehouse or storage place.

storm *n.* 1 a sudden disturbance of the air with thunder, strong wind, heavy rain or snow. 2 a sudden, violent attack.
STORM *v.* 1 to attack suddenly and violently. 2 to display violent anger. STORMY *adj.*

story *n.* an account of real or imaginary happenings. *pl.* STORIES.

stout *adj.* 1 strong and thick. 2 fat. 3 brave.

stove *n.* an apparatus used for cooking or heating.

stow *v.* to pack and store something away.

stowaway *n.* a person who hides in a ship or aircraft to avoid paying the fare.

straggle *v.* to fall behind or wander away from the main party. STRAGGLER *n.*

straight *adj.* 1 without a bend or curve. 2 neat and tidy. 3 honest; direct. STRAIGHTEN *v.*

straightforward *adj.* direct; uncomplicated; honest.

strain *v.* 1 to filter or sift. 2 to weaken by overwork.
STRAIN *n.* 1 a stretching. 2 an injury caused by straining. STRAINED *adj.*

strait *n.* a narrow channel of water connecting two seas. STRAITS *n.pl.* difficulty or hardship.

strange *adj.* 1 unusual; not familiar or well known. 2 odd; peculiar. STRANGELY *adv.*

stranger *n.* 1 person not known before. 2 a person in unfamiliar surroundings.

strategy *n.* the planning of a campaign.

straw *n.* 1 the dry cut stalks of cereal grasses. 2 a thin tube for drinking through.

stray *v.* to wander; to lose the way.
STRAY *n.* a lost person or animal.

streak *n.* a line or stripe of contrasting color.
STREAK *v.* 1 to mark with stripes. 2 to move quickly. STREAKY *adj.*

stream *n.* 1 a small river or brook. 2 a flow of water, light, air, people, traffic, etc.
STREAM *v.* to move or flow freely.

street *n.* a road lined with buildings.

strength *n.* being strong; power. STRENGTHEN *v.*

strenuous *adj.* needing great effort; vigorous.

stress *n.* 1 pressure; tension; strain.
2 emphasis; importance. STRESS *v.* to emphasize.

stretch *v.* 1 to make (something) wider, longer or tighter by pulling. 2 to strain; to extend; to spread.
STRETCH *n.* 1 the act of stretching or being stretched. 2 a continuous length of time or space.

stretcher *n.* a light, folding framework with handles at each end for carrying a sick or injured person.

strict *adj.* 1 exact; precise. 2 severe; stern.
STRICTNESS *n.*

stride *v.* to walk with long steps.

strife *n.* conflict; struggle.

strike *v.* 1 to hit; to attack suddenly.
2 to refuse to work because of a dispute.
3 to sound.
STRIKE *n.* 1 a hit. 2 a refusal to work because of a dispute. STRIKING *adj.*

string *n.* 1 a thin cord used for tying things.
2 a series of things linked together.
STRING *v.* 1 to put on a string. 2 to provide with a string. STRINGED *adj.*

strip *v.* 1 to remove the outer covering from.
2 to undress. 3 to deprive of.
STRIP *n.* a narrow piece.

stripe *n.* 1 a long narrow mark. 2 a marking on a uniform indicating the rank of the wearer.
STRIPE *v.* to mark with stripes. STRIPED *adj.*

stroke *n.* 1 a blow. 2 a sweep of an oar in rowing; a movement of the arms in swimming.
3 a mark made with a pencil, brush or pen.
3 a sudden paralysis.
STROKE *v.* to smooth with the hand.

strong *adj.* 1 having great power; not easily broken or damaged. 2 very powerful in flavor or smell. 3 glaring; dazzling.

structure *n.* 1 something that has been built.
2 the way in which something is built or put together.

struggle *v.* 1 to make great efforts.
2 STRUGGLE WITH or AGAINST to fight.
STRUGGLE *n.* an effort; a fight.

stubble *n.* 1 short stalks of grain left in the ground after reaping. 2 short growth of hair.

stubborn *adj.* obstinate; inflexible.
STUBBORNNESS *n.*

student *n.* a person who studies.

studied *adj.* deliberate; carefully planned.

studio *n.* 1 a workroom for an artist or photographer. 2 a place for making records, films or broadcasts.

study *v.* 1 to give time and thought to acquiring information, knowledge and learning.
2 to examine carefully.
STUDY *n.* 1 the learning of a subject.
2 a private room used when studying.
STUDIOUS *adj.*

stuff *v.* to fill tightly. STUFFED *adj.*

stumble *v.* 1 to trip up. 2 to move or speak hesitatingly. STUMBLE *n.* a trip; a fall.

stump *n.* 1 the projecting part of a felled or fallen tree. 2 the remaining part of a cut or broken pencil, tooth, etc.

stun *v.* 1 to knock senseless. 2 to amaze; to confuse.

stunt *v.* to check the growth or development of.
STUNT *n.* something done to attract attention or to gain publicity. STUNTED *adj.*

stupid *adj.* foolish; lacking intelligence.
STUPIDLY *adj.* STUPIDITY *n.*

sturdy *adj.* robust; strong; vigorous.
STURDILY *adv.*

stutter *v.* to stammer. STUTTER *n.* a stammer.

style *n.* 1 the way or manner in which something is done, written or spoken. 2 fashion in dress, furnishing, etc. STYLISH *adj.*

subconscious *adj.* 1 not fully conscious. 2 about those mental activities of which a person is not fully aware.

subject *adj.* (pron. SUB-jekt) 1 under the power of another. 2 liable to or conditional upon.
SUBJECT *v.* (pron. sub-JEKT) to subdue.
SUBJECT *n.* 1 a member of a particular state or country. 2 a topic of conversation; a theme.

submarine *n.* a ship which can travel under water.
SUBMARINE *adj.* living or growing under the sea.

submerge *v.* to go under water or beneath the surface of a liquid; to cause something to do this.

submission *n.* a surrender; obedience.

submit *v.* 1 to surrender; to yield. 2 to suggest; to propose.

subordinate *adj.* lower in rank or importance.
SUBORDINATE *n.* a person who is lower in rank or importance.
SUBORDINATE *v.* to regard as less important; to put into a subordinate position.

subscribe *v.* to make a contribution; to help towards something.
SUBSCRIBER *n.* SUBSCRIPTION *n.*

subsequent *adj.* following; coming later.

subside *v.* to sink or settle down; to grow less. SUBSIDENCE *n.*

subsidy *n.* a financial grant or aid.

substance *n.* 1 any kind of matter; anything that is real and not imaginary. 2 wealth and possessions. 3 the meaning or importance of something. SUBSTANTIAL *adj.*

substitute *v.* to use (something or someone) in place of (another). SUBSTITUTE *n.* something or someone used in place of another. SUBSTITUTION *n.*

subterranean *adj.* underground.

subtle *adj.* 1 fine and delicate. 2 ingenious; clever. SUBTLY *adv.*

subtract *v.* to take one number or quantity from another; to deduct. SUBTRACTION *n.*

subway *n.* an underground railway.

succeed *v.* 1 to be successful; to achieve a purpose. 2 to come after; to take the place of; to inherit.

success *n.* 1 achievement; prosperity. 2 a person who achieves success. SUCCESSFUL *adj.* SUCCESSFULLY *adv.*

successive *adj.* coming one after another in turn.

successor *n.* a person or thing coming after another.

such *adj.* 1 of the same kind as. 2 denoting a particular person or thing. 3 so great.

suck *v.* to draw (liquid or air) into the mouth.

suction *n.* a sucking or drawing of liquid or air from something.

sudden *adj.* happening or done quickly and unexpectedly. SUDDENLY *adv.* SUDDENNESS *n.*

sue *v.* to plead; to take legal action against.

suffer *v.* 1 to undergo pain or experience loss, grief or punishment. 2 to tolerate; to allow. SUFFERER *n.* SUFFERING *n.*

sufficient *adj.* enough; adequate. SUFFICIENTLY *adv.*

suffocate *v.* 1 to have difficulty in breathing. 2 to smother or choke. SUFFOCATION *n.*

sugar *n.* a sweet, energy-giving substance obtained from plants, esp. sugarcane and sugar beet.

suggest *v.* 1 to put forward an idea or proposal. 2 to hint. SUGGESTION *n.*

suicide *n.* intentional self-killing.

suit *n.* 1 a set of clothes of the same material and color. 2 one of the four sets in a pack of playing cards. 3 an action in a law court. SUIT *v.* 1 to meet the needs of. 2 to look well on; to be good for.

suitable *adj.* appropriate for the purpose or occasion. SUITABLY *adv.*

suite *n.* 1 set of furniture. 2 a set of rooms. 3 a musical composition in several parts.

sulk *v.* to be sullen and silent. SULKY *adj.*

sullen *adj.* morose and gloomy.

sum *n.* the total obtained when adding numbers, quantities or items. SUM *v.* to add together.

summary *n.* a short account of a story, book, article, speech, etc.

summer *n.* the warmest season of the year.

summit *n.* the highest point; the top; the highest degree.

summon *v.* 1 to call together; to command someone to appear. 2 to order to appear in court.

summons *n.* an order to appear in court. SUMMONS *v.* to serve with a summons.

sun *n.* the heavenly body giving light and heat to the Earth.

Sunday *n.* the first day of the week.

sunken *adj.* 1 submerged; below ground level. 2 hollow.

sunlight *n.* the light given by the sun. SUNLIT *adj.*

sunshine *n.* the sun's heat and light rays.

superb *adj.* splendid; magnificent.

superficial *adj.* on the surface; shallow; not thorough.

superfluous *adj.* more than needed or required.

superior *adj.* greater, higher or better than others. SUPERIOR *n.* a person of higher rank or better than others. SUPERIORITY *n.*

supermarket *n.* a large self-service store selling goods of all kinds.

supersede *v.* to take the place of (another); to replace.

superstition *n.* a belief in magic and supernatural powers. SUPERSTITIOUS *adj.*

supervise *v.* to direct and control work of performance. SUPERVISION *n.*

supervisor *n.* a person who supervises; a manager.

supper *n.* an evening meal.

supple *adj.* easily bent; flexible.

supplement *v.* to add something to; to assist. SUPPLEMENT *n.* an addition.

supply *v.* to provide what is needed. SUPPLY *n.* 1 a stock of something. 2 something which is supplied. *pl.* SUPPLIES.

support *v.* 1 to hold up; to keep in place. 2 to provide for. 3 to encourage. SUPPORT *n.* a person or thing that supports.

suppose v. 1 to assume; to think. 2 to imagine. SUPPOSED adj.

suppress v. 1 to crush; to put an end to. 2 to hold back; to keep secret.

supreme adj. highest in authority, rank or power. SUPREMELY adv.

sure adj. 1 certain; confident. 2 safe; reliable.

surface n. the outside of something; the exterior. SURFACE v. to come to the surface.

surge v. to move up and down or to and fro. SURGE n. a surging motion.

surgeon n. a doctor who performs operations.

surgery n. the treatment of disease and injury by operations on the body.

surly adj. sullen; morose; sulky.

surmise v. to suppose; to imagine. SURMISE n. something that is supposed; a guess.

surmount v. to overcome (difficulties).

surname n. a family name.

surpass v. to outdo; to exceed.

surplus n. the amount left over when the required amount has been used; the excess. SURPLUS adj. needless; unnecessary.

surprise n. 1 an unexpected happening. 2 the feeling a person has about an unexpected happening. SURPRISE v. to cause a feeling of surprise in; to startle. SURPRISING adj.

surrender v. 1 to give in to; to yield. 2 to give up possession of. SURRENDER n. the act of surrendering.

surround v. to encircle; to be around (something) on all sides.

surroundings n.pl. the things and places which are around a person or place; a neighborhood.

survey v. (pron. sur-VEY) 1 to look at and consider. 2 to measure. 3 to make a map or a plan. SURVEY n. (pron. SUR-vey) 1 a view or inspection. 2 a map or plan of an area.

surveyor n. a person qualified to survey land and buildings.

survive v. to remain alive or to outlive. SURVIVOR n.

suspect v. 1 to have suspicions or doubts about (someone or something). 2 to suppose; to imagine. SUSPECT n. a suspected person. SUSPECT adj. arousing suspicion.

suspend v. 1 to hang (something) up. 2 to delay or postpone. SUSPENSION n.

suspense n. uncertainty; strain; doubt.

suspicion n. 1 a feeling that something is wrong. 2 a slight trace; a very small amount.

suspicious adj. doubtful; distrustful. SUSPICIOUSLY adv.

sustain v. 1 to support; to maintain. 2 to give strength to.

swallow n. 1 a swift-flying, migratory bird with a forked tail. 2 a gulp. SWALLOW v. 1 to allow food or drink to pass down the throat. 2 to believe readily.

swamp v. to flood; to sink; to overwhelm. SWAMP n. a marsh; boggy land.

swan n. a large, white, long-necked water bird.

swarm n. 1 a large group of insects. 2 a crowd or multitude. SWARM v. to move in a large group.

sway v. 1 to move or swing from side to side. 2 to control; to influence. SWAY n. 1 a swinging movement. 2 control; influence.

swear v. 1 to take an oath. 2 to use bad language. SWEARING n.

sweat v. to perspire. SWEAT n. perspiration; condensation.

Swedish adj. belonging to Sweden or its people. SWEDISH n. the language of Sweden.

sweep v. 1 to clean with a brush. 2 to travel over quickly. 3 to clearly everything away quickly or forcefully. SWEEP n. 1 a long, swift movement. 2 a person who cleans chimneys. SWEEPING adj.

sweet adj. 1 having a taste like sugar. 2 pleasant; attractive. SWEET n. 1 a small piece of something sweet made from sugar or chocolate. 2 a pudding. SWEETNESS n.

sweetheart n. a loved one.

swell v. 1 to grow larger or louder. 2 to rise and fall like waves. SWELLING n.

swerve v. to change direction suddenly. SWERVE n. a sudden change of direction.

swift adj. fast; speedy; quick. SWIFT n. a small, swift-flying, migratory bird in the swallow family.

swim v. 1 to move through the water by moving limbs or fins. 2 to cross water by swimming. 3 to feel dizzy.

swindle v. to cheat; to defraud. SWINDLE n. a fraud. SWINDLER n.

swine n. a pig or pigs.

swing v. 1 to move to and fro. 2 to turn suddenly. SWING n. 1 a swinging movement. 2 a suspended seat for swinging on.

Swiss n. an inhabitant of Switzerland. SWISS adj. belonging to Switzerland or its people.

switch *n*. 1 device for turning electricity on or off. 2 a sudden change.
SWITCH *v*. 1 to operate a switch. 2 to change direction suddenly.

swoop *v*. 1 to descend steeply and swiftly. 2 to make a sudden attack.
SWOOP *n*. a sudden descent or attack.

sword *n*. a weapon with a long, steel blade and hilt.

sycamore *n*. a large deciduous tree.

syllable *n*. a whole word or part of a word containing one vowel sound.

syllabus *n*. the program for a course of study.

symbol *n*. a sign or mark which represents something else; an emblem.

symmetry *n*. 1 the state of being equally balanced on each side. 2 a balance; harmony.

sympathy *n*. 1 sharing the feelings of others. 2 understanding; agreement. SYMPATHETIC *adj*.

symphony *n*. a musical composition in several movements for orchestra.

symptom *n*. 1 a change in a person's condition that indicates illness. 2 a sign; an indication.

synagogue *n*. a building for Jewish worship and teaching.

synthetic *adj*. produced artificially.

syringe *n*. an instrument for squirting or injecting liquids. SYRINGE *v*. to squirt; to spray

syrup *n*. 1 a thick fluid obtained in the refining of sugar. 2 a solution of sugar in water or fruit juice.

system *n*. 1 a regular method or planned way of doing things. 2 a number of things working together for a purpose.
SYSTEMATIC *adj*. SYSTEMATICALLY *adj*.

T

table *n*. 1 a piece of furniture with a flat top supported on legs. 2 a statement of facts or figures set out in columns.

tablet *n*. 1 a flat piece of stone with words cut on it. 2 a small pill.

tabulate *v*. to arrange figures or words in a table or index. TABULATION *n*.

tacit *adj*. permitted and understood but not spoken. TACITLY *adv*.

taciturn *adj*. in the habit of saying very little.

tack *n*. 1 a short, broad-headed nail. 2 a long, loose stitch. 3 a zigzag course against the wind in sailing.
TACK *v*. 1 to fasten with tacks.
2 to stitch loosely. 3 to sail a zigzag course.

tackle *n*. 1 equipment needed for a particular activity. 2 an arrangement of ropes and pulleys for lifting loads. 3 the grasping or holding of an opponent.
TACKLE *v*. 1 to deal with a problem or task. 2 to grasp; to hold.

tact *n*. the ability to speak and act without causing offense TACTFUL *adj*. TACTLESS *adj*.

tactics *n.pl*. 1 the management of military forces in battle. 2 the plan for achieving a purpose.
TACTICIAN *n*.

tadpole *n*. a frog or toad in the first stage after hatching.

tail *n*. 1 the projecting part at the rear end of the bodies of animals, birds and fish.
2 anything sticking out behind or at the rear.

tailor *n*. a person who makes suits and other garments. TAILOR *v*. to make garments.

taint *v*. to infect; to currupt.
TAINT *n*. a trace of something unpleasant or bad.

take *v*. 1 to get hold of. 2 to grasp; to seize. 3 to guide; to accompany.

tale *n*. 1 a true or fictitious story.
2 a mischievous report.

talent *n*. a special skill or ability. TALENTED *adj*.

talk *v*. 1 to speak; to express in spoken words. 2 TALK OVER or ABOUT to discuss.
TALK *n*. 1 conversation or discussion.
2 a lecture. 3 gossip.

tall *adj*. 1 of more than average height. 2 of a particular height.

tame *adj*. 1 not wild; domesticated 2 gentle and obedient.
TAME *v*. to make tame; to subdue. TAMELY *adv*.

tamper (with) *v*. to meddle with; to interfere.

tan *v*. to make an animal skin into leather by treating with acid. 2 to become brown by exposure to the sun.
TAN *n*. 1 oak bark used for tanning. 2 sunburn.
3 a yellowish-brown color. TANNED *adj*.
TANNING *n*.

tangent *n*. a straight line which touches a curve at a point but does not cross it.

tangerine *n*. a small, sweet orange.

tangible *adj*. 1 that can be touched. 2 real; definite.

tangle *v*. 1 to become confused and muddled.
2 to twist or jumble together.
TANGLE *n*. a muddle; a mix-up.

tank *n*. 1 container for a liquid or a gas.
2 an armored fighting vehicle moving on caterpillar tracks.

tanker *n*. a ship or road vehicle for carrying liquids.

tantrum *n*. a fit of bad temper.

tap *n*. 1 a device for controlling the flow of a liquid or gas. 2 a light pat or touch.
TAP *v*. 1 to draw off liquid by means of a tap. 2 to pat or touch.

tape *n*. 1 narrow strip of fastening material. 2 a magnetic ribbon used to make sound and/or video recordings.
TAPE *v*. 1 to fasten with tape. 2 to record (sound and/or video) on tape.

taper *v*. 1 to become narrower toward one end. 2 to make thinner toward one end.
TAPER *n*. 1 a narrowing. 2 a long thin candle.

tapestry *n*. a piece of cloth with patterns or pictures woven into it.

tar *n*. a thick, black substance obtained from coal and used for road surfacing and wood preservation. TAR *v*. to coat with tar.

target *n*. 1 a mark or object for shooting at. 2 something to be aimed at.

tarnish *v*. to make or become dull and discolored. TARNISHED *adj*.

tart *n*. a piece of pastry containing fruit or jam; a shallow pie. TART *adj*. sharp or sour in taste.

task *n*. a piece of work set to be done.

taste *n*. 1 the ability to taste. 2 flavor. 3 a person's judgment in liking things. 4 a small quantity.
TASTE *v*. 1 to distinguish a taste or flavor. 2 to test a small quantity.
TASTEFUL *adj*. TASTELESS *adj*. TASTY *adj*.

tattoo *n*. a design on the skin made by pricking it and applying dyes.
TATTOO *v*. to prick a design into the skin.

taunt *v*. to mock or sneer at; to ridicule.
TAUNT *n*. mockery; ridicule.

taut *adj*. tightly stretched. TAUTLY *adv*.

tax *n*. a contribution levied on a person, property or business by a government (local, state, or federal). TAX *v*. 1 to demand or impose a tax. 2 to accuse; to charge. TAXATION *n*.

taxable *adj*. liable to be taxed.

taxi *n*. an automobile and driver that may be hired. TAXI *v*. to move an aircraft along the ground before or after flying.

taxidermy *n*. the art of stuffing the skins of animals, birds and fish to make them look lifelike. TAXIDERMIST *n*.

tea *n*. 1 the dry leaves of a shrub grown in Asia. 2 a hot drink made by pouring water on these leaves. 3 an afternoon meal at which tea is usually drunk.

teach *v*. 1 to pass on knowledge or skill. 2 to give instruction in a particular subject.
TEACHING *n*.

teacher *n*. a person who teaches.

teak *n*. 1 a tree from the Far East. 2 its timber.

team *n*. 1 a group of people playing or working together. 2 two or more animals harnessed together.

tear *v*. (pron. TARE) 1 to pull apart by force; to pull to pieces. 2 to rush along.
TEAR *n*. a rip; a vent. TEARING *adj*.

tear *n*. (pron. TEER) a drop of water in or flowing from the eye. TEARFUL *adj*.

tease *v*. 1 to make fun of or to annoy and torment somebody. 2 to separate the fibers of wool or other material using a comb or teasel.

technical *adj*. concerning some particular art, craft or science.

technicality *n*. a technical detail or point.

technique *n*. 1 the way of doing something. 2 the skill required by an artist, musician, etc.

technology *n*. the practical uses of scientific knowledge.

tedious *adj*. wearisome; long and boring.
TEDIOUSLY *adv*.

telegram *n*. a message sent by telegraph.

telegraph *n*. an electrical apparatus for sending messages or signals over long distances.

telephone *n*. an electrical apparatus for transmitting sound and speech over long distances. TELEPHONIC *adj*.

telescope *n*. an instrument fitted with lenses for making distant objects seem nearer and larger.
TELESCOPE *v*. to make (something) shorter by sliding one section inside another.
TELESCOPIC *adj*.

television *n*. 1 the radio transmission of a picture which is reproduced on a screen. 2 the apparatus for receiving such pictures.
TELEVISION *adj*. concerned with television.

tell *v*. 1 to give an account of; to relate. 2 to reveal. 3 to order; to command. 4 TELL THINGS APART to distinguish one thing from another.

temper *n*. 1 a person's state of mind or mood. 2 the degree of hardness in metal. 3 a fit of anger or annoyance.
TEMPER *v*. 1 to toughen and harden (metal) by heating and cooling. 2 to make less severe; to calm.

temperament *n*. a person's nature, character and state of mind.

temperate *adj*. 1 moderate; avoiding extremes. 2 neither very hot nor very cold.

temperature *n*. the hotness or coldness of something as shown by a thermometer.

temple *n*. 1 a place of religious worship.
2 the part of the head between the forehead and
the ear.

temporary *adj*. lasting only for a short time.
TEMPORARILY *adv*.

tempt *v*. 1 to try to persuade; to entice.
2 to attract; to allure. TEMPTING *adj*.

temptation *n*. 1 tempting or being tempted.
2 an attraction; a bait.

ten *n*. the number one more than nine; the
symbol 10.

tenacious *adj*. holding firmly; clinging tightly.
TENACITY *n*.

tenant *n*. a person who rents a building, house or
land.

tend *v*. 1 to look after; to take care of.
2 to move or be directed in a certain direction;
to incline toward.

tendency *n*. a leaning toward; a trend.

tender *n*. 1 a small supply vehicle or vessel.
2 an offer to do work or to supply goods at a
fixed price. TENDER *v*. to make an offer.
TENDER *adj*. 1 soft; easily damaged. 2 easily cut
or chewed. 3 loving; kindly. 4 sore; painful.
TENDERNESS *n*.

tendon *n*. a strong cord connecting a bone to a
muscle.

tennis *n*. a game for two or four players played
with rackets and a ball on a grass or hard court.

tenor *n*. 1 the male voice between baritone and
alto. 2 the musical part for a tenor voice; a man
with such a voice. 3 a general course of
direction.

tense *adj*. stretched tight; strained.
TENSE *n*. the form taken by a verb to indicate
time—past, present and future.

tension *n*. 1 stretching or being stretched.
2 mental strain or excitement.

tent *n*. a portable shelter, made of canvas or
nylon and supported by poles and ropes.

tentacle *n*. the long slender feeler of certain
animals and insects.

tentative *adj*. done as a trial; experimental.
TENTATIVELY *adv*.

term *n*. 1 period of time. 2 a division of the
school or university year. 3 a word having a
precise meaning.
TERMS *n.pl*. conditions; tone of expression.
TERM *v*. to name; to describe.

terminal *n*. 1 a connecting point for electrical
apparatus. 2 an airport, container depot or
railway station at which journeys begin or end.
TERMINAL *adj*. occurring at the end.

terminate *v*. to stop; to bring to an end.
TERMINATION *n*.

terrestrial *adj*. 1 living on the ground.
2 belonging to the Earth.

terrible *adj*. 1 causing great fear or terror.
2 awful; dreadful. TERRIBLY *adv*.

terrier *n*. a small, lively dog that will dig to reach
its prey.

terrific *adj*. very great; excellent.
TERRIFICALLY *adv*.

terrify *v*. to frighten; to fill with terror.

territory *n*. 1 large area of land. 2 land belonging
to an individual or to a particular country; an
area dominated by certain animals or birds.
TERRITORIAL *adj*.

terror *n*. 1 great fear. 2 a terrifying thing or
person.

terse *adj*. short and concise. TERSELY *adv*.

test *n*. an examination of something or
somebody.
TEST *v*. to examine or try the qualities, nature or
ability of (someone or something). TESTED *adj*.

testament *n*. 1 a will; a written statement.
2 one of the two main parts of the Bible.

testify *n*. to give evidence; to declare.

testimonial *n*. 1 a written statement giving an
opinion about a person's character and abilities.
2 a gift presented as a token of appreciation and
respect.

testimony *n*. evidence; a written or oral
statement made under oath.

text *n*. 1 the actual words spoken or written by
someone. 2 a short passage from the Bible,
quoted as the subject for a sermon.

textile *n*. woven material, cloth or fabric.
TEXTILE *adj*. concerned with fabrics and
weaving.

texture *n*. 1 the manner in which something is
woven. 2 the quality of something according to
taste or feel.

than *conj*. a word used when making
comparisons.

thank *v*. to express gratitude to. THANKFUL *adj*.

thanks *n.pl*. an expression of gratitude.

that *pron. & adj*. the person or thing already
named. *pl*. THOSE

thaw *v*. 1 to become unfrozen; to unfreeze
(something). 2 to become more relaxed and
genial.

theater *n*. 1 a place where plays are performed.
2 a room where surgical operations are
performed. THEATRICAL *adj*.

theft *n*. stealing; robbery.

their *pron.pl*. belonging to them.

them *pron.pl*. persons already spoken about.

theme *n.* 1 a subject or topic. 2 a repeated melody, with variations.

then *adv.* 1 at that time. 2 after that; next. 3 for this reason.
THEN *conj.* in that case; therefore.

theology *n.* the study of God and religion.

theorem *n.* an idea or statement which needs to be proved by reasoning.

theory *n.* 1 a suggested explanation. 2 the general ideas and principles of some activity.

therapy *n.* healing; the treatment of disease or illness.

there *adv.* at, in or to that place.

thermal *adj.* of heat; determined, operated or measured by heat.
THERMAL *n.* a rising current of warm air.

thermometer *n.* an instrument for measuring temperature.

thermostat *n.* an automatic device for controlling temperature.

these *pron.pl.* plural of this.

thick *adj.* 1 of great or specified depth from one side to the other. 2 crowded; packed. 3 dense; hard to see through. 4 stiff; flowing slowly.
THICKLY *adv.* THICKNESS *n.*

thicken *v.* to make or become denser; stiffer or thicker.

thief *n.* a person who steals.

thigh *n.* the part of the leg between the hip and the knee.

thimble *n.* a small metal or plastic cap to protect the finger when sewing.

thin *adj.* 1 having opposite surfaces close together. 2 of small diameter; not thick; narrow. 3 slim; slender. 4 weak; watery.
THIN *v.* 1 to make or become thin. 2 to reduce in bulk or number.

thing *n.* 1 an object; an article. 2 an action or happening.

think *v.* 1 to reason; to have an opinion. 2 to consider; to imagine. THINKING *n.*

third *adj.* the next after second; the last of three.
THIRD *n.* one of three equal parts.

thirst *n.* a strong desire or need to drink.
THIRST (FOR or AFTER) *v.* to desire strongly.
THIRSTY *adj.*

thirteen *n.* the number one more than twelve. the symbol 13.

thirty *n.* three times ten, the symbol 30.

this *pron. & adj.* the person or thing near or just mentioned. *pl.* THESE.

thorn *n.* 1 a sharp, pointed growth on a plant. 2 a prickly shrub or tree.

thorough *adj.* 1 complete; with attention to every part or detail. 2 careful; conscientious.
THOROUGHLY *adv.* THOROUGHNESS *n.*

thoroughbred *adj.* of pure breed.

those *pron.pl.* plural of that.

though *adv.* however; nevertheless.
THOUGH *conj.* although; in spite of the fact that.

thought *n.* 1 the process of thinking or reasoning. 2 an idea or opinion.

thoughtful *adj.* 1 thinking deeply. 2 considerate.

thousand *n.* ten times a hundred, the symbol 1,000.

thrash *v.* 1 to beat and hit repeatedly. 2 THRASH ABOUT to move about violently.
THRASHING *n.*

thread *n.* 1 a length of cotton, silk or nylon. 2 the spiral ridge on a screw or inside a nut. 3 the connection between points in a talk or story.
THREAD *v.* 1 to pass thread through a needle or opening. 2 to find a way through.

threat *n.* 1 a warning sign of trouble or danger. 2 a source of trouble or danger.
THREATEN *v.* THREATENING *adj.*

three *n.* the number one more than two, the symbol 3.

thresh *v.* to separate grain seed from the plant.

thrift *n.* careful management of goods or money in order to save. THRIFTY *adj.*

thrill *n.* a sudden feeling of excitement.
THRILL *v.* to cause excitement in someone; to feel excitement.

thrive *v.* to grow vigorously; to prosper.
THRIVING *adj.*

throat *n.* the front of the neck; the gullet and the windpipe.

throne *n.* the seat of a king, queen, or bishop.

throttle *v.* 1 to strangle; to choke. 2 to regulate the flow of.
THROTTLE *n.* valve for regulating the flow of air or steam.

through *prep.* 1 from end to end; from the beginning to the end of. 2 as a result of.
THROUGH *adv.* all the way.

throughout *adv.* in every part.
THROUGHOUT *prep.* from end to end of.

throw *v.* to fling or hurl.
THROW *n.* 1 the act of throwing. 2 the distance something is thrown.

thrush *n.* a songbird having a brown back and speckled breast.

thrust *v.* to push suddenly or violently; to pierce.
THRUST *n.* a sudden or violent push.

thumb *n*. the short, thick finger of the hand.
THUMB *v*. to handle or mark with the thumb.

thunder *n*. 1 the loud sound that follows lightning. 2 any loud rumbling noise.
THUNDER *v*. to make a sound like thunder; to roll; to rumble loudly.

Thursday *n*. the fifth day of the week.

thus *adv*. in this or that way.

thyme *n*. (pron. TIME) a sweet-smelling herb used in cookery.

tick *n*. a light, regular sound; the sound made by a watch or clock.
TICK *v*. to make a ticking sound.

ticket *n*. a piece of card or paper giving the right to be admitted, travel. etc.

tickle *v*. 1 to touch a person's skin lightly, often producing laughter. 2 to amuse.
TICKLE *n*. 1 the act of tickling. 2 an irritation.

tidal *adj*. affected by or concerned with the tides.

tide *n*. 1 the regular rise and fall of the sea. 2 a time or season. 3 something which ebbs and flows.

tidy *adj*. neat; carefully arranged.
TIDILY *adv*. TIDINESS *n*.

tie *v*. 1 to fasten with a string or cord. 2 to score equally in a competition or game.
TIE *n*. 1 a link or connection. 2 an equal score. 3 a necktie. TIED *adj*.

tiger *n*. a large, fierce, striped animal of the cat family. *fem*. TIGRESS.

tight *adj*. 1 firmly fastened or stretched. 2 closely fitted or crowded together. TIGHTEN *v*.

tile *n*. a thin piece of baked clay or other material for covering roofs, floors or walls.
TILE *v*. to cover with tiles.

till *v*. to plow and cultivate the land.

tilt *v*. to slope to one side; to lean.
TILT *n*. a slope; a slant.

timber *n*. 1 wood used in building, carpentry, etc. 2 trees providing such wood. TIMBERED *adj*.

time *n*. 1 the measure or duration of the past, present and future. 2 a particular moment in time. 3 a period of time. 4 the rhythm and speed of a piece of music.
TIME *v*. to measure the time taken to do something. TIME *adj*. concerned with time.

timid *adj*. shy; easily frightened. TIMIDLY *adv*.

tin *n*. 1 a soft, silvery-white metal. 2 a can or container made of tin-plate.
TIN *v*. 1 to pack something into tins. 2 to coat with tin.

tingle *v*. to have a prickly sensation on the skin.

tint *n*. a shade of color; a hue.
TINT *v*. to color; to tinge.

tiny *adj*. very small.

tip *n*. 1 the point or end of something. 2 a useful piece of advice. 3 a gratuity for service.
TIP *v*. 1 to tilt or overturn. 2 to give a gratuity to. 3 to touch lightly.

tirade *n*. a long outburst or speech.

tire *n*. 1 an air-filled rubber tube around a vehicle wheel. 2 a metal or rubber rim around a wheel.

tire *v*. 1 to become or to make weary. 2 TIRE OF to lose interest in.
TIRED *adj*. TIREDNESS *n*.

tireless *adj*. never becoming weary; never resting. TIRELESSLY *adv*.

tiresome *adj*. annoying; making weary.

tissue *n*. 1 a fine woven fabric. 2 the substance of which living things are made.

tithe *n*. 1 a tax of one tenth of the produce of a farm, formerly paid to support the clergy and the church. 2 a tenth part.

title *n*. 1 the name of a book, play, film or piece of music. 2 a word which shows a person's rank, position or profession. TITLED *adj*.

toad *n*. a warty amphibian of the frog family.

toadstool *n*. an umbrella-shaped kind of fungus, often poisonous.

toast *v*. 1 to make (food) crisp and brown by grilling it. 2 to drink to a person's health.
TOAST *n*. 1 toasted bread. 2 the act of drinking a toast.

tobacco *n*. the dried leaves of the tobacco plant prepared for smoking in cigarettes, cigars and pipes. TOBACCONIST *n*.

toboggan *n*. a long, narrow sledge for use in snow. TOBOGGAN *n*. to travel in a toboggan.

today *n*. this present day.

toe *n*. 1 a digit of the foot. 2 the front part of a shoe, sock or boot.

together *adv*. 1 in company; side by side. 2 at the same time.

toil *v*. to work hard. TOIL *n*. heavy work; labor.

toilet *n*. 1 a lavatory. 2 the act of washing, dressing, etc.

tolerable *adj*. 1 that can be borne or endured. 2 fairly good.

tolerant *adj*. willing to tolerate opinions and behavior different from one's own.
TOLERANCE *n*.

tolerate *v*. to put up with; to endure.
TOLERATION *n*.

toll *n*. 1 a charge made for the use of some roads and bridges. 2 loss and suffering.
TOLL *v*. to ring a bell slowly.

tomato *n.* a red, pulpy edible fruit. *pl.* TOMATOES.

tomb *n.* a grave; a burial place.

tomorrow *n.* the day after today.

ton *n.* a measure of weight. 2,000 pounds (about 907 kilograms).

tone *n.* 1 a musical sound. 2 a quality indicating the character of something. 3 a shade or tint of color. TONE *v.* to give tone or color to.

tongue *n.* 1 the movable, fleshy organ in the mouth used in speaking, tasting and swallowing. 2 a language.

tonight *n.* this night

tonsil *n.* one of the two small organs at the back of the throat. TONSILITIS *n.*

too *adv.* 1 also; in addition. 2 more than is wanted.

tool *n.* an instrument or implement required for doing work.

tooth *n.* 1 one of the bonelike structures rooted in the gums and used for biting and chewing. 2 toothlike projection on a comb, gear wheel or saw. *pl.* TEETH.

toothache *n.* a pain in a tooth or the teeth.

top *n.* 1 the highest part of anything. 2 the upper surface. 3 the person or thing in the highest position. 4 a spinning toy.

topic *n.* a subject for discussion, study or writing. TOPICAL *adj.*

topography *n.* the physical features of a district or landscape.

torch *n.* 1 a small portable electric lamp. 2 a piece of blazing material carried to give light.

torment *v.* (pron. tor-MENT) to torture; to cause great suffering. TORMENT *n.* (pron. TOR-ment) severe physical or mental suffering. TORMENTOR *n.*

tornado *n.* a violent whirlwind.

torpedo *n.* a self-propelled underwater missile. *pl.* TORPEDOES. TORPEDO *v.* to attack with torpedoes.

torrent *n.* 1 a rushing stream. 2 a heavy downpour of rain. 3 a rush of words. TORRENTIAL *adj.*

torso *n.* the human body without head or limbs; the trunk.

tortoise *n.* a four-legged slow-moving reptile with a hard body shell.

tortuous *adj.* 1 full of twists or turns. 3 devious; not straightforward.

torture *n.* the infliction of severe bodily or mental pain. TORTURE *v.* to inflict such pain upon.

toss *v.* 1 to throw lightly, easily or carelessly. 2 to move restlessly from side to side. TOSS *n.* the act of tossing.

total *n.* the full amount; the total number. TOTAL *v.* to find the total; to add up. TOTAL *adj.* whole; complete. TOTALLY *adv.*

touch *v.* 1 to be in contact with; to feel. 2 to obtain the sympathy of. TOUCH *n.* 1 the act of touching. 2 the sense enabling a person to feel. TOUCHING *adj.*

tough *adj.* 1 strong; not easily broken. 2 hard to bite or cut. 3 rough; violent. 4 difficult. TOUGHEN *v.* TOUGHNESS *n.*

tour *n.* a journey from place to place returning to the starting place. TOUR *v.* to travel from place to place. TOURIST *n.*

tournament *n.* 1 a series of games or contests. 2 formerly, a combat on horseback.

tow *v.* to pull along using a rope or chain. TOW *n.* 1 anything towed. 2 coarse flax.

toward, towards *prep.* in the direction of; approaching.

towel *n.* a cloth for drying things.

tower *n.* a tall, narrow building rising high above others, often part of a church or fortress. TOWER *v.* to rise high above others.

town *n.* 1 place, larger than a village, with houses, shops, churches, schools, etc. 2 the people living in a town.

toy *n.* a child's plaything. TOY (WITH) *v.* to play with.

trace *v.* 1 to seek and find. 2 to copy by using transparent paper. TRACE *n.* 1 a mark, sign or piece of evidence. 2 a small quantity.

track *n.* 1 a path or trail made by regular use. 2 a railway line. 3 a series of marks left by a person, animal or vehicle. TRACK *v.* to follow tracks.

traction *n.* the power used in pulling something.

tractor *n.* a motor vehicle for pulling heavy loads.

trade *n.* 1 the buying, selling or exchanging of goods. 2 commerce. 3 a particular craft or occupation. TRADE *v.* to buy, sell, or deal. TRADER *n.*

tradesman *n.* 1 a shopkeeper. 2 a man skilled in a particular trade or craft.

tradition *n.* the ideas, customs, music and stories passed on from one generation to another. TRADITIONAL *adj.* TRADITIONALLY *adv.*

traffic *n.* 1 the movement of people, ships and aircraft. 2 trading and dealing. TRAFFIC *v.* to trade.

tragedy *n.* 1 a tragic event or misfortune. 2 a play with an unhappy ending. *pl.* TRAGEDIES.

tragic *adj.* concerned with tragedy and sadness. TRAGICALLY *adv.*

trail *v.* 1 to drag or pull along. 2 to walk wearily behind. 3 to follow the tracks of. TRAIL *n.* 1 the track left by something. 2 a rough path.

trailer *n.* 1 a vehicle pulled by another. 2 extracts from a film shown to advertise it.

train *v.* 1 to give (to someone) instruction and practice in doing something. 2 to prepare for a particular activity. TRAIN *n.* 1 number of coaches or wagons drawn by a locomotive. 2 the trailing part of a long dress.

trained *adj.* skilled and efficient through training.

trainer *n.* a person who prepares athletes, horses, etc., for races.

training *n.* practical instruction and education.

trait *n.* a feature of a person's character or personal habits.

traitor *n.* a person who betrays a trust or his country.

tramp *v.* 1 to walk heavily. 2 to walk for a long distance. TRAMP *n.* 1 a long walk. 2 a homeless person who walks from place to place. 3 a cargo ship without a regular route.

trance *n.* a sleeplike state; a hypnotic state.

tranquil *adj.* peaceful; quiet; untroubled. TRANQUILLY *adv.* TRANQUILLITY *n.*

transact *n.* to do; to carry through; to carry out (business). TRANSACTION *n.*

transcend *v.* 1 to rise above; to exceed. 2 to go beyond.

transept *n.* an arm of a cross-shaped church, at right angles to the nave.

transfer *v.* (pron. trans-FER) 1 to move a person or thing from one place to another. 2 to give legal possession (of something) to another. TRANSFER *n.* (pron. TRANS-fer) 1 a movement from one place to another. 2 a change of ownership. 3 a small picture that can be transferred from one surface to another.

transform *v.* to make a considerable change in the appearance or shape of. TRANSFORMATION *n.*

transformer *n.* a device that changes electrical voltage.

transfuse *v.* 1 to transfer liquid from one thing to another. 2 to transfer blood from one person's body to that of another person. TRANSFUSION *n.*

transgress *v.* to break the law; to go beyond the limit.

transient *adj.* brief; passing quickly.

transistor *n.* an electronic device used in radio, television, etc.

transit *n.* 1 a passing across. 2 the carrying of passengers, goods, etc., from one place to another.

translate *v.* to turn what is said or written from one language into another. TRANSLATION *n.* TRANSLATOR *n.*

transmission *n.* 1 the act of sending from one person to another. 2 a radio or television broadcast program.

transmit *v.* 1 to pass on; to communicate. 2 to send out radio or television signals. TRANSMITTER *n.*

transparency *n.* 1 being transparent. 2 a photograph on a transparent film.

transparent *adj.* 1 easily seen through. 2 clear; obvious.

transplant *v.* to plant in another place; to remove to another place.

transport *v.* (pron. trans-PORT) 1 to convey from one place to another. 2 to carry away by strong emotion; to delight. TRANSPORT *n.* (pron. TRANS-port) 1 the act of transporting. 2 vehicles ships or aircraft used for carrying passengers or goods.

trap *n.* 1 a device for catching wild animals. 2 a plan or trick for catching a person unawares. 3 a small horse-drawn carriage with two wheels. TRAP *v.* to catch in a trap.

trapeze *n.* a swinging bar used by gymnasts and acrobats.

trapper *n.* a person who traps wild animals.

trash *n.* refuse.

travel *v.* 1 to make a journey. 2 to move. TRAVEL *n.* 1 movement. 2 a journey. TRAVELED *adj.* TRAVELING *n.*

trawler *n.* a fishing boat which drags a trawl.

tray *n.* a flat piece of wood, metal or plastic, with raised edges, for carrying things.

treacherous *adj.* 1 deceptive; unreliable. 2 disloyal; not to be trusted.

treachery *adj.* betrayal; disloyalty.

tread *v.* 1 to walk; to step. 2 TREAD UPON to trample. TREAD *n.* 1 the act of stepping. 2 the horizontal part of a step or a stair. 3 the molded part of a tire which touches the road.

treason *n.* 1 disloyalty to a cause or friend. 2 the betrayal of a country or its secrets to an enemy.

treasure *n.* 1 a store of valuables. 2 anything of great value. TREASURE *v.* to value highly.

treasurer *n.* a person responsible for the funds and accounts of a club, society or business.

treasury *n.* 1 a storage place for valuables. 2 a government department which is responsible for the nation's finances.

treat *v.* 1 to deal with in a certain way. 2 to give medical attention to somebody. 3 to pay for food, drink or entertainment for (somebody).

treatment *n.* 1 particular way in which anything is dealt with. 2 the method of treating a patient or disease.

treaty *n.* an agreement between nations.

treble *n.* 1 the highest part in music. 2 a boy with a high singing voice. TREBLE *v.* to multiply by three. TREBLE *adj.* three times as much; three times as many.

tree *n.* a large plant having a single wooden trunk from which leaf-bearing branches grow.

trek *v.* to make a long and exhausting journey. TREK *n.* a long and exhausting journey.

tremble *v.* to shake; to shudder with anger, cold, fear, etc. TREMBLE *n.* a shake, a shudder.

tremendous *adj.* 1 very great or powerful. 2 dreadful; fearful.

tremor *n.* a shudder; a vibration; a quiver.

trench *n.* a long narrow ditch cut in the ground.

trend *n.* the general direction or tendency; a fashion.

trespass *v.* 1 to sin. 2 TRESPASS UPON to enter (another person's property) without permission. 3 to intrude upon. TRESPASS *n.* 1 an act of trespassing. 2 a sin. TRESPASSER *n.*

trial *n.* 1 a test; an experiment. 2 a law-court hearing. 3 an affliction or hardship.

triangle *n.* 1 a figure with three sides and three angles. 2 a percussion instrument shaped like a triangle. TRIANGULAR *adj.*

tribe *n.* a group of families or a race of people ruled by a chief. TRIBAL *adj.*

tribunal *n.* 1 a court of justice. 2 a court appointed to deal with a particular type of problem or a specific question.

tributary *n.* a stream or river flowing into another. TRIBUTARY *adj.* paying tribute.

tribute *n.* 1 something said, done or given to show respect or admiration. 2 a tax paid by one nation to another.

trick *n.* 1 a deceitful act or scheme. 2 a clever act meant to amuse or entertain. 3 the cards played in one round of bridge, etc. TRICK *v.* to deceive by a trick; to cheat.

tricky *adj.* 1 artful; cunning. 2 difficult. TRICKILY *adv.*

tricycle *n.* a cycle with three wheels.

trident *n.* a spear with three prongs.

tried *adj.* tested and proved.

trifle *n.* 1 something of very little importance. 2 a small amount. 3 a sweet dish made of cake, jam, cream, custard, etc. TRIFLE (WITH) *v.* to treat (something) lightly.

trigger *n.* the catch or lever which fires a gun.

trigonometry *n.* the branch of mathematics dealing with the relationship between the sides and angles of a triangle.

trim *adj.* neat and tidy. TRIM *v.* 1 to make neat and tidy. 2 to decorate. 3 to balance a boat or aircraft. TRIM *n.* fitness; condition.

trio *n.* a group or set of three.

trip *v.* 1 to stumble. 2 to step lightly and quickly. TRIP *n.* 1 a stumble. 2 a light, quick step. 3 a journey; an outing.

triple *adj.* 1 having three parts. 2 three times as much or as many. TRIPLE *v.* to multiply by three.

triplet *n.* one of three children born to the same mother at one birth.

tripod *n.* a stand or support having three legs.

triumph *n.* victory; a great success. TRIUMPH *v.* to win a victory; to be very successful. TRIUMPHAL *adj.*

triumphant *adj.* victorious; successful. TRIUMPHANTLY *adv.*

trivial *adj.* of small value of importance. TRIVIALITY *n.*

trombone *n.* a large musical instrument with a sliding tube for changing notes.

troop *n.* 1 a group of people or animals. 2 a company of soldiers. TROOP *v.* to move in a large group.

trophy *n.* 1 a prize. 2 something kept as a souvenir of a victory or success.

tropic *n.* one of the two imaginary circles around the Earth between the equator and the poles. TROPICS *n.pl.* the hot regions between the Tropic of Cancer and the Tropic of Capricorn.

trot *v.* to run at a moderate pace. TROT *n.* 1 a moderate run. 2 a horse's pace between a walk and a gallop.

trouble *n.* 1 worry; vexation. 2 grief; difficulty. 3 disburbance; discontent. TROUBLE *v.* 1 to worry or be worried. 2 to disturb or be disturbed. TROUBLED *adj.* TROUBLESOME *adj.*

trough *n.* 1 a long, narrow receptacle for animals to drink or feed from. 2 the hollow between two waves. 3 an area of low barometric pressure.

trousseau *n.* (pron. TROO-so) a bride's outfit of clothes.

trout *n.* a small freshwater fish, held in high regard as food and game.

trowel *n.* 1 a flat-bladed tool used for laying bricks. 2 a small hand tool for use in a garden.

truant *n.* a pupil who is absent from school without permission.

truce *n.* an agreement to cease fighting for a time.

truck *n.* 1 a heavy-goods motor vehicle. 2 a rectangular-framed, two-wheeled barrow.

true *adj.* 1 real; genuine; in accordance with fact. 2 loyal; faithful. 3 reliable; trustworthy. TRULY *adv.*

trumpet *n.* a brass wind instrument.

truncate *v.* to cut the top or end off.

trunk *n.* 1 the main stem of a tree. 2 a torso; a body without head or limbs. 3 a large chest or box with a hinged lid. 4 the long nose of an elephant.

truss *n.* 1 a bundle of hay or straw. 2 a bandage for support. 3 supporting structure of a roof or bridge. TRUSS (UP) *v.* to tie up in a bundle.

trust *v.* 1 to rely upon; to believe in. 2 to hope. TRUST *n.* 1 confidence or faith in. 2 responsibility. 3 property placed in the care of a trustee.

truth *n.* whatever is true; reality; fact. TRUTHFUL *adj.*

try *v.* 1 to attempt; to make an effort. 2 to test or examine (something). 3 to put on trial. TRYING *adj.*

tube *n.* 1 hollow length of metal or flexible material for carrying water, gas, etc. 2 a soft container for toothpaste, ointment, etc., which can be squeezed out.

tuck *v.* to fold in or under. TUCK *n.* a fold made in a garment or a piece of material.

Tuesday *n.* the third day of the week.

tuft *n.* a bunch of feathers, hair or grass growing together.

tug *v.* 1 to give a sudden pull. 2 to pull along. to drag. TUG *n.* 1 a sudden pull. 2 small, powerful boat which tows larger vessels.

tulip *n.* a bell-shaped flower which grows from a bulb.

tumble *v.* 1 to fall. 2 to perform acrobatics. TUMBLE *n.* a fall.

tumbler *n.* 1 an acrobat. 2 a drinking glass.

tumor *n.* a swelling; a growth in the body.

tumult *n.* an uproar; a great disorder. TUMULTUOUS *adj.*

tundra *n.* a vast, treeless plain with arctic climate and vegetation.

tune *n.* a musical melody or air. TUNE *v.* 1 to correct the pitch of (a musical instrument) 2. to adjust (an engine or other mechanism) to give maximum performance. TUNEFUL *adj.* TUNELESS *adj.*

tunic *n.* 1 a uniform jacket worn by policemen, members of the forces, etc. 2 a loose garment hanging from the shoulders to the hips.

tunnel *n.* an underground passage. TUNNEL *v.* to dig or bore a tunnel; to burrow. TUNNELING *n.*

turban *n.* a man's headdress made by winding a long cloth around the head as worn by Muslims and Sikhs.

turbine *n.* an engine which is operated by a jet of gas, steam or air.

turf *n.* a layer of soil with grass growing on it. TURF *v.* to cover with turf.

turkey *n.* a large variety of poultry.

Turkish *adj.* belonging to Turkey or its people. TURKISH *n.* the language of the Turks. TURK *n.*

turmoil *n.* agitation; tumult; confusion.

turn *v.* 1 to change direction. 2 to revolve; to rotate. 3 to alter; to convert. 4 TURN ON to switch on. TURN *n.* 1 a change of direction. 2 a revolution; a rotation. TURNING *n.*

turnip *n.* a large root vegetable.

turquoise *n.* 1 a precious stone, greenish-blue in color. 2 a greenish-blue color.

turtle *n.* a four-legged, slow-moving reptile with a hard shell.

tusk *n.* a long, pointed tooth projecting beyond the mouth as in the elephant, walrus, etc.

tutor *n.* a teacher, an instructor. TUTORIAL *adj.*

tweed *n.* a heavy, woven, woolen cloth.

tweezers *n.pl.* small pincerlike instrument for picking up small objects or plucking out hairs.

twelve *n.* the number one more than eleven, the symbol 12; one dozen.

twenty *n.* the number one more than nineteen, the symbol 20.

twice *adv.* two times; on two occasions.

twig *n.* a small shoot or branch of a shrub or tree.

twilight *n.* the faint light before sunrise and after sunset.

twin *n.* one of two children born to the same mother at one birth.

twinkle *v.* 1 to sparkle. 2 to shine with a light that comes and goes.
TWINKLE *n.* a sparkle or shine.

twirl *v.* to whirl or spin around rapidly.
TWIRL *n.* a whirling or rapid spin.

twist *v.* 1 to turn (something) around. 2 to turn and curve. 3 to bend out of shape.
TWIST *n.* twisting or being twisted.

two *n.* the number one more than one; the symbol 2.

type *n.* 1 a kind; a sort; a species. 2 an example; a specimen. 3 a letter or symbol, usually in metal, for printing. TYPE *v.* to use a typewriter.

typewriter *n.* a machine with a keyboard, for printing letters on paper.

typhoid *n.* an infectious disease, producing a fever, caused by germs in contaminated water or food.

typhoon *n.* a violent hurricane or whirlwind.

typhus *n.* a dangerous disease transmitted by small parasitic insects.

typical *adj.* serving as an example or type; normal; usual.

tyranny *n.* the rule of a tyrant.
TYRANNICAL *adj.* acting like a tyrant.

tyrant *n.* a cruel, harsh ruler or person.

U

udder *n.* the bag or glands of a cow, goat or sheep where the milk is made and stored.

ugly *adj.* 1 unpleasant or repulsive in appearance. 2 dangerous; threatening. UGLINESS *n.*

ulcer *n.* an open sore on the external or internal surface of the body.

ultimate *adj.* the last of all; final.
ULTIMATELY *adv.*

ultimatum *n.* a final offer or demand.

ultrasonic *adj.* beyond the normal hearing range.

umbrella *n.* 1 a light, folding, metal framework covered with fabric to give protection against rain. 2 a protective canopy or covering.

umpire *n.* 1 a referee in certain games. 2 a person appointed to decide a question or dispute. UMPIRE *v.* to referee; to judge.

unable *adj.* not able to; powerless.

unabridged *adj.* complete; not shortened or censored.

unacceptable *adj.* not acceptable; unwelcome.

unaccompanied *adj.* alone; not escorted.

unaccustomed *adj.* not used to; unusual; strange.

unaltered *adj.* unchanged; remaining the same.

unanimous *adj.* with the agreement of everyone; all of one mind. UNANIMOUSLY *adv.*

unarmed *adj.* without weapons.

unassuming *adj.* modest; humble.

unattached *adj.* independent; free.

unavoidable *adj.* certain; not able to be avoided.
UNAVOIDABLY *adv.*

unaware *adj.* not knowing; ignorant of.

unbearable *adj.* that cannot be borne or endured. UNBEARABLY *adv.*

unbelieving *adj.* not believing; doubting.
UNBELIEVABLE *adj.*

unbroken *adj.* 1 continuous; uninterrupted. 2 whole; entire.

unceasing *adj.* continual; endless.
UNCEASINGLY *adv.*

uncertain *adj.* doubtful; not reliable; changeable.
UNCERTAINLY *adv.* UNCERTAINTY *n.*

unchanging *adj.* fixed; consistent.

uncivilized *adj.* primitive; rough.

uncle *n.* the brother of a mother or father; the husband of an aunt.

unclean *adj.* dirty; impure.

uncomfortable *adj.* lacking comfort; uneasy.
UNCOMFORTABLY *adv.*

uncommon *adj.* rare; unusual; remarkable.
UNCOMMONLY *adv.*

unconditional *adj.* without conditions; complete.
UNCONDITIONALLY *adv.*

unconscious *adj.* 1 not conscious. 2 not aware.
UNCONSCIOUSLY *adv.* UNCONSCIOUSNESS *n.*

uncontrollable *adj.* unmanageable; beyond control; unruly. UNCONTROLLABLY *adv.*

unconvincing *adj.* uncertain; not easy to believe.
UNCONVINCINGLY *adv.*

uncouth *adj.* clumsy; awkward; vulgar; rough.

uncover *v.* to expose; to reveal; to remove a cover.

undaunted *adj.* fearless; not dismayed.

undecided *adj.* 1 not decided; not certain. 2 hesitating; doubtful.

undeniable *adj.* that cannot be denied; certain.
UNDENIABLY *adv.*

under *prep.* beneath; below. UNDER *adv.* in a lower position. UNDER *adj.* lower.

undercurrent *n.* a current flowing beneath the surface.

undergo. *v.* to suffer; to bear.

underground *adj.* 1 below the ground. 2 secret or concealed.
UNDERGROUND *n.* 1 an underground railway. 2 a secret movement.

undergrown *adj.* not fully grown; undersized.

undergrowth *n.* shrubs or small trees growing under larger ones.

underline *v.* 1 to draw a line under (a word). 2 to emphasize; to stress.

undermine *v.* 1 to dig beneath and weaken. 2 to weaken or wear out slowly.

underneath *adv.* beneath; below; lower. UNDERNEATH *prep.* beneath; below.

understand *v.* 1 to know the meaning of. 2 to have a thorough knowledge of. 3 to comprehend.

understandable *adj.* 1 clear; easily understood. 2 excusable; forgivable.

understanding *n.* 1 the ability to see the full meaning; intelligence. 2 an agreement.

understatement *n.* 1 an insufficient description. 2 less than the truth.

understudy *n.* a person who is able to take the part or place of another.

undertake *v.* 1 to promise to do something. 2 to attempt.

undertaking *n.* 1 something which is being attempted. 2 a business. 3 a promise.

undeserved *adj.* not deserved.

undesirable *adj.* not wanted; unpleasant; unwelcome. UNDESIRABLY *adv.*

undisciplined *adj.* unruly; lacking discipline.

undisturbed *adj.* 1 not altered. 2 not troubled; calm.

undivided *adj.* complete; whole.

undo *v.* 1 to untie or unfasten. 2 to reverse; to destroy.

undoubted *adj.* certain; without any doubt or question. UNDOUBTEDLY *adv.*

undulating *adj.* 1 having the appearance of waves. 2 gently rising and falling.

unearned *adj.* not earned; not gained by work or service.

uneasy *adj.* restless; uncomfortable. UNEASILY *adv.* UNEASE *n.*

unemployed *adj.* 1 out of work. 2 not being used.

uneven *adj.* 1 not smooth or level. 2 not of the same length. 3 not of the same quality throughout.

unexpected *adj.* 1 not expected or foreseen. 2 surprising. UNEXPECTED *adv.*

unfair *adj.* unjust; not impartial. UNFAIRLY *adv.*

unfaithful *adj.* disloyal; deceitful.

unfamiliar *adj.* strange; uncommon; not well known.

unfavorable *adj.* not encouraging; adverse. UNFAVORABLY *adv.*

unfit *adj.* 1 not suitable. 2 not fit; unhealthy.

unfold *v.* 1 to open out. 2 to tell; to reveal.

unfortunate *adj.* 1 unlucky; unhappy. 2 unsuccessful. UNFORTUNATELY *adv.*

unfounded *adj.* 1 without foundation; not based on facts. 2 untrue.

ungainly *adj.* clumsy; awkward.

ungrateful *adj.* showing no gratitude or thanks. UNGRATEFULLY *adv.*

unguarded *adj.* 1 without a guard; unprotected. 2 careless; heedless.

unhappy *adj.* 1 sad; sorrowful. 2 unfortunate; unsuitable. UNHAPPILY *adv.*

unhealthy *adj.* 1 damaging to health. 2 sickly; diseased.

unheeded *adj.* ignored; not noticed.

unhesitating *adj.* 1 without hesitation. 2 prompt; ready. UNHESITATINGLY *adv.*

uniform *adj.* always the same; not changing. UNIFORM *n.* the official clothing worn by members of a team, the police, military forces, etc.

uninhabited *adj.* not lived in; deserted.

unintelligible *adj.* not able to be understood.

unintentional *adj.* not intended; accidental. UNINTENTIONALLY *adv.*

union *n.* 1 the joining together as one; being united. 2 an association of workers.

unique *adj.* being the only one of its kind; having no likeness or equal. UNIQUELY *adv.*

unison *n.* a tune in which everyone sings the same notes; agreement.

unit *n.* 1 a single thing or person; one. 2 a quantity or amount used as a basis for measurement.

unite *v.* 1 to join together. 2 to make or become one; to combine. UNITED *adj.*

unity *n.* 1 one; oneness; being one, single or individual. 2 harmony; agreement.

universal *adj.* concerning everything and everybody. UNIVERSALLY *adv.*

universe *n.* all existing things; the whole of creation.

university *n.* a place of learning and research. *pl.* UNIVERSITIES.

unkind *adj.* not kind; harsh; cruel. UNKINDNESS *n.*

unknown *adj.* 1 undiscovered; unexplored. 2 not identified.

unlawful *adj.* not permitted by law; illegal. UNLAWFULLY *adv.*

unless *conj.* if not; except when.

unlike *adj.* not like; different from.

unlikely *adj.* improbable.

unlimited *adj.* very numerous; without limits.

unlucky *adj.* unfortunate; unsuccessful.
UNLUCKILY *adj.*

unmanageable *adj.* unruly; difficult to control or handle.

unmentionable *adj.* not fit to be spoken of; unspeakable.

unmerciful *adj.* cruel; inhuman

unmistakable *adj.* certain; undoubted; obvious.
UNMISTAKABLY *adv.*

unmoved *adj.* firm; calm; not affected by emotion.

unnecessary *adj.* not needed; superfluous.
UNNECESSARILY *adv.*

unnerve *v.* to frighten; to weaken.

unnoticed *adj.* not seen; ignored; overlooked.

unobtrusive *adj.* modest; not prominent; reserved.

unperturbed *adj.* calm; not upset.

unpleasant *adj.* disagreeable; not pleasing.

unpopular *adj.* disliked; not in favor.
UNPOPULARITY *n.*

unpromising *adj.* not showing promise; unfavorable.

unquestionable *adj.* certain; beyond doubt.

unravel *v.* to disentangle; to solve a problem.

unreasonable *adj.* 1 absurd; foolish. 2 excessive.

unreliable *adj.* not trustworthy; uncertain.

unrest *n.* a state of trouble or discontent; disturbance.

unruly *adj.* disorderly; badly behaved; hard to control. UNRULINESS *n.*

unsatisfactory *adj.* poor; not good enough.
UNSATISFACTORILY *adv.*

unscrupulous *adj.* without any regard for rightness, honesty or detail.

unseen *adj.* unnoticed; invisible.

unselfish *adj.* generous; showing concern for others.

unsettle *v.* to upset; to disturb; to make restless.

unsightly *adj.* ugly; not pleasing to see.

unskilled *adj.* not trained, experienced or skilled.

unstable *adj.* not steady; not secure.

unsuspecting *adj.* having no suspicion; trusting.

unsympathetic *adj.* lacking sympathy; unkind.

untidy *adj.* not neat and orderly; careless.

until *conj.* till; up to the time when.
UNTIL *prep.* till; up to the time of.

untiring *adj.* persistent; tireless.

unto *prep.* to.

untrue *adj.* 1 false; inaccurate. 2 not faithful. 3 not straight, level or exact. UNTRULY *adv.*

untruth *n.* a lie; a falsehood. UNTRUTHFUL *adj.*

unusual *adj.* uncommon; remarkable; strange.
UNUSUALLY *adv.*

unwary *adj.* incautious.

unwind *v.* to undo; to uncoil.

unwise *adj.* foolish; showing bad judgment.

unworthy *adj.* without merit; dishonorable.
UNWORTHILY *adv.* UNWORTHINESS *n.*

unwrap *v.* to undo; to take out of the wrapping.

unyielding *adj.* firm; determined.

up *adv.* 1 to a higher place; in a high place. 2 out of bed and dressed. 3 completely; absolutely. 4 finished.

uphold *v.* to defend; to support; to maintain.

upholster *v.* to pad and cover chairs and other seats. UPHOLSTERY *n.* UPHOLSTERER *n.*

upon *prep.* on.

upper *adj.* higher in place.
UPPER *n.* the upper part of a shoe or boot.

uppermost *adj.* the highest in rank or place.

upright *adj.* 1 vertical; erect. 2 honest; honorable.
UPRIGHT *n.* a vertical post or support.

uprising *n.* a revolt; a mutiny.

uproar *n.* shouting; disturbance; tumult.

uproot *v.* to pull out by the roots.

upset *v.* 1 to overturn. 2 to disarrange; to confuse. 3 to disturb the temper or digestion.
UPSET *n.* disorder; confusion.

upstairs *adv.* on a higher floor.

upward *adj.* going up toward something higher or overhead.
UPWARD *adv.* in an upward direction; more.

uranium *n.* a radioactive metal used as a source of atomic energy.

urban *adj.* belonging to a city or large town.

urge *v.* 1 to drive on. 2 to try to persuade.
URGE *n.* a strong desire; a longing.

urgent *adj.* needing immediate attention or action. URGENTLY *adv.*

urine *n.* a pale-yellow liquid, containing bodily waste, filtered from the blood by the kidneys and discharged via the bladder.

usable *adj.* that can be used.

usage *n.* 1 the method of using. 2 the custom or habit.

use *v.* (pron. YOOZ) 1 to do something with; to employ. 2 to consume.
USE *n* (pron. YOOS) 1 the work done; employment. 2 the ability or right to use.
USEFUL *adj.* USEFULNESS *n.*

useless *adj.* 1 serving no useful purpose. 2 having no effect.
USELESSLY *adv.* USELESSNESS *n.*

usual *adj.* common; normal; happening often.
USUALLY *adv.*

utensil *n.* an instrument; a tool; a dish or pan.

utility *n.* 1 usefulness. 2 something useful.

utilize *v.* to make use of.

utmost *adj.* 1 the farthest; the most distant. 2 the greatest; the strongest.

utter *adj.* complete; total.
UTTER *v.* to speak. UTTERANCE *n.*

utterly *adv.* fully; completely.

V

vacancy *n.* 1 emptiness. 2 an unfilled job.

vacant *adj.* 1 empty; not filled or occupied. 2 dreamy; stupid.

vacate *v.* 1 to leave empty. 2 to give up possession of.

vacation *n.* a holiday.

vaccinate *v.* to inoculate with a vaccine to obtain protection against smallpox and other diseases.
VACCINATION *n.*

vaccine *n.* a substance containing a virus introduced into the body by inoculation to obtain immunity to a disease.

vacuum *n.* a space that is completely empty; a space from which all air has been removed.

vagrant *n.* a wanderer; a tramp or beggar.

vague *adj.* not clear; not certain.
VAGUELY *adv.* VAGUENESS *n.*

vain *adj.* 1 useless; unsuccessful. 2 proud and conceited. VAINLY *adj.*

valentine *n.* a card sent anonymously on St. Valentine's Day, February 14th; a sweetheart chosen on this day.

valiant *adj.* brave; courageous. VALIANTLY *adv.*

valid *adj.* 1 sound; good. 2 legally acceptable.

valley *n.* lowland between hills or mountains.

valor *n.* personal courage, esp. in battle; bravery.

valuable *adj.* 1 of great value. 2 precious; very useful.

value *n.* 1 the amount something is worth in money. 2 the importance or worth of something.
VALUE *v.* 1 to estimate the worth of (something). 2 to have a high opinion of. VALUED *adj.*
VALUELESS *adj.*

valve *n.* a device for controlling the flow of air, gas or liquid through a pipe.

vampire *n.* 1 a legendary spirit that sucked the blood of sleeping people. 2 a species of bat.

van *n.* 1 a vehicle for carrying goods. 2 *abbrev.* of VANGUARD *n.* the leading part of an army or a fleet.

vandal *n.* a person who deliberately spoils or destroys things. VANDALISM *n.*

vanilla *n.* the flavoring obtained from the pod of vanilla, a tropical plant, used in cakes, ice cream and chocolate.

vanish *v.* to disappear; to pass out of sight.

vanity *n.* conceit; excessive pride.

vanquish *v.* to defeat; to overcome.

vapor *n.* 1 the gas into which most liquids and solids can be turned by heat. 2 steam; mist.

variable *adj.* changeable.

variation *n.* change; alteration.

varied *adj.* different; of various sorts.

variety *n.* 1 the absence of monotony or sameness. 2 a number of different things.
VARIETY SHOW an entertainment consisting of singing, dancing, comedy, etc.

various *adj.* 1 different. 2 of many kinds.
VARIOUSLY *adj.*

varnish *n.* a clear liquid which gives a hard, glossy surface to canvas, wood, etc.
VARNISH *v.* to coat with varnish.

vary *v.* 1 to make or become different. 2 to differ; to disagree.

vase *n.* a jar of glass, pottery, etc., used as an ornament or for holding cut flowers.

vast *adj.* immense; huge; very great.
VASTNESS *n.*

vault *n.* 1 an arched ceiling. 2 a cellar. 3 a leap or spring over something.
VAULT *v.* to leap or spring over (something).
VAULTED *adj.*

veal *n.* the meat of a calf.

veer *v.* to change direction. VEERING *adj.*

vegetable *n.* a plant grown for food. VEGETABLE *adj.* having to do with or made from plants.

vegetarian *n.* a person who eats no meat.

vegetation *n.* plant life.

vehicle *n.* 1 any conveyance that carries passengers or goods over land. 2 the means by which something is done.

veil *n.*1 a piece of light material used to hide or protect the face. 2 a curtain.
VEIL *v.* to conceal; to cover.

vein *n.* 1 a blood vessel through which blood flows back to the heart. 2 the small rib of a leaf. 3 a seam of mineral in rock.

velocity *n.* 1 speed. 2 rate of motion in a given direction.

vendetta *n.* a quarrel or feud between families, often started by a murder.

vengeance *n.* revenge; infliction of punishment for wrong done.

venom *n.* 1 the poison from snakes and other poisonous animals. 2 spite; hatred.

ventilate *v.* 1 to allow fresh air to circulate freely. 2 to discuss (something) freely. VENTILATION *n.* VENTILATOR *n.*

ventriloquist *n.* a person who can make his/her voice appear to come from some other person or place. VENTRILOQUISM *n.*

venture *n.* an adventurous or risky undertaking. VENTURE *v.* to risk; to dare.

Venus *n.* 1 a bright planet which moves around the sun. 2. in Roman mythology, the goddess of beauty and love.

veranda *n.* an open platform, running alongside a house, with a roof supported on pillars.

verb *n.* the word in a sentence that tells what a thing does or what is done to it.

verbal *adj.* spoken; not written. VERBALLY *adv.*

verdict *n.* 1 the decision given by a jury in a court of law. 2 a decision; a judgment.

verify *v.* to prove the truth or accuracy of (a statement, evidence, etc.) VERIFICATION *n.*

vermilion *n.* a bright red color.

vermin *n.* small destructive animals, such as mice, rats, fleas, lice, etc. VERMINOUS *adj.*

versatile *adj.* turning easily from one subject or task to another; adaptable. VERSATILITY *n.*

verse *n.* 1 a group of rhymed lines in a poem or song. 2 poetry.

version *n.* 1 a description; an account. 2 a translation of a book.

versus *prep.* against.

vertebra *n.* each of the segments forming the backbone or spine. *pl.* VERTEBRAE.

vertebrate *n.* an animal which has a backbone or spine.

vertical *adj.* upright; perpendicular. VERTICALLY *adv.*

very *adj.* real; true. VERY *adv.* to a great extent; extremely.

vessel *n.* 1 container for holding liquids. 2 a ship or boat.

vest *n.* 1 an undergarment worn next to the skin. 2 a waistcoat.

veteran *n.* a person who has had long experience or service, as in the military. VETERAN *adj.* old and experienced.

veterinary *adj.* concerned with the diseases and injuries of domestic animals.

veto *v.* to forbid or reject. VETO *n.* the power or right to forbid or reject a legal instruction or proposed law.

via *prep.* by way of; through.

viaduct *n.* a long bridge built on a series of arches to carry a road or railway.

vibrate *v.* to throb; to tremble; to quiver. VIBRATION *n.*

vice *n.* 1 evil; wickedness. 2 a sin; a wicked habit. 3 an appliance with two jaws which can grip and hold tightly. VICE *(prefix)* in place of; second in rank e.g., vice-president, vice-admiral, vice-captain, etc.

vicinity *n.* the surrounding area; the neighborhood.

vicious *adj.* spiteful; evil, VICIOUSLY *adv.*

victim *n.* 1 a killed or injured person or creature. 2 a person who suffers injury or loss.

victory *n.* success in a contest or battle. VICTORIOUS *adj.* VICTORIOUSLY *adv.*

videophone *n.* a telephone equipped for transmitting pictures of the speakers.

videotape *n.* a magnetic tape used to record pictures.

view *n.* 1 a scene; a sight of anything. 2 an opinion. VIEW *v.* to look at; to examine.

vigil *n.* a time of watching and waiting.

vigilant *adj.* watchful; wakeful; cautious.

vigor *n.* 1 strength; energy. 2 healthy growth. VIGOROUS *adj.* VIGOROUSLY *adv.*

Viking *n.* a Scandinavian sea-adventurer of the eighth to tenth centuries.

vile *adj.* 1 shameful; disgusting. 2 unpleasant; bad.

village *n.* a group of houses in a country area. VILLAGER *n.*

vindicate *v.* to clear of blame; to prove (someone or something) to be right, just or innocent. VINDICATION *n.*

vindictive *adj.* revengeful; spiteful.

vine *n.* any climbing plant with a slender stem, but esp. one that bears grapes.

vinegar *n.* an acid liquid obtained from wine, malt, etc., and used for flavoring and pickling food. VINEGARY *adj.*

vineyard *n.* a plantation of grapevines.

viola *n.* 1 a stringed, musical instrument like a large violin. 2 the family of plants to which violets and pansies belong.

violate *v.* 1 to break an agreement or treaty. 2 to break in upon.

violence *n.* 1 brutal conduct or physical force. 2 intense force.

violent *adj.* 1 using or having great physical force. 2 strong; wild. VIOLENTLY *adv.*

violet *n.* a small, purplish-blue flower.

violin *n.* a musical instrument with four strings, played with a bow. VIOLINIST *n.*

viper *n.* a small poisonous snake; an adder.

virtue *n.* goodness; excellence. VIRTUOUS *adj.*

virus *n.* a microscopic organism that causes many diseases.

visa *n.* an official mark on a passport allowing the holder to enter or leave a country.

visibility *n.* 1 being visible; the possibility of being seen determined by the conditions of light and atmosphere. 2 the distance at which something can be seen under particular weather conditions.

visible *adj.* that can be seen. VISIBLY *adv.*

vision *n.* 1 the power of seeing; sight. 2 imagination. 3 something seen in a dream or a trance.

visit *v.* 1 to go to see (a person or place). 2 to stay with a person or at a place. VISITOR *n.*

visor *n.* the movable front part of a helmet, protecting the face.

visual *adj.* to do with sight. VISUALLY *adv.*

vital *adj.* 1 essential to life. 2 very important. VITALLY *adv.*

vitamins *n.pl.* any of a number of substances occurring in foods which are essential for health and normal growth.

vivid *adj.* 1 bright; intense. 2 lively; clear. VIVIDLY *adv.*

vocabulary *n.* 1 the words used in a language or by a person. 2 a list of words with their meanings.

vocal *adj.* to do with the voice; spoken or sung. VOCALIST *n.*

voice *n.* 1 sound that comes from the mouth in speaking, shouting, singing, etc. 2 an opinion. VOICE *v.* 1 to speak. 2 to give an opinion.

void *adj.* 1 empty; vacant. 2 not valid. VOID *n.* an empty space.

volcano *n.* a mountain with openings through which ash, lava and gases sometimes erupt or flow. *pl.* VOLCANOES. VOLCANIC *adj.*

volley *n.* 1 a shower of missiles. 2 a sudden rush of words, questions, etc. 3 in ball games, the return of the ball before it touches the ground.

volt *n.* a unit for measuring electricity. VOLTAGE *n.*

volume *n.* 1 a book or one of a set of books. 2 the amount of space occupied. 3 the amount of sound produced.

voluntary *adj.* done willingly, freely and without compulsion. VOLUNTARILY *adv.*

volunteer *n.* a person who voluntarily offers services. VOLUNTEER *v.* to offer to serve without being asked.

vomit *v.* to reject food from the stomach through the mouth; to be sick.

vote *v.* to express an opinion or choice. VOTE *n.* 1 an opinion or choice. 2 the right to vote. VOTER *n.*

vouch (for) *v.* to confirm; to guarantee.

voucher *n.* a receipt; a ticket.

vow *n.* a promise or oath. VOW *v.* to promise.

vowel *n.* a simple speech sound—a,e,i,o,u.

voyage *n.* a journey by sea. VOYAGE *v.* to go on a journey by sea.

vulgar *adj.* coarse in manners; rude. VULGARLY *adv.* VULGARITY *n.*

vulnerable *adj.* 1 defenseless; open to attack. 2 easily damaged or wounded.

vulture *n.* a large bald-headed bird of prey that feeds on decaying meat.

W

wade *v.* to walk through water, mud, etc.

wage *n.* a regular payment for work done. WAGE *v.* to carry on (war or a battle).

wager *n.* a bet. WAGER *v.* to bet.

wagon *n.* a large four-wheeled cart.

wail *v.* to cry out or moan loudly. WAIL *n.* a long, loud cry or moan.

waist *n.* the part of the body between the hips and the ribs.

wait *v.* 1 to remain in place. 2 to delay doing something. 3 WAIT UPON to serve food. WAIT *n.* time spent in remaining at one place. WAITING *n.*

waiter *n.* a man who serves food or drink in a restaurant, hotel, etc. *fem.* WAITRESS.

wake *v.* 1 to rouse from sleep. 2 to cease sleeping. WAKE *n.* the track left by a ship in the water. WAKEN *v.* WAKENING *n.*

walk *v.* to travel on foot.
WALK *n.* 1 the act of walking. 2 a journey on foot. 3 a pathway. 4 WALK OF LIFE occupation; profession. WALKER *n.*

wall *n.* a side of a house, room or building; a stone or brick fence. stone or brick fence.

wallet *n.* a folding case for holding papers and money, and carried in the pocket or handbag.

wallow *v.* to roll about in mud or water.

walnut *n.* a tree whose wood is used for making furniture; the edible nut of this tree.

walrus *n.* a large, furry sea mammal with two large tusks, and of the seal family.

waltz *n.* a dance with a graceful, flowing melody. WALTZ *v.* to dance a waltz.

wander *v.* 1 to roam aimlessly. 2 to stray from the point. WANDERER *n.* WANDERING *adj.*

want *v.* 1 to need or require. 2 to wish for; to desire. 3 to be without.
WANT *n.* 1 shortage; scarcity. 2 a need.

war *n.* an armed struggle and fighting between military forces or countries.
WARFARE *n.* WARLIKE *adj.*

ward *n.* 1 a room for patients in a hospital. 2 a child in the care of a guardian. 3 a division of a town or area for election purposes.
WARD (OFF) *v.* to protect (oneself or someone else) from.

wardrobe *n.* 1 a large cupboard in which clothes are hung. 2 all of a person's clothes.

ware *n.* a general name for manufactured articles.

warehouse *n.* a building for the storage of goods.

warm *adj.* 1 containing heat; fairly hot. 2 enthusiastic; affectionate.
WARM *v.* to make or become warm. WARMTH *n.*

warn *v.* 1 to give notice or caution of danger. 2 to give advance notice to. WARNING *n.*

warp *v.* 1 to twist or distort. 2 to haul a ship with a rope. WARP *n.* 1 a twist or distortion. 2 a rope. 3 the lengthwise threads in woven material. WARPED *adj.*

warrant *n.* an official document giving authority. WARRANT *v.* to authorize; to guarantee.

warrior *n.* a soldier; a fighting man.

wart *n.* a small, hard growth on the skin.

wary *adj.* cautious; watchful. WARILY *adv.*

wash *v.* 1 to clean with water. 2 to flow against. 3 WASH AWAY to be carried away by water. WASH *n.* 1 the act of washing. 2 things to be washed. 3 the action and sound of water. 4 a thin covering of paint. WASHING *n.*

washer *n.* a rubber or metal ring that seals a joint or fits under a nut to keep it tight.

wasp *n.* a small black and yellow winged insect with a sting.

waste *v.* 1 to spend carelessly; to squander; to use extravagantly. 2 to become thinner or weaker.
WASTE *n.* 1 refuse; rubbish. 2 uncultivated or barren land. 3 extravagance. WASTEFUL *adj.*

watch *v.* 1 to look at (something) closely. 2 to guard. 3 to be wakeful.
WATCH *n.* 1 the act of watching. 2 a small type of clock for the wrist or pocket. 3 a spell of duty on board a ship, etc. WATCHFUL *adj.*

watchman *n.* a person employed to guard property.

watchword *n.* a password; a slogan.

water *n.* 1 colorless, tasteless, odorless liquid. 2 an expanse of lake, sea or river.
WATER *v.* 1 to supply or provide with water. 2 to add water to. WATERY *adj.*

waterfall *n.* a stream or river of water falling over a ledge of rock.

waterfowl *n.* birds which live and nest near water, esp. swimming and diving birds.

waterlogged *adj.* saturated or filled with water.

waterproof *adj.* not allowing water to pass through.
WATERPROOF *v.* to make something proof against water.

watershed *n.* the area of high land dividing two river basins.

watt *n.* a unit of electrical power.

wave *n.* 1 a moving ridge of water. 2 something shaped like a wave. 3 a sign made with the hand. 4 a vibration of electricity, heat, light or sound.
WAVE *v.* 1 to move up and down or to and fro. 2 to make a waving movement with the hand. 3 to curl (the hair).

waver *v.* to hesitate; to move unsteadily.
WAVERING *adj.*

wax *n.* 1 a fatty substance produced by bees. 2 any of various substances resembling beeswax. WAX *v.* 1 to smear with wax. 2 to increase in size or strength.

way *n.* 1 a road, track, path or route. 2 distance traveled. 3 a method, plan, habit, custom or manner of behaving.

weak *adj.* 1 feeble; fragile; frail. 2 having little willpower. 3 watery; thin.
WEAKLY *adv.* WEAKNESS *n.*

weaken *v.* to make or to become weak.

wealth *n.* riches; large possessions. WEALTHY *adj.*

wean *v.* 1 to accustom a baby to food other than its mother's milk. 2 to break away from a habit.

weapon *n.* an instrument used in fighting.

wear *v.* 1 to have something on the body; to be clothed in. 2 to attach something to the clothes. 3 to last a long time. 4 WEAR OUT to use up or be used up. WEAR *n.* 1 clothing. 2 damage from continual use.

weary *adj.* exhausted; tired. WEARY *v.* to exhaust or tire. WEARILY *adv.* WEARINESS *n.*

weasel *n.* a small, fierce carnivorous mammal.

weather *n.* the conditions of rain, sunshine, wind, etc., in a particular place at a certain time.
WEATHER *v.* 1 to wear by exposure to the weather. 2 to come successfully through some difficulty.

weave *v.* 1 to make fabric by interlacing threads, etc. 2 to operate a loom. 3 to wind in and out. WEAVER *n.*

web *n.* 1 anything that is woven. 2 the skin joining the toes of water birds, bats, etc.

wed *v.* to marry.

wedding *n.* a marriage ceremony; a marriage.

wedge *n.* a V-shaped piece of wood or metal used for splitting, forcing open or fastening. WEDGE *v.* to fix or fasten with a wedge. WEDGED *adj.*

Wednesday *n.* the fourth day of the week.

weed *n.* a wild plant growing where it is not wanted. WEED *v.* to remove weeds.

week *n.* a period of seven days.

weekly *adj.* happening once a week.
WEEKLY *n.* a newspaper or magazine published once a week.

weep *v.* to cry; to shed tears. WEEPING *adj.*

weigh *v.* 1 to find out how heavy something is by using scales. 2 to have a certain heaviness.

weight *n.* 1 the heaviness of something. 2 a piece of metal of known weight used in weighing articles. 3 importance; influence. WEIGHTY *adj.*

weird *adj.* uncanny; very strange. WEIRDLY *adv.*

welcome *v.* to greet with pleasure.
WELCOME *n.* a friendly greeting.
WELCOME *adj.* 1 giving pleasure. 2 freely permitted.

weld *v.* 1 to join two pieces of metal together by heat and pressure or by fusing the joint. 2 to unite firmly.
WELD *n.* a joint made by welding.

welfare *n.* happiness; health; prosperity; well-being.

well *n.* 1 a deep hole or shaft sunk into the earth to obtain water or oil. 2 a space in a building enclosing a staircase or elevator.
WELL (UP) *v.* to flow or gush out.
WELL *adj.* 1 in good health. 2 in a good and satisfactory manner.
WELL *adv.* in a thorough and satisfactory manner.

west *n.* the point on the horizon where the sun sets. WEST *adj.* toward the west.
WESTWARD *adv.* toward the west.

western *adj.* in the west.

wet *adj.* 1 covered or saturated with water or other liquid. 2 rainy; showery.
WET *v.* to make wet or to moisten. WETNESS *n.*

whale *n.* a large sea mammal often hunted for its oil, whalebone, etc.

whaler *n.* a ship or person that hunts whales. WHALING *n.* hunting whales.

wharf *n.* a platform where ships are loaded or unloaded.

what *pron.* that which; whatever.
WHAT *adj.* 1 which. 2 how much. 3 the amount, kind, etc.

wheat *n.* a cereal plant; its grains.

wheel *n.* a circular frame or disc which revolves on an axle.
WHEEL *v.* 1 to move (something) on wheels. 2 to turn around like a wheel.

wheelbarrow *n.* a container with one wheel and a pair of handles.

when *adv.* 1 at what time. 2 how long ago. 3 as soon as.
WHEN *conj.* 1 at the time. 2 although.

where *adv.* 1 in or to what place. 2 in the place which.

whether *pron.* which of the two.
WHETHER *conj.* if; which.

which *pron.* who, of a number of persons; what one, of a number of things.

while *n.* a period of time.
WHILE *conj.* at the time that.
WHILE (AWAY) *v.* to pass time.

whim *n.* a sudden fancy or impulse.

whimper *v.* to whine; to make feeble crying sounds. WHIMPER *n.* a feeble crying sound.

whine *n.* 1 complaining tone. 2 continuous high-pitched sound.
WHINE *v.* to make a whining sound.

whip *v.* 1 to lash with a whip. 2 to beat. WHIP *n.* a cord or leather thong attached to a handle.

whipping *n.* a beating or thrashing.

whirl *v.* to rotate quickly; to spin.
WHIRL *n.* a spinning motion.

whirlpool *n.* a strong and rapid circular movement of water in a sea or a river.

whirlwind *n.* a violent and spinning wind or air current.

whisk *n.* 1 a quick sweeping movement. 2 an implement for beating eggs, cream, etc. WHISK *v.* 1 to sweep lightly. 2 to beat.

whisker *n.* a hair growing on the face.

whisky *n.* an alcoholic drink distilled from fermented malt, barley, rye, etc.

whisper *v.* 1 to speak very softly. 2 to make a soft murmuring sound. WHISPER *n.* 1 a softly made sound. 2 a hint or a rumor. WHISPERING *adj.*

whistle *n.* 1 a shrill sound produced by blowing air through the lips. 2 an instrument for making a shrill sound. WHISTLE *v.* 1 to produce a shrill sound by blowing air through the lips or an instrument. 2 to make a tune or signal by whistling. WHISTLING *n.*

white *adj.* the color of fresh snow. 2 pale. WHITE *n.* 1 the color white. 2 the part of an egg surrounding the yoke. WHITEN *v.* WHITENESS *n.*

whitewash *n.* a mixture of lime and water used for whitening. WHITEWASH *v.* 1 to coat with a mixture of lime and water. 2 to cover up guilt or faults intentionally.

whole *adj.* 1 entire and complete. 2 in one piece; perfect. WHOLE *n.* the complete or total amount.

wholesale *n.* the buying and selling of goods in large quantities. WHOLESALE *adj.* in large quantities; extensive. WHOLESALER *n.*

wholesome *adj.* favorable to health; nourishing.

wholly *adv.* completely; entirely.

why *adv.* for what reason; for what purpose.

wick *n.* a cotton thread or woven cord in a lamp or candle which draws up the oil or molten wax to the flame.

wicked *adj.* 1 evil; sinful. 2 mischievous. WICKEDLY *adv.* WICKEDNESS *n.*

wicker *n.* anything made of woven willow twigs, reeds or cane.

wide *adj.* broad; stretching far. WIDE *adv.* 1 to the full extent. 2 off the target. WIDENESS *n.* WIDELY *adv.*

widen *v.* to make or become wider or broader.

widespread *adj.* extensive; distributed over a large area.

widow *n.* a woman whose husband is dead and who remains unmarried.

widower *n.* a man whose wife is dead and who remains unmarried.

width *n.* the distance or measurement from side to side; the breadth.

wield *v.* 1 to hold and use (a weapon, etc.); to brandish. 2 to exercise (power and authority).

wife *n.* a married woman. *pl.* WIVES.

wig *n.* an artificial covering of hair for the head.

wild *adj.* 1 living freely and naturally; untamed. 2 not cultivated or inhabited. 3 savage. WILDNESS *n.*

wilderness *n.* a desert; an uncultivated or a desolate area.

wile *n.* a cunning trick or deception.

willful *adj.* obstinate; intentional, deliberate. WILLFULLY *adv.*

will *n.* 1 a person's power to make decisions. 2 determination; resolve. 3 desire; intention. 4 a document showing what a person wishes to be done with his/her property after death. WILL *v.* to direct or bequeath.

willing *adj.* ready and eager to help. WILLINGLY *adv.* WILLINGNESS *n.*

willow *n.* a tree with slender, flexible branches usually growing near water.

wilt *v.* to droop; to become limp

win *v.* 1 to gain or earn. 2 to be victorious. 3 to gain affection. WIN *n.* a victory; a success.

wince *v.* to draw back from; to flinch. WINCE *n.* a sudden movement or expression of pain.

winch *n.* a machine for pulling or lifting loads by a rope wound around a drum. WINCH *v.* to move by means of a winch.

wind *n.* 1 a current of air; a breeze. 2 breath.

wind *v.* (pron. WYND) 1 to turn or twist. 2 to make into a coil or ball. 3 to tighten. WINDING *adj.*

windmill *n.* a mill operated by the action of the wind on sails or vanes.

window *n.* an opening in the wall of building, usually filled with glass, to let in light and air.

wine *n.* a drink made from the juice of grapes or other fruits.

wing *n.* 1 the part of a bird, bat or insect by which it flies. 2 the plane, or flat surface, which supports an aircraft in flight. 3 a side extension to a building. WING *v.* 1 to fly. 2 to wound in the wing.

wink *v.* 1 to close and open an eyelid quickly. 2 to flicker or flash. WINK *n.* 1 a quick closing and opening of an eyelid. 2 a flicker of light. WINKING *n.*

winner *n.* a person who wins.

winning *adj.* 1 victorious. 2 charming; attractive. WINNING *n.* the gaining of a prize or victory.

winter *n.* the cold season of the year between autumn and spring.
WINTER *v.* to spend the winter.

wipe *v.* to clean or dry by rubbing with a cloth.
WIPE *n.* the act of wiping.

wire *n.* 1 a metal thread. 2 a telegram.
WIRE (UP) *v.* to fit electrical wiring. WIRED *adj.*

wisdom *n.* possession of experience and knowledge, with the ability to use them in making good judgments and decisions.

wise *adj.* having experience, knowledge and good judgment. WISELY *adv.*

wish *v.* to long for; to desire.
WISH *n.* a longing or desire. WISHFUL *adj.*

wit *n.* 1 the power of understanding and intelligence. 2 the ability to say or to see something that is amusing. 3 a person who has this ability.

witch *n.* a woman supposed to have evil magical powers. WITCHCRAFT *n.*

with *prep.* 1 in company of. 2 because of. 3 having or possessing.

withdraw *v.* 1 to go back or away; to retreat. 2 to take back. WITHDRAWAL *n.*

wither *v.* to become dry and shriveled.
WITHERED *adj.*

withhold *v.* to keep back; to refuse to grant.

within *prep.* inside; not beyond.
WITHIN *adv.* indoors; inwardly.

without *prep.* 1 outside or out of. 2 in the absence of.
WITHOUT *adv.* out of doors; outwardly.

withstand *v.* to resist; to oppose.

witness *n.* 1 an observer of an incident. 2 a person who gives evidence in court. 3 evidence; testimony.
WITNESS *v.* 1 to see (something) happen. 2 to give evidence.

wizard *n.* a magician; a conjurer.

wobble *v.* 1 to move unsteadily from side to side. 2 to quiver; to shake.

woe *n.* sorrow; grief.

wolf *n.* a fierce wild animal which hunts in packs and belongs to the dog family. 2 a greedy person.
pl. WOLVES. WOLF *v.* to eat greedily.

woman *n.* an adult female human being.
pl. WOMEN.

wonder *n.* 1 a feeling of surprise and admiration. 2 anything which causes surprise or amazement.
WONDER *v.* to marvel at; to be filled with surprise. WONDERFUL *adj.* WONDERING *adj.*

wood *n.* 1 an area of land covered by growing trees. 2 timber. WOODED *adj.* WOODLAND *n.*

wooden *adj.* 1 made of wood. 2 stiff; dull.

woodpecker *n.* a bird that pecks the bark of trees in searching for insects.

wool *n.* 1 the soft wavy hair of sheep and some other animals. 2 thread or cloth made from this hair. WOOLEN *adj.* WOOLLY *adj.*

word *n.* 1 any sound or combination of sounds forming a single part of speech. 2 news; information. 3 a speech or conversation. 4 a promise. WORD *v.* to express in words.

work *n.* 1 action which needs bodily or mental activity. 2 a person's employment. 3 something produced by effort.
WORK *v.* 1 to be involved in action needing bodily or mental activity. 2 to be employed. 3 to produce by effort.
WORKER *n.* WORKING *adj.*

works *n.pl.* 1 a factory, mill, etc. 2 the moving parts of machinery.

world *n.* 1 the Earth and all it contains. 2 the universe and all creation. 3 any planet or star. 4 an area of activity or interest.

worm *n.* 1 a long, soft, limbless, creeping animal, without a backbone, such as the earthworm. 2 the thread of a screw.

worn *adj.* 1 showing signs of damage from use. 2 WORN OUT tired and weary.

worry *n.* anxiety; trouble.
WORRY *v.* 1 to cause anxiety or trouble to.
WORRIED *adj.*

worse *adj.* more bad; more ill.
WORSE *adv.* more badly.

worship *n.* 1 reverence; honor and respect. 2 admiration.
WORSHIP *v.* to revere, honor and respect.

worst *adj.* most bad, WORST *adv.* most badly.

worth *n.* 1 the value or cost of something. 2 the importance or merit.
WORTH *adj.* 1 equal in value to. 2 deserving of.
WORTHY *adj.*

wound *n.* (pron. WOOND). an injury caused by a blow or cut to the body.
WOUND *v.* to injure or hurt. WOUNDED *adj.*

wrangle *v.* to argue angrily.
WRANGLE *n.* a noisy quarrel.

wrap *v.* to fold up or put a covering around (something).
WRAP *n.* a shawl or similar covering.
WRAPPER *n.* WRAPPING *n.*

wrath *n.* violent anger; rage.

wreath *n.* flowers and leaves woven together into a ring.

wreck *n.* 1 the broken remains of something destroyed. 2 the destruction of something.
WRECK *v.* to ruin or destroy. WRECKAGE *n.*

wren *n.* a very small bird.

wrench *v.* to twist or pull violently.
WRENCH *n.* 1 a violent burst or pull.
2 a tool for gripping and turning nuts and bolts.

wrestle *v.* 1 to struggle with an opponent and try to throw him to the ground. 2 to struggle with a problem or some difficulty. WRESTLING *n.*

wretched *adj.* 1 sad; miserable. 2 of poor quality.

wring *v.* to twist and squeeze.

wrinkle *n.* a small fold or crease in the skin or in the surface of something.
WRINKLE *v.* to make small folds or creases.

wrist *n.* the joint between the hand and arm.

write *v.* 1 to set down letters, words on paper or other material. 2 to be an author or composer. 3 to communicate by letter.
WRITING *n.* WRITTEN *adj.*

writer *n.* 1 person who writes. 2 an author.

wrong *adj.* 1 incorrect; unsuitable. 2 not according to rule or law. 3 not working properly. WRONG *v.* to be unfair or unjust to.
WRONG *n.* an injustice; unfairness.

wry *adj.* twisted out of shape; turned to one side.

X

Xmas *n. abbrev.* Christmas.

X-ray *n.* 1 a ray of short waves which can penetrate solid things. 2 a photograph taken by X-rays. X-RAY *v.* to photograph by X-rays.

xylophone *n.* (pron. ZYLO-phone). a musical percussion instrument made up of a number of plates which vibrate to give different notes when struck with a small hammer.

Y

yacht *n.* (pron. YOT). a sailing boat built for racing or cruising.
YACHT *v.* to race or cruise a yacht. YACHTING *n.*

yak *n.* a long-haired ox of central Asia.

yam *n.* a tropical climbing plant and its edible root.

yank *v.* to give a sudden, sharp pull or jerk to.
YANK *n.* a sudden, sharp pull or jerk.

yard *n.* 1 a measure of length, 36 inches or 3 feet. 2 a wooden spar supporting a sail. 3 an enclosed, unroofed space near a building.

yarn *n.* 1 a thread which has been spun and prepared for knitting or weaving. 2 a tale or story. YARN *v.* to tell a story.

yawn *v.* 1 to gape; to be wide open. 2 to open the mouth wide and take a deep breath when tired or bored.
YAWN *n.* the act of yawning. YAWNING *adj.*

year *n.* 1 the time taken by the Earth to travel once around the sun, 365¼ days. 2 a unit of time, 12 months.

yearly *adj.* once a year; lasting a year.

yearn (for) *v.* to long for or to desire something.
YEARNING *n.*

yeast *n.* a microscopic plant which causes fermentation, used in making beer, wine and bread.

yell *v.* to shout or cry out loudly.
YELL *n.* a loud shout or cry.

yellow *n.* a bright golden or lemon color.
YELLOW *adj.* of a bright golden or lemon color.

yes *adv.* word which expresses agreement or consent.

yesterday *n.* the day before today.

yet *adv.* 1 up to the present time. 2 still; further.
YET *conj.* however; nevertheless.

yield *v.* 1 to give in; to surrender. 2 to produce (a crop) or give (a profit).
YIELD *n.* the crop; the profit. YIELDING *adj.*

yoga *n.* a Hindu method of meditation and self-control.

yogurt *n.* a semisolid food made from fermented milk.

yoke *n.* 1 a curved wooden beam placed across the shoulders of oxen when working together. 2 a frame supported on a person's shoulders and carrying a pail at each end.
YOKE *v.* to couple, or link, together.

yolk *n.* (pron. YOKE). the yellow part of an egg.

you *pron.* the person or persons spoken to.

young *adj.* 1 not old. 2 not far advanced in life, growth or development.

youth *n.* 1 being young. 2 the early part of life. 3 a young man. YOUTHFUL *adj.*

Z

zeal *n.* great enthusiasm; eagerness.
ZEALOUS *adj.*

zebra *n.* a wild, horselike African animal with a striped body.

zero *n.* 1 the figure or symbol 0; nothing; nought; nil. 2 the starting point of calculating on a scale of measurement.

zest *n.* 1 great enthusiasm. 2 enjoyment.

zigzag *n.* a series of sharp alternate turns like those in the letter Z.
ZIGZAG *v.* to make Z-like turns. ZIGZAG *adj.*

zipper *n.* a sliding fastener, with interlocking toothed strips, for clothes, bags, etc.

zone *n.* 1 a region or area with particular features or purposes. 2 one of the five belts into which the Earth is divided according to climate.

zoo *n.* a place where wild animals are kept and exhibited.

zoology *n.* the scientific study of animals. ZOOLOGICAL *adj.* ZOOLOGIST *n.*

Zulu *n.* a member or the language of one of the South African Bantu peoples.

APPENDICES

Parts of Speech
Capital Letters
Common Abbreviations
Calendar
Roman Numerals

Parts of Speech

noun	the name of a person, place or thing, whether real or abstract. e.g. book, nurse, star, greed, truth, army, team, Boston, Susan.
pronoun	used in place of a noun. e.g. I, me, he, him, she, her, it, we, us, you, they, them. who, whom, whose, which, what, that. myself, himself, herself, itself, ourselves, yourself, yourselves, themselves.
adjective	qualifies a noun; that is, it tells more about a noun. e.g. easy, green, horrible.
verb	shows the action of a sentence or a clause; tells of being, doing or having. e.g. (to) accept, burn, come, worship, yawn.
adverb	modifies a verb; that is, it tells more about the verb; tells how, when or where something is done. e.g. eagerly, fast, well. daily, never, soon. anywhere, here, nowhere. An adverb can sometimes modify an adjective. e.g. It is a **very** cold day.
conjunction	joins words, phrases and clauses together. e.g. and, as, but, until, if, either ... or, neither ... nor.
preposition	names a special relationship between one word and another, where one thing is in relationship to another. e.g. after, around, beside, between, by, from, in, off, over. through, to, under, up, with.
interjection	an exclamation. e.g. ah, golly, hurrah, oh, wow.

Capital Letters

Capital letters are used:

1 to begin sentences:
   e.g. The house is on the right-hand side of the road.

2 to begin the names of people and places.
   Notice the capital letters in an address:

   Miss Joan Brown
   23 Main St.
   Madison, CT 06443

   John Smith, President
   ABC Company
   Suite 411
   2800 Hillbrook Lane, N.W.
   Washington, DC 20016

3 to begin the names of relations:
   e.g. Aunt Christine, Uncle Bob
   and titles:
   e.g. President William Clinton

4 for the pronoun I:
   e.g. Last week I was nine.

5 for exclamation words such as "Oh," "Ah," etc.

6 to begin the names of days, special days and months:
   e.g. Come and see me on Tuesday.
        Christmas Day is in December.

7 when speech marks (inverted commas) are used for the first time:
   e.g. We said, "We shall go to the cricket match tomorrow."

8 at the beginning of lines of poetry:
   e.g. The Pobble who has no toes
        Had once as many as we;
        When they said, "Some day you may lose them all"
        He replied: 'Fish fiddle-de-dee!'

9 for the important words in titles of books, stories, poems, etc.
   e.g. A Tale of Two Cities
        Jack and the Beanstalk

Common Abbreviations

A	ampère
AAA	American Automobile Association
ABC	The alphabet
AC	alternating current
a/c	account
A.D.	(*L.* Anno Domini) in the year of our Lord
advt.	advertisement
AEC	Atomic Energy Commission
A.M.	(*L.* ante meridiem) before midday
anon.	anonymous or unknown
approx.	approximately
Apr.	April
Assoc.	Association
Asst.	Assistant
Aug.	August
B.A.	Bachelor of Arts
B.C.	Before Christ
B.Mus.	Bachelor of Music
bros.	brothers
B.S.	Bachelor of Science
C	Celsius
Capt.	Captain
ch., chap.	chapter
CIA	Central Intelligence Agency
cm	centimeter
Co.	Company; County
C.O.	Commanding Officer
c/o	care of
COD	cash on delivery
Col.	Colonel
co-op	co-operative society
Cpl.	Corporal
DC	direct current
D.D.	Doctor of Divinity
Dec.	December
Dept.	Department
D.F.C.	Distinguished Flying Cross
dia.	diameter

D.J.	disc jockey
D.Litt.	Doctor of Letters
doz.	dozen
D.Phil.	Doctor of Philosophy
Dr.	doctor
D.S.C.	Distinguished Service Cross
D.S.	Doctor of Science
D.S.M.	Distinguished Service Medal
E	East
ed.	edition; editor
EC	European Community
e.g.	(*L.* exampli gratia) for example
Esq.	Esquire
ETA	estimated time of arrival
etc.	(*L.* et cetera) and the rest; and so on
exam.	examination
f.	(forte) loud
FBI	Federal Bureau of Investigation
Feb.	February
ff.	(fortissimo) very loud
Fri.	Friday
g	gram(s)
gal.	gallon
G.B.	Great Britain
geog.	geography
geol.	geology
G.I.	enlisted soldier
Gov.	governor
G.P.	general practitioner (doctor)
h.	hour
h. and c.	hot and cold
H.F.	high frequency
H.Q.	headquarters
i.e.	(*L.* id est) that is
IMF	International Monetary Fund
Inc.	Incorporated
IOU	"I owe you"
I.Q.	intelligence quotient
ital.	italic
Jan.	January

Jr.	Junior
J.P.	Justice of the Peace
Jul.	July
Jun.	June
kg	kilogram(s)
km	kilometer(s)
KO	knockout
kW	kilowatt(s)
l	liter(s)
lat.	latitude
Lieut., Lt.	Lieutenant
LL.B.	Bachelor of Laws
LL.D.	Doctor of Laws
long.	longitude
m	meter(s)
M.A.	Master of Arts
Maj.	Major
Mar.	March
math.	mathematics
max.	maximum
M.D.	Doctor of Medicine
min.	minute(s)
misc.	miscellaneous
ml	milliliter(s)
mm	millimeter(s)
Mon.	Monday
MPH	miles per hour
Mr.	Mister
Mrs.	Mistress
M.S.	Master of Science
MS (s)	manuscript(s)
N	north
NASA	National Aeronautics and Space Administration
NATO	North Atlantic Treaty Organization
N.B.	(*L.* note bene) note well
NCO	noncommissioned officer
NE	northeast
no.	number
Nov.	November
NW	northwest

N.Y.	New York
N.Y.C.	New York City
Oct.	October
oz.	ounce
p.a.	(*L.* per annum) yearly
par.	paragraph
P.E.	physical education
percent	(*L.* per centum) in every hundred
P.M.	(*L.* post meridiem) after midday
PO	Post Office
pop.	population
POW	prisoner of war
pp.	pages
Pres.	President
pro	professional
Prof.	Professor
pro tem	(*L.* pro tempore) for the time being
prox.	(*L.* proximo) in the next month
PS(s)	(*L.* post scriptum); postscript(s)
P.T.	physical training
PTA	Parent-Teacher Association
Pvt.	Private (soldier)
R.C.	Roman Catholic
Rd.	road
recd.	received
retd.	retired
Rev.	Reverend
R.I.P.	(*L.* requiescat in pace) May (he or she or they) rest in peace
R.N.	Registered Nurse
RPM	revolutions per minute
R.S.V.P.	(*Fr.* répondez s'il vous plâit) Please reply
S	south
Sat.	Saturday
SE	southeast
secy.	secretary
Sr.	senior
Sept.	September
Sgt.	Sergeant
Soc.	Society

SOS	Save our Souls (Morse Code)
sq.	square
SS	Social Security
St.	saint; street
Sun.	Sunday
Supt.	Superintendent
SW	southwest
tel.	telephone
Thurs.	Thursday
Tues.	Tuesday
T.V.	Television
UFO	unidentified flying object
UHF	ultra-high frequency
UN	United Nations
UNESCO, Unesco	United Nations Educational, Scientific and Cultural Organization
UNICEF	United Nations International Children's Emergency Fund
Univ.	University
U.S.	United States
U.S.A.	United States of America
U.S.S.R.	Union of Soviet Socialist Republics
V	volt(s); Roman numeral (5)
v	(*L.* versus) against
VHF	very high frequency
V.I.P.	very important person
viz.	(*L.* videlicet) namely
VTOL	vertical take-off and landing
W	watt(s)
W	west
Wed.	Wednesday
WHO	World Health Organization
WO	Warrant Officer
wt.	weight
X	Roman numeral (10)
YMCA	Young Men's Christian Association
yr.	year
YWCA	Young Women's Christian Association

Calendar

January	31 days
February	28 days (+ 1 day in a leap year)
March	31 days
April	30 days
May	31 days
June	30 days
July	31 days
August	31 days
September	30 days
October	31 days
November	30 days
December	31 days

Here is a very old rhyme that may help you remember the number of days in each month:

Thirty days have September,
April, June, and November.
All the rest have thirty-one
except February,
which has twenty-eight days each year
and twenty-nine each leap year.

Roman Numerals

I	1	XIV	14	LXXX	80
II	2	XV	15	XC	90
III	3	XVI	16	C	100
IV	4	XVII	17	CC	200
V	5	XVIII	18	CCC	300
VI	6	XIX	19	CD	400
VII	7	XX	20	D	500
VIII	8	XXI	21 etc.	DC	600
IX	9	XXX	30	DCC	700
X	10	XL	40	DCCC	800
XI	11	L	50	CM	900
XII	12	LX	60	M	1000
XIII	13	LXX	70	MM	2000